BIRTH OF DEMOCRATIC CITIZENSHIP

BIRTH OF DEMOCRATIC CITIZENSHIP
Women and Power in Modern Romania

Maria Bucur and Mihaela Miroiu

Indiana University Press

This book is a publication of

Indiana University Press
Office of Scholarly Publishing
Herman B Wells Library 350
1320 East 10th Street
Bloomington, Indiana 47405 USA

iupress.indiana.edu

© 2018 by Indiana University Press

All rights reserved

No part of this book may be reproduced or utilized in any form or by any means, electronic or mechanical, including photocopying and recording, or by any information storage and retrieval system, without permission in writing from the publisher.

The paper used in this publication meets the minimum requirements of the American National Standard for Information Sciences—Permanence of Paper for Printed Library Materials, ANSI Z39.48-1992.

Manufactured in the United States of America

Cataloging information is available from the Library of Congress.

ISBN 978-0-253-02564-7 (hardback)
ISBN 978-0-253-03846-3 (pbk.)
ISBN 978-0-253-03847-0 (web PDF)

1 2 3 4 5   23 22 21 20 19 18

To our 101 coauthors from Hunedoara County

Contents

Acknowledgments	ix
List of Abbreviations	xi
Introduction	1
1 Women from Romania's Past into the Present: A Short Historical Overview	18
2 Men: Working through Gender Norms at Home	41
3 Children: The Most Beautiful Accomplishment of My Life	63
4 Work and Personal Satisfaction	79
5 Communities: Beyond the Family	93
6 Communism as State Patriarchy	112
7 Facing Capitalism and Building Democracy	135
Conclusion	161
References	169
Index	181

Acknowledgments

THIS BOOK CAME into being because of the kindness of the 101 women we interviewed in Hunedoara County. They opened their homes and hearts to us and patiently answered every question we posed. Knowing how valuable their few moments of spare time are in their busy lives, we are grateful for the generosity they extended to us. We are thankful especially to Emilia Bîrsan and Otilia David for all their help with the focus groups. We will treasure the memories of the whole experience far beyond the scholarly goals of our research.

Our research was made possible by grants from the National Endowment for the Humanities and the International Research and Exchanges Board (IREX). All errors, factual and interpretive, are those of the authors.

We owe a debt of gratitude to our research assistants, Diana Neaga and Cristina Rădoi, who interviewed many of our respondents and labored over the transcriptions of the interviews. For assistance with transcriptions, we express our thanks also to Valentin Niculescu Quintus. Crisia Miroiu, Andrei Miroiu, and Elena Popa were very helpful with translations. Alex Tipei provided invaluable work editing the translations and providing critical feedback. We are very grateful to Jeffrey Isaac for his comprehensive and critical reading of the manuscript. We wish to thank our peer reviewers and the editorial team of Indiana University Press, who contributed significantly to the improvement of the manuscript.

Finally, two men sustained us through their affectionate support over the decade-long path of this project from idea to final manuscript. As with our previous work, we couldn't have done it without Dan Deckard and Adrian Miroiu.

Abbreviations

BOB	Bureau of the Base Organization
CCEO	County Councils for Equal Opportunity
CYU	Communist Youth Union
DLP	Democratic Liberal Party
DP	Democratic Party
EIGE	European Institute for Gender Equality
EU	European Union
IMF	International Monetary Fund
IUFR	International Union of Free Romanians
NATO	North Atlantic Treaty Organization
NCCD	National Council for Combating Discrimination
NCW	National Council of Women
NGO	Nongovernmental organization
NLP	National Liberal Party
NPP	National Peasant Party
NSF	National Salvation Front
PISA	Program for International Student Assessment
RCP	Romanian Communist Party
SDP	Social Democratic Party

BIRTH OF DEMOCRATIC CITIZENSHIP

Introduction

THROUGHOUT MODERN HISTORY, women have pushed for recognition as full human beings, morally and intellectually, and as full citizens, politically and civically.[1] Globally, countless women still do not enjoy full citizenship or gender equality. This book examines women's road toward democratic citizenship over the past seventy years in one country—Romania. It explores this history through the stories of 101 women from Hunedoara County, a region thoroughly transformed by the communist regime. Some were born in the 1920s, an era when women in Romania had very limited civil and political rights. These women subsequently saw the total suppression of democracy under communism—a loss that more dramatically impacted their male counterparts. Most of our subjects were born during the communist period (1947–89). This regime served as a context for a significant portion of their adult lives. Before the fall of communism, moreover, none of the women we interviewed understood their political and civic rights in terms of feminist self-positioning.[2]

For the 101 women we interviewed, democratic citizenship began on May 20, 1990, when, for the first time in Romanian history, women gained unrestricted access to the vote and participated in free multiparty local and national elections. When we conducted our research in 2009–10, these women already had a two-decade-long experience of democratic citizenship. A handful of them had assumed feminist positions, engaging as active citizens and political critics.

Democratic Citizenship

Our study begins with a normative definition of democracy and democratic citizenship. We define *democracy* broadly as a political system in which all members of the community have the same rights and responsibilities in relation to political decision-making and policy implementation, enjoy the same legal protections against discrimination, and succeed in maintaining this equality through active engagement in the life of the polis. Historically, eligibility for membership has differed based on age, education, race, ethnicity, place of birth, religion, and gender. In such cases, one can speak about limited democratic regimes. It is also true that historically, formal democratic measures (e.g., voting rights) have not necessarily translated into actual power, as can be seen in the history of one-party states like communist Romania.

Finally, there are cases where communities with democratic institutions that facilitated the exercise of democratic rights have brought about nondemocratic or illiberal outcomes. In an illiberal democracy, there is a tendency for political parties to develop as cartels and capture state institutions. Economic inequalities are high, and the freedom of association and collective action become very limited for most people. Freedom of expression, even if it exists, is also limited by private and public media oligopolies and monopolies. Economic inequalities are deep enough to generate enormous insecurity and result in a low capacity to fully exercise legal rights for many segments of society. Even if the necessary legal provisions for gender equality exist as a matter of principle, society remains patriarchal in its politics and practices. Finally, politicians treat national security as more important than democracy (Krastev 2016).

In a consolidated democracy, where eligibility is based only on reaching the age of maturity, and both institutions and individuals are assumed to participate in bolstering the democratic goals of that political regime, we define *democratic citizenship* as an individual's membership in a community, whether national or multinational (such as the European Union [EU]) where he or she has full political and civil rights. The citizenry exercises its will through electoral votes in a pluralist political regime, referenda, pressure group lobbying, protests, and other means of political expression. Laws and public policy result from this process of negotiation in which citizens play an active, essential role. The people's will is bound, however, by a respect for human rights, fundamental freedoms (e.g., of self-expression), and the rule of law. The legitimacy of representatives and institutions in a liberal democracy derives from the will of the people to protect these rights. Being monist and authoritarian, communist regimes are incompatible with this definition of democratic citizenship.

In addition to constitutional and voting rights, democratic citizenship requires that access to the economic, social, and civic life of the community be free of gender or biologically based discrimination. To be a democratic citizen is to accept and act according to the principles of tolerance and human rights and to shoulder the moral-political duty of actively protecting these values in the polis. Democratic citizens assume rights and responsibilities. They balance what the state rightfully owes them (in a liberal-individualist view) and what they offer as citizens to the political community (in a communitarian-republican view), two modes of engagement that go "hand in hand" (Walzer 1995, 217).

Democratic citizenship begins to flourish only when all citizens have the opportunity to translate their personal experiences into a political agenda and offer policy solutions. Human agency rests at the heart of this concept of democracy. The feminist sociologist Ruth Lister, whose work has greatly informed our approach, distinguishes between being and acting as a citizen. Being a citizen, she contends, simply requires access to political participation: "To act as a citizen involves fulfilling the full potential of the status. Moreover, in practice, political participation tends to be more of a continuum than an all or nothing affair; it can fluctuate during the individual's life-course, reflecting, in part, the demands of caring obligations which can also be interpreted as the exercise of citizenship obligations" (1998, 35–36). Thus, as our interviews in Hunedoara illustrate, when a retired widow betters her neighborhood by keeping the sidewalks clean, she acts as a citizen. When a doctor seeks elected office to fund improvements to her village's public dispensary, she acts as a citizen.

A Feminist Perspective

When it comes to women's access to political power (and that of other groups marginalized by race, religion, ethnicity, class, and sexuality), a dramatic gap exists between the ideal and the reality.[3] Leaving aside a few notable exceptions,[4] important forms of gender inequality persist in even the most democratic of states. Women's civic activity is valued differently and their contributions to the socioeconomic well-being are rewarded unequally compared to men's. When women propose uses for public/state resources, their recommendations become, at best, marginalized as "women's issues" or, at worst, fail to receive a full vetting.[5] Given this, how can the interests of this category of individual citizens and their elected representatives harmoniously coexist? How can the political class go beyond catering to perceived state interests to better represent the citizenry?

A feminist perspective provides us with tools to critique gender power relations and the development of democratic citizenship. As Lister writes, "'Feminist' is a political identity that is rooted in a broad understanding of what constitutes 'the political.' It means that politics has implications for how we live our lives and for our personal relationships and it illuminates gendered power relationships and inequality in the private as well as the public sphere. . . . For many women who claim feminism as an identity it is a political identity that does not recognize a rigid division between the public and the private" (2005, 443–44). Drawing on this broad understanding of politics and specific definition of feminism, our research focused on everyday forms of citizenship, not just explicit political activity. Regardless of ideology, all modern political regimes connect the familial, private sphere with the public sphere. We cannot neatly separate private from public or personal from political when we discuss men's and especially women's daily activities (Mouffe 1993; Okin 1987, 1998, 2004).

Under the authoritarian regimes of the twentieth century, the political entirely determined the personal. Our respondents grew up subject to overwhelming state control of their private lives. For women who outlived communism, the road to democratic citizenship has been a novel enterprise, particularly in claiming the personal as political. This is a historical experience foreign to the development of Western feminism.[6]

Western feminists of various orientations[7] agree that social programs act as correctives to the historical and structural discrimination that has blocked women's access to political power and resources. Without such programs, women cannot fully exercise their civic and political rights as citizens. In this view, social rights and the welfare state are preconditions of women's full political agency (Phillips 1998, 2003; Shapiro 1998; Young 1990). This position identifies contemporary neoliberalism as a threat to the exercise of women's rights and, by extension, to democratic citizenship. It logically and predictably derives from a specific historical context.

Women who lived in communist Romania had a radically divergent historical experience. They assign value to social and political rights differently than their Western counterparts do. Under communism, social rights took precedence over political rights. The state was a paternalist entity that provided for its citizens. The state apparatus (and its policies), however, were predicated on a denial of the individual as a rational being, one capable of understanding and acting in accordance with his or her own self-interest, a concept central to democracy. Thus, while the communist regime facilitated the economic independence of women from men, it aimed to eradicate women's—and men's—capacity for autonomous action as citizens. Until the fall of communism, the fundamental ingredients of democratic citizenship, recognizing the need for and facilitating the exercise of autonomous action, were missing (M. Miroiu 2004b).[8]

Given all of this, we have chosen a normative theoretical approach that descends from Immanuel Kant's, John Stuart Mill's, and more recently John Rawls's work on political ethics as a component of ethical liberalism. Our approach is closely linked to liberal feminism—both its nineteenth-century Anglophone and Romanian versions and its contemporary manifestations, especially strains that view welfare liberalism as a condition for equal opportunity.[9] Communitarian feminists, such as J. B. Elshtain (1981), and socialist feminists, like Iris M. Young (1990), H. Hartman (1981), and Sofia Nădejde in Romania (Mihăilescu 2002), have also considerably influenced us.

In addition to a deep familiarization with scholarly and ideological discourses on communism, our own lived experiences of the Romanian communist regime (seventeen years for Maria Bucur and thirty-four for Mihaela Miroiu) proved advantageous when carrying out our research. Likewise, the substantial part of our lives spent in the United States (Maria Bucur) and postcommunist Romania (Mihaela Miroiu) has enhanced our intellectual engagement with the relevant scholarship on neoliberalism.[10] We do not claim that our personal histories have brought us greater objectivity but rather that they have augmented our comprehensive approach, one that reaches beyond scholarly expertise into experiential knowledge. Along with our respondents, we weathered a regime that severely limited personal freedom, regardless of gender. Consequently, we see this historical background as fundamental to fully understanding democratic citizenship in the Romanian context. Our case study supplements these historical experiences and enriches a diverse scholarship on gender and democratic citizenship (Dietz 1998).

Scholarship

Until recently, only a small and dedicated network of feminist sociologists, anthropologists, and historians devoted their attention to the impact of Eastern European communist regimes on women's perceptions of citizenship and everyday politics (Bucur 2008a; Verdery 1996). Historians like Sheila Fitzpatrick or Marianne Kemp, and anthropologists like Nancy Ries and Sarah Phillips, have provided excellent insights and initiated more nuanced discussions about gender and everyday politics in the Soviet Union and its successor states. Over the past decade, welcome additions to the scholarship on women's perceptions of the communist regimes come from historians such as Jill Massino and Luciana Jinga for Romania, Krassimira Daskalova and Kristen Ghodsee for Bulgaria, and Malgorzata Fidelis and Anna Muller for Poland, among others (Daskalova 2007; Fidelis 2010; Ghodsee 2004; Jinga 2015; Massino 2007; A. Muller 2013).[11] Yet there are still very few multigenerational, qualitative studies encompassing those who came of age from the early postwar years through the postcommunist transition. This is true for all of the Eastern European communist regimes.

An obsession with new beginnings dominated the scholarship on Romania during the first postcommunist decade. Few people wanted to look back at the traumatic recent past. Historians of Romanian communism, furthermore, demonstrated little interest in how women articulated their own relationship to discourses, policies, and cultural artifacts. Rather, it was political scientists, sociologists, and anthropologists who posed gendered questions about the population's perceptions of the radical political shifts of the past fifty years (Kligman 1998; Miroiu 2004b; Verdery 1996). Yet since 2000, historians have grown increasingly interested in understanding gendered aspects of the communist regimes (Jinga 2015; Rostaș and Văcărescu 2008). These works have pointed to women as a less controversial, accepted category of study for both feminist scholars and researchers uncomfortable with feminism (Pasti 2003).

Background to This Project

Both of us have studied gender relations and power regimes in Romania for decades, using the tools of history (Maria Bucur) and political science and sociology (Mihaela Miroiu). Within the framework of our disciplines, we each employ normative, philosophically inspired, and primarily ethical approaches. Prior to this project, Mihaela Miroiu coordinated a series of quantitative, national-scale studies, including *Barometrul de gen* (Gender barometer) (Open Society Foundation 2000), *Gen: Interese politice, și inserție europeană* (Gender: Political interests and European insertion) (CNCSIS 2006–8), and a contribution to the comparative study *Gender in Central and Eastern Europe: Feminism and Poverty* (ERSTE 2009–10).

Mihaela Miroiu's research program provided a jumping off point. First, the statistical evidence in *Barometrul de gen* demonstrated that communism played an insignificant part in rolling back the traditional and symbolic patriarchal order, in so far as women's emancipation through paid work was concerned. This research showed that treating men as the "head" (this term and its uses will be addressed in-depth in the chapter on men) in both the political and the private spheres remained a historical constant across the twentieth century. Next, *Gen. Interese politice si insertie europeana* shed light on women's priorities in terms of good governance and state-funded services. Specifically, the findings highlighted a mismatch between women's concerns and the agendas of contemporary political parties. Our own interviews fully bore out these findings, with a wealth of qualitative detail about the reasons why women are still reluctant to participate more directly in party politics. Finally, though the collapse of planned economies had a more direct adverse impact on male (as opposed to female) workers' status and income, *Gender in Central and Eastern Europe* revealed a clear trend in the feminization of poverty after 1989.

From these findings, we turned to European and international statistical data on women's income, participation in the labor force, leisure, decision-making, and domestic violence.[12] These quantitative studies—in conjunction with qualitative research on gender and education,[13] gender and the labor market, and intersectional work on gender, ethnicity, and citizenship—provided not only data but also a scholarly context for a coherent formulation of the questions we sought to answer.

We began work on this book in 2009–10, two decades after women in Romania began to exercise their political rights in a neoliberal democratic regime. At the time, the literature lacked a sense of how women thought about, explained, and performed their gender roles. There were few nuanced narratives authored by women not directly engaged in the public sphere as opinion makers or politicians about how they understood their impact in society and especially their relationship to gender roles in the family, informal communities, and politics, from the local to the international. Qualitative studies also primarily dealt with women who participated actively in politics, whether at the national or European level (Paul 2011), and almost completely neglected those who took part only locally or were inactive.

Those who voiced their political opinions included women leaders of non-governmental organizations (NGOs), such as Renate Weber (Open Society Foundation) and Monica Macovei (APADOR, the Romanian affiliate of the Helsinki Committee). In time, both were elected to the EU Parliament and played prominent roles in Romanian politics, as special counsel to the president (Weber) and minister of justice (Macovei). Other prominent women include public intellectuals like Doina Cornea, best known as a dissident in the 1980s; the poet Ana Blandiana; the writer and journalist Gabriela Adameşteanu; and Rodica Palade, the editor in chief of the most important intellectual weekly during the first postcommunist decade, 22. Younger public intellectuals, such as Oana Băluţă, have continued to shape the evolving landscape of civic activism.

We felt the need to move away from such exceptionalism to more in-depth research, even if that implied limiting the study to 101 women respondents. The relatively small size of our sample has been mitigated by our selection, which aimed to be representative of the "average person" (Iluţ 1997). The women in our research live in average-sized cities (Hunedoara and Simeria) for Romania and a village (Sâncrai) that experienced the economic and social transformation brought on by the communist regime in dramatic, yet representative ways, as our chapter on historical background shows. For example, Sâncrai experienced collectivization full force and saw the disbanding of collectivized agriculture after 1989, followed more recently by a move toward privatized production for personal and, to a smaller extent, commercial uses.

At the same time, we wanted our participants to reflect the ethnoreligious diversity of Romania. The proportion of ethnic minorities in Romania has hovered around 10 percent since 1990, down from 28 percent at the end of the interwar period (Gusti 1938; Institutul Naţional de Statistică 2013). This change is connected largely to the emigration of a significant number of the two most important minorities, the Hungarians and the Germans, and to the Hungarian and Romanian governments' genocidal policies against the Jewish population during World War II. The Roma population was also subjected to a similar murderous policy but has made a comeback. In 2011, Hungarians made up 6.5 percent of the population (down by 200,000 individuals from the previous census in 2002) and the Roma 3.3 percent (up by over 16.0 percent from the 2002 census). The growth of the Roma population is even more exceptional in the context of Romania's overall negative nuptiality. In Hunedoara County, the 2002 census showed a similar percentage of minorities vis-à-vis the 92.0 percent ethnic Romanian majority.

The religious diversity of Hunedoara presented another important advantage in terms of illustrating larger social realities. The 2011 census revealed that this county's population was 76.5 percent Orthodox, notably smaller than the 86.5 overall percentage in Romania yet still the vast majority of believers. Catholics (primarily ethnic Hungarians) made up 6.4 percent of the population, slightly higher than the national average of 4.6 percent. Compared to the 0.8 national percentage, a small but significant minority of 2.7 percent were Greek Catholic or Uniate (ethnic Romanians).[14] Other religious minorities among the region's inhabitants include Pentecostals (2.3 percent versus 1.9 percent nationally) and Seventh-Day Adventists (a little over 1.0 percent), denominations that attracted followers largely since 1990. A slightly higher percentage of Baptists reside in Hunedoara County compared to the national average of 0.6 percent. Calvinists are significantly absent from the Hunedoara region, though they make up around 3.2 percent of the national average. This population is concentrated in other parts of Transylvania, generally north of Hunedoara (Institutul Național de Statistică 2013). In designing our project, we intentionally sought a breadth of interlocutors who represented these religious differences, especially the presence of Catholic respondents.

We chose the Hunedoara region not only for its representative historical experience and demographic makeup but also because Mihaela Miroiu is a native of the area, which gave us better access to the participants. Her personal connections facilitated our initial contact with respondents and encouraged their willingness to express themselves freely and extensively. Funding from the National Endowment for the Humanities' National Council for Eastern Europe and Russia for Maria Bucur's transnational project *The Everyday Experience of Women's Emancipation in the U.S. and Romania in the Twentieth Century and Beyond: A Transnational Study* made our research possible.

We chose a qualitative, oral history method appropriate for the study of everyday life, with a special focus on citizenship (Pawluch, Shaffir, and Miall 2005). Both of us have extensive experience with these methods. Mihaela Miroiu began participant observation research as an undergraduate student in the 1970s, an approach she has continued to pursue in her sociological work. During her four decades of research, she has both designed and implemented many sociological questionnaires and qualitative interviews. Maria Bucur previously completed two oral history projects, one focused on memory and war and the other on reading under communism. She used open-ended questionnaires and life stories as her main interview and data collection tools in both projects.[15] Our experiences with sociological, ethnographic, and oral history methods led us to rely on focus groups and individual interviews, using the focus groups as a springboard to further elaborate our research questions and design (Bulai 2000). The individual interviews provided the means for more nuanced and open-ended data collection (King, Keohane, and Verba 1994; Rubin and Rubin 2005; Schatz 2009).

Three Focus Groups

The first focus group involved eight participants and took place on August 1, 2009, in the city of Hunedoara.[16] Other than a nurse and an auditor at the Ministry of Finance, the participants were retired women aged sixty to seventy-seven. They had worked as teachers, lab assistants, and electricians. The composition is fairly typical for this generation of urban women. Most had high school diplomas and professional qualifications that enabled them to work until retirement age. All were first-generation urban dwellers. All but two had adult children; some participants had grandchildren as well. The meeting took place in the apartment of one of the participants, a retired elementary school teacher. They were communicative, positive, and expressed themselves with humor and sometimes self-irony. Six were Romanians (Orthodox), one Hungarian (Unitarian), and one German (religiously indifferent).

The second focus group also took place in Hunedoara city, on August 4, 2009, in the home of one of the eight participants. Various professions were represented in this group: medical doctors, economists, a secretary, a nurse, and a judge. They belong to the first focus group's daughters' generation and had access to higher education and qualifications. Their ages ranged between forty-two and fifty-eight. With a single exception, they had children, most already grown. Four were married and three divorced, while one woman had always been single and had no children. Five were Romanians (Orthodox), two Hungarians (Catholics), and one Greek Romanian (Orthodox). Most of them knew each other. As a result, the atmosphere was relaxed and the tone somewhat confessional, occasionally veering toward a community brainstorming session where they both reflected critically on and sought solutions to their problems.

The third focus group, held in Sâncrai, a village ten miles outside Hunedoara city, brought together seven women aged forty-eight to eighty-three. Six of them were retired, while one worked in a nearby bread factory. All had children, and most were also grandparents. One had four children, while the others had one or two, a number more consistent with the national average. This group's main concern was their grandchildren, particularly the dearth of jobs available in 2009 due to the impact of the global economic crisis on Romania. Four of the women were widows and had very modest incomes, having worked primarily in the cooperative farm established during the communist period, which ceased to exist after 1990. All of them were Romanian and active in the Orthodox Church. In addition, four belonged to the Lord's Army.[17] The focus group took place in a shed familiar to the participants, creating a relaxed and easygoing atmosphere, reminiscent of the get-togethers of their youth.

They recalled family experiences, traditions, life under communism, and their relationships with their neighbors, the local administration, and the political parties. While the discussion started with complaints about how bad things were, there were notable moments of empowerment that highlighted how these women managed to survive in hostile times and project solutions for current problems, often by reaching out to each other rather than relying on government or outside resources. Each came dressed in her Sunday best, treating the meeting as an event she had long been waiting for: someone who would listen to her opinions on public affairs. These participants had no illusions about our ability to solve their problems but were happy to chat about them and "set the

Fig. 0.1 Sâncrai in 2017. Many houses are from the precommunist period, some still well maintained and others decaying. Paving the main road and bringing electricity to the entire village were accomplished during the communist period. Photo by Maria Bucur.

country straight" (as the local idiom goes) with "ladies" from the United States and Bucharest.

All focus group participants were later interviewed in-depth and suggested other women who subsequently became part of our sample. The initial participants' familiarity with the issues and with us, as well as our research assistants, Diana Neaga and Cristina Rădoi, who conducted most of the individual interviews, fostered a relaxed atmosphere. The focus group participants gave us their unanimous and explicit consent to film them and use their real names.

The main issues that came up in these three group conversations may be clustered around several themes, and each presented clear questions warranting further inquiry:

1. Family: How do these women understand gender norms and how have they shaped their own gender roles? What differences emerge among respondents? Variables included participation in work in and outside the home, participation in community rituals, and views on gender roles.
2. Close relations: Neighbors, relatives, and friends. Who are they close to and what do these relationships offer in terms of solidarity and support?

3. Surrounding community: Are they involved in professional and informal relationships with their neighbors, at church, or in town? How do these relations impact their lives as citizens?
4. Local political administration, from the village and neighborhood to the city and county levels: What does local political representation and participation consist of? How do elected officials engage with the needs and interests of these female citizens?
5. National political community: What does national political representation and participation consist of?
6. European and international political community: How do they perceive the impact of Romania's accession to the EU and of international politics more broadly on personal problems and concerns?

We used the focus group findings to develop our questionnaires for individual interviews. Indeed, the focus groups allowed us to pilot our original interview guide and then improve it, revising questions for relevance and language with the aim of enhancing and nuancing the information elicited and increasing the validity of the responses (Bulai 2000; Rubin and Rubin 2005). In the interviews, we formulated questions about these themes in a language that was direct and accessible for all the participants. We never used the term *gender* in our questions but rather referred to relations between men and women or between various institutions (e.g., government, work, religious) and women or men.

101 Interviews

The 101 life story interviews began in August 2009, one week after the last focus group meeting, and continued through March 2010. The weeklong hiatus enabled us to adapt our research hypotheses and interview guide in response to trends that emerged in discussions with the twenty-three focus group participants. Of the total, 96 interviews were audio recorded, mostly by our research assistants. We video recorded another 5 interviews with key persons in the relevant communities.

We selected interviewees through snowballing rather than probability sampling, by choosing participants who, in our estimation, could help test our research hypotheses, provide a rich content in their answers, and assist in adjusting our questions (Atkinson 2006). To a considerable extent, we followed the recommendations of our focus group participants, who were of great help in finding other participants. Our secondary goal in selecting the subsequent interviewees was to increase diversity in terms of age, residential area, education, ethnicity, religion, and occupational status.

Most interviews took place at the home of the respondent at a previously agreed-on time, and a few were conducted at the respondent's workplace. We did not impose a time limit on the interviews, so the women could delve as deeply into the topics as they wanted. The interviews lasted two hours on average, with a few taking up only one hour while several were four to five hours long. The longer interviews came from self-reflexive interlocutors who were willing to canvass their reactions to their own life histories and who expressed their views on politics in greater detail than the rest. With one exception, when a woman's husband continually interceded to correct her, all respondents were alone with the interviewer. The length of the interviews underscored a sense that many respondents were eager to have the opportunity to voice their opinions, especially on political matters; explain the nature of their experiences under communism; and analyze family and work life. The material gathered from the focus groups and interviews proved particularly rich and required laborious transcription work, completed in the fall of 2010. Subsequently, we returned to Hunedoara (2011–16) for informal follow-ups.

We collected explicit personal identification data: name, age, marital status, children, and profession/occupation.[18] We also gathered other implicit identification data, such as place of work, religion, ethnicity, and financial status. This enabled us to examine several correlations while interpreting the qualitative data. In terms of the construction of democratic citizenship, the strongest correlations were among age, residential area (urban/rural), and occupation. Educational level, marital status, children,[19] and financial standing were moderately correlated. Ethnicity and specific religious denomination turned out to have the weakest correlation to democratic citizenship, though religiousness shows up as a significant element.[20]

Consequently, while analyzing the data, we focused primarily on differences in age, residential area, and occupation. The group we identify as the "communist generation," aged sixty to eighty-three and comprising twenty-three urban and four rural dwellers, offered particularly rich perspectives on politics under communism and articulated their frustration vis-à-vis their limited involvement in subsequent changes as retirees.[21] The "transition generation," aged forty to fifty-nine, were still very active professionally, sometimes civically, but rarely politically. We interviewed fifty urban and six rural women in this category. They provided abundant interpretative detail on changes brought on by democracy and the exercise of democratic citizenship. The respondents aged twenty-four to thirty-nine most clearly saw democracy as a given, rather than an aspiration, presenting it as unproblematic, even banal.[22] We interviewed sixteen urban and two rural women in this category. We identify them as the "democracy generation." The demarcations among generations are not clear-cut. One cross-generational commonality was the time and interest participants allocated to the interview topics.

In the interviews, we pursued essentially the same themes as in the focus groups. We were interested in the significance women ascribed to their status as citizens and how they exercised their citizenship in conjunction with other roles in their daily lives, as mothers, wives, daughters, neighbors, coworkers, and friends. In other words, we were interested in the ways gender roles shape citizenship: the extent to which the former become a hindrance in practicing citizenship or, conversely, how new attributes of citizenship have impacted women's political interests and agendas. We looked at the relationship between political culture, on the one hand, and political and social structures, on the other hand, and the effects newly created economic and political institutions had on women's civic and political involvement, both locally and nationally.

Like men, women experienced radical change in political institutional structures between 1945 and 2010. In a nutshell, political institutions, in the institutionalist sense of the term (A. Miroiu 2016), went through successive mutations as regimes changed: transition from war to peace (1945–47); dictatorship of the proletariat (1948–65); so-called communism with a humane face (1965–71); national communism, a Stalinist-style dictatorship (1972–89); the postcommunist transition, marked by democratic pluralism and a market economy that triggered radical changes in professional status, widespread unemployment (especially for men), and retreat of state involvement in childcare (1990–99); EU and NATO accession and the adoption of Western institutions (2000–7); and EU membership and institutional consolidation (2007–10). For the communist generation, these changes spanned their entire lifetimes. The transition generation was marked by institutional changes after the dictatorship of the proletariat ended (Vincze 2006), while the democracy generation was primarily touched by post-1990 transformations. Thus, we were particularly interested in participants who, based on their personal experience, could comment on the impact of these historical changes on their daily lives and in the multiple roles they had or chose to assume.

We did not predetermine this generational selection. It emerged from the substance of the interviews, the participants' responses, and their interest in a critical and comprehensive inquiry into their lives as women, mothers, wives, colleagues, and citizens. Especially for the first two generations, the interviews were a chance to review their lives and create a record that could reach readers in other parts of the world. Sometimes women explicitly mentioned that they saw having their stories and opinions as citizens preserved as an opportunity.

Organization and Findings

Birth of Democratic Citizenship is the fruit of our effort to analyze the findings of the research we have outlined. We were deeply impressed with the lively discussions in the focus groups and interviews. The stories that the participants told were rich, and many were artfully rendered. In the following chapters, we quote many of these interviews extensively because we want to give our respondents the opportunity to speak for themselves and provide substantial testimony on their perceptions of life and gender roles under the communist and postcommunist regimes. In a sense, therefore, the book does not have just two authors but dozens—our respondents, who proved essential in crafting the final narrative. This book is the history of an implicit coauthorship.

We intersperse these rich qualitative sources with brief incursions into the realm of quantitative analysis, which helps situate the stories in this book in the larger national context, from participation in politics to attitudes regarding state institutions. We return time and again to the past and various historical contexts or processes that are relevant for understanding specific responses or attitudes. We revisit history with a theoretical goal in mind, to better understand why democracy emerged so late in Romania and what the historical conditions and forces were (or are) that seem to have both initially prevented and more recently enabled democracy to take root.

We begin our analysis with a chapter that outlines in broad strokes the history of women in Romania from the late eighteenth century until today, focusing on civil and political rights, economic practices, and education. This chapter provides an essential historical framework for understanding the gender norms that anchored the actions and perceptions of our respondents. The book then proceeds in the concentric fashion of our interviews, moving via key words from intimate and private spaces to wider communities. In order to simplify the great diversity of topics addressed in the open-ended life histories, we focused on the words these women used most frequently in the interviews, treating them as key concepts in their understanding and shaping of citizenship in theory and practice. We start with *men*, which allows us to delve into women's understanding of gender norms in the private sphere and how they themselves translated them into personal aspirations beyond the family, involvement in relations with others, and public roles. We move to *children* as a key word for how women discuss the intergenerational shaping of gender roles, especially with regard to moral values, as well as their understanding of the state's role in molding their own parenting responsibilities. This chapter also touches on the impact of predominantly female parenting on younger generations and its implications in public life, from early education onward.

With the chapter on *work*, we move out of the familial circle and into the relations women developed in their professional lives. This chapter shows most clearly the huge impact of the communist regime on women's expectations as active and autonomous participants in the public sphere. Our discussion also highlights the limits of women's economic empowerment under communism and into the postcommunist period as a result of government policies and a lack of regard for the double burden women had to assume as both workers and primary caretakers at home.[23] The chapter on *communities* details the lesser development of informal communities of interest, from neighborhood associations to religious communities and NGOs. In our last two chapters, dedicated to politics before and after 1989, respectively, we connect findings from previous chapters concerning informal, everyday forms of citizenship to women's attitudes toward the realm of direct participatory citizenship and their opinions on the political environment.

Our conclusions are that in Romania, average citizens have a nuanced understanding of the standards of liberal democracy. In the case we present here, we found many important similarities between these women's opinions about politics and rights as citizens, and the views and attitudes of their counterparts living in consolidated Western democracies. However, their experiences under communism and the short period they have lived as democratic citizens contributed to different forms of exercising these rights. Instead of appealing to government institutions to resolve problems and disputes, our respondents prefer to work through informal interpersonal networks first and to view themselves and others as responsible for their own well-being. They seldom claim rights without bringing up citizens' duties toward their community.

Ultimately, in this region, many men lost their economic and social status during the first decade of transition, and politicians, overwhelmingly male, are not engaged in addressing the common good but remain focused primarily on party and personal financial interests of those who helped fund their campaigns. Women have been left to their own devices to administer and develop both private goods and public ones. In this equation, these women see other people neither as an electorate nor as statistical "heads" that need counting but rather as individuals with specific unmet needs connected primarily to those they care about: children, husbands, parents, and neighbors. The notion of keeping political power in check is, for the time being, still foreign to them. The concept of empowering others through their efforts, however, is familiar. These women evaluate politics in normative terms, close to the liberal model of citizenship. Left on their own by all political parties, women closely associate their understanding of citizenship with their self-identification as caretakers. Overall, women have remained an undervalued and underused category of citizens in terms of generating greater levels of direct participation and vesting in the political processes of democratization. Our book points to the reasons that nurturing greater participation by women in politics would benefit all citizens living in Romania.

Notes

1. The 1948 United Nations (UN) Universal Declaration of Human Rights put the principle of full gender equality in the realm of politics on a global agenda for the first time. The UN took further steps in 1979 when it established an international convention for eliminating all forms of discrimination against women.

2. This is not to say that a feminist movement did not exist in Romania before 1990, an issue we discuss further in the next chapter.

3. As simultaneous members of these minority categories, women tend to be further marginalized based on their gender.

4. The Scandinavian countries and New Zealand come to mind as notable exceptions.

5. Child- and elderly care are two such key issues.

6. In the United States or Great Britain, for example, the feminist movement of the nineteenth century grew out of the experiences of white women. Their own conditions often informed their political goals. For African American or Native American women, the American political regime in the nineteenth century (and, in many regards, through the civil rights movement) appeared more authoritarian than democratic (Solinger 2016).

7. Including liberal, socialist, Marxist, communitarian, radical, and eco-feminists (Jaggar 1983; Millett 1970; Nussbaum 2001; Okin 1987, 1998; Pateman 1989, 2006; Plumwood 1993; Tronto 1993).

8. The individualist versus relational elements in the definition of *autonomy*, as articulated by feminist theorists with regard to the notion of internalized oppression, are beyond the scope of our discussion here (Lister 2008; Mackenzie and Stoljar 1999).

9. Including the works of Mary Wollstonecraft ([1792] 2004), J. S. Mill and Harriet Taylor Mill (1982), and, in Romania, Adela Xenopol, Eugenia de Reuss-Ianculescu, Maria Buțureanu, and Calypso Botez (Mihăilescu 2002, 2006). Other contemporary studies that have impacted our research are those from Nussbaum (2001), Okin (1998), Phillips (1998, 2003), and Tronto (1993).

10. Here, we refer to the form of globalized neoliberalism that developed following the fall of communism (Steger 2002).

11. The journal *Aspasia* began a comparative conversation on this topic in 2007, with the forum "Is Communist Feminism a Contradictio in Terminis?" (*Aspasia* 2007) and returned to it in 2016, with the forum "Ten Years After: Communism and Feminism Revisited" (*Aspasia* 2016).

12. See reports by the European Institute for Gender Equality (EIGE) and the *Global Gender Gap Report* referenced herein.

13. Braga 2014; Gheorghe 2014; M. Miroiu 2004a; Morteanu 2014; Vincze, 2011.

14. Greek Catholics (Uniates) represented a sizeable minority in the 1930 census, and almost all of them lived in Transylvania. In 1948, the communist regime forcefully drove the Uniate Church underground. Believers had to choose between converting to Orthodoxy, which was tolerated by the Romanian Communist Party (RCP), or maintaining an illicit affiliation with the Uniate Church (Stan and Turcescu 2007). After 1990, the state recognized the Uniate Church, leading believers to return to this congregation. In the Hunedoara region, a decline in the Orthodox population can be linked to this history as well as to the growth of Pentecostal and Seventh-Day Adventist congregations, largely made up of ethnic Romanian converts from Orthodoxy.

15. These projects were team-based collaborations with Ștefan Ungureanu, a sociologist at Transylvania University in Brașov.

16. The group originally included nine members, but one woman, intimidated by public speaking, left early.

17. For a more in-depth discussion about the Lord's Army, see the chapter on communities.

18. A handful of respondents did not wish to be identified by name and/or provide their age. For those individuals we did not provide two initials, using A. instead.

19. Family care of children negatively impacted active citizenship. The mothers of grown children had a greater tendency toward civic activism outside the family and workplace.

20. A clarification is in order about the absence of Roma participants in our study, even though they represent a growing proportion of the total Romanian population (3.3 percent in 2011) and are well represented in Hunedoara. The Roma population in Hunedoara can be grouped in three categories: (1) assimilated Roma families who do not self-identify as Roma publicly or in censuses; (2) less assimilated Roma families who live in state-assisted living arrangements, a sort of ghetto, mentioned in some interviews; and (3) unassimilated newcomers from Poland who live in a tight-knit community at the city limits. The first category is invisible, and therefore we were not able to identify them. Moreover, though our research assistant who has an interest in Roma issues attempted to contact women in the second and third categories, she was ultimately unsuccessful. Many in these communities, especially those who belong to the third category, have significant interdictions against mixing with non-Roma populations. While it is possible that for some of these groups, ethnicity would have shown a stronger correlation with active political citizenship, we were ultimately unable to test this hypothesis.

21. Throughout the book, we identify the ages of the participants at the time of the interview. Where the age does not appear in parenthesis, it is because the interlocutor did not wish to provide it. In those cases we simply estimated their age in terms of the generational divisions we define further on.

22. The youngest of the women in this group were sixteen during the revolution. We separated women who were fourteen and younger at the end of the communist period because they were never fully integrated into in the regime's institutions, such as the Communist Youth Union (CYU), and did not experience anything beyond elementary school prior to 1990.

23. By double burden, we mean the responsibility placed on women's shoulders as a matter of socially and politically sanctioned gender norms to be the primary caretakers in the home (of children, the household, the elderly) while also working full time. By contrast, men are not expected to participate in caretaking in the home in any significant way. Some refer to this situation as the double workday. Others define the double burden as a triple burden under communism, the third element being the regime's mandate that all citizens become politically active. As our discussion indicates, most women faced insurmountable time limitations to becoming politically active, given their double burden.

1 Women from Romania's Past into the Present: A Short Historical Overview

IN THE LAST two decades, historians and other scholars have started to delve into the history of women in Romania. Some have published research on the feminist movement, while others started to integrate gender into their social and political analyses of the recent past (Bolovan et al. 2009; Bucur 2017; Cheșchebec 2005; Jinga 2015; Massino 2007; Văcărescu 2014). However, to date, no comprehensive history of women in Romania exists. Therefore, what follows provides specific context for our study and offers a sketch of what a history of women in modern Romania might look like. This overview examines the institutions (political, religious, legal, and cultural) and practices (social, economic, and cultural) that structured women's participation in Romanian society from the eighteenth century through the end of the twentieth century. Without this context, the institutional framework that helped define gender norms and limited women's agency remains obscure. Throughout the rest of the book, we will reference moments on this timeline that help clarify our interviewees' responses.

Pre-1859 Wallachia and Moldavia: Women's Legal Subordination

Before 1859, when the Great Powers recognized the Romanian principalities' autonomy, there was no political entity named Romania. In the eighteenth century, the principalities of Moldavia and Wallachia paid a tribute to the Ottoman Empire and in return the Porte left their internal administration and elites relatively untouched. During the same period, Transylvania, which became part of Romania after World War I, was a territory of the Habsburg Empire. While Transylvania enjoyed some autonomy, it was thoroughly integrated in Habsburg administrative structures. These political regimes used religious identity, as well as class/economic status and ethnicity, to define women's legal personhood, their rights and property protections, and the social expectations placed on them.

In Wallachia and Moldavia, the state's interests were closely linked to those of the ruling prince and local elites.[1] As in most of the Ottoman Empire, notables here displayed little enthusiasm for women's education, rights, or any form of fundamental social change. In addition, the state apparatus was weak and its functions personalized and limited in scope (Vintilă-Ghițulescu 2004).[2] For most individuals in the principalities, the Orthodox Church represented the main, if not the only, institution in their daily lives. Thus, while women's fortunes hinged on the whims of the male ruling class, they depended even more on the teachings of the Orthodox Church—a veritable bastion of tradition and male privilege.

Church doctrine was the basis for laws governing all aspects of an individual's life, including marriage, property, and inheritance. The church gathered its teachings on these subjects into a compendium in 1652: *Îndreptarea legii: Pravila cea mare* (Setting the law: The great codex) (Rădulescu et al. 1962). These laws pertained only to Orthodox Christians in the principalities, the majority of the population. They did not apply to Jews, Catholics, or Muslims. (Protestants had a significant presence only in Transylvania.) Implicitly, members of these religious minorities were subject to the traditions and restrictions of their respective denominations.

Îndreptarea legii represented women as a fundamentally different category of people than men, in terms of their nature, identity, obligations, and rights as members of this flock. The church described women's nature as weak and bent on sinning. It taught that women's reproductive functions and sexuality drove their behavior and that they possessed an inferior ability to reason (Rădulescu et al. 1962). The gender norms and regulations that governed every aspect of human interaction, from marriage to economic activity, stemmed from these assumptions.

The church stipulated that all individuals marry and that this represented the most important contract they would enter over the course of their lives. Marriage also served as a means of controlling women. Consequently, the church recommended steering girls toward marriage early on—it deemed a twelve-year-old to be adequately grown-up, as menstruation often begins at this age, while by sixteen the bride's purity might come into question (Rădulescu et al. 1962). By advising parents to marry their daughters young, the church made sexual activity the decisive element in determining female gender norms. It implicitly reduced women to their biology. In contrast, the church counseled men to marry later, ideally between ages eighteen and twenty-four. As heads of their household, men needed to demonstrate good judgment and Christian moderation, moral qualities they were implicitly considered capable of developing, unlike women. By contrast, the church and society seem to have placed little importance on women's emotional or intellectual capacities.

As heads of their households, men legally controlled the fortunes of minors and wives in their homes. Women entered marriages as their husbands' obedient followers, bringing a dowry with them to cover their expenses. Though the dowry technically belonged to the wife, the law obliged her to relinquish control of it to her husband, as he was responsible for her economic welfare. More generally, women had little or no legal power over the wealth/property of their marital home. For example, though a wife could directly inherit property left to her by a deceased parent, she could not sign contracts or exercise other forms of legal expression without her husband's consent (Vintilă-Ghițulescu 2004, 2009).[3]

Divorce was not a realistic option for most women. In Wallachia, fewer than two hundred divorce cases were filed in the eighteenth century. Since the principality's population had grown to 700,000 inhabitants by the end of that century, this statistic suggests that divorce was greatly frowned on and seldom attempted.[4] Women, however, initiated far more of these cases than men. They generally brought charges of abandonment (e.g., the husband had disappeared for years and the woman was unable to sell her dowry or other property) or abuse (e.g., the husband beat his wife). Women's complaints tended to fall on the deaf ears of the priests (and occasionally princes, if the aggrieved party was a boyar) who adjudicated such matters. Wives were often told to patch things up with their abusers, some of their accounts were questioned, and sometimes women were publicly humiliated; none had recourse to appeal. In rare cases when a woman prevailed in court, there was no reliable enforcement of the decision. To pursue her husband, the aggrieved wife had to draw on her personal finances. If she could pay a *vătaf*[5] to successfully return her properties, the divorcée could attempt to start her life over, though she would still have to contend with the general opprobrium against divorce and especially divorced women.

As most women married early and never divorced, they remained legally and economically dependent on their fathers, husbands, and occasionally sons. *Îndreptarea legii* dictated that women could only dwell under the roof of either their father or their husband (Rădulescu et al. 1962, 243). Only widows could hope to inherit their own houses. Thus, for most of their lives, women were relegated to a subordinate status in their own homes. Any authority women might have had within the household was informal and transitory, as it lacked legal recognition.[6] The Orthodox Church, moreover, advised men to beat their wives often both to remind them of their inferior social position and to eliminate evil ideas from their minds (Rădulescu et al. 1962, 119).[7] No church teachings advocated for women to become self-sustaining human beings.

Women received very little education. Illiteracy rates among women were extremely high in the principalities and did not dip below 90 percent until the twentieth century (Murgescu 2010). Nearly all rural women were illiterate, as were most men. When educational institutions began to develop in the early nineteenth century, they were designed exclusively for boys (Tipei 2016). Only after the founding of a Romanian state in the second half of the nineteenth century (1859) did girls' education become a matter of public concern and policy. Consequently, women possessed very little knowledge of the law, state institutions, or written culture. The knowledge communicated by Orthodox priests on Sundays was likely the closest most women came to formal education.

Women's days were filled with the work of production and reproduction. Well into the twentieth century, women worked the fields, producing a variety of agricultural goods ranging from cheese to țuică (plum brandy). A small number of landowners controlled most of the land, and those dwelling on such properties, regardless of gender, toiled day in and day out (Hitchins 1996). In some communities, peasants held land, and there women worked next to men in the fields and at home (Stahl 1980). Some women participated in the cash economy through small-scale artisan work, including weaving, embroidery, and foodstuff. But profits reaped from market transactions belonged to the household and, therefore, to the husband.

The kind of live-in service work that provided young women in Western Europe greater social and economic autonomy starting in the early modern era did not develop in the principalities. Such arrangements violated Orthodox moral codes that mandated women live with their fathers or husbands. Among women, only slaves and serfs worked in the homes of others.[8] The church condoned the institution of slavery and was the largest slave owner in the principalities. Though we have partial body counts, travelers' observations, and some court documents about beatings, these women left no records. Consequently, we know very little about the daily lives of slaves, the quality of their existence, or the abuses they suffered (Achim 1998).[9]

Slaves, who were almost exclusively Roma, were traded and used for various forms of labor, including sex work (Achim 1998). Roma women worked in households and fields owned by boyars, the Orthodox Church, and the state. *Îndreptarea legii* and a number of other church records refer to the legal and moral status of slaves in terms of marriage, inheritance, and property rights. Women who were born or fell into slavery had no protection whatsoever from rape or any other form of physical abuse. In contrast, their owners could act as aggrieved parties if another free person damaged their "property."

Toward a Modern State: Women's Explicit Exclusion from the Polis

Though in the mid-eighteenth century Constantin Mavrocordat abolished serfdom in the Romanian principalities, illegal practices continued to tie propertyless peasants to the land until 1864. Consequently, on the large estates that dominated the countryside, men and women used for their labor were often abused.

Despite recorded abuses, serfdom and slavery persisted until after the election of the abolitionist Alexandru Ioan Cuza as prince of both Wallachia and Moldavia in 1859 (Hitchins 1996). In 1864 Cuza pushed through a civil code that emancipated the slaves, outlawed any means for continuing informal serfdom, and expropriated much of the Orthodox Church's land. Cuza was deposed five years later largely due to the unpopularity of these reforms and his disregard of the church's economic and political power.

However, Cuza was no friend of women's rights. The civil code he helped pass remained largely intact until the communist takeover. It more explicitly rendered women second-class citizens—further limiting their property rights and granting them no political rights. It was only in 1932 that married women in Romania gained the ability to control their property and sign contracts without their husbands' approval (Ciocalteau 1936).

While the legal and political situation of women did not improve between 1864 and the 1930s, they enjoyed new educational opportunities thanks to the efforts of feminists like Eugenia Reuss Ianculescu (1866–1938). Women's schools (primary and secondary) opened in larger urban centers like Bucharest and Iași, and affluent families sent their daughters abroad to receive further training. For example, Alexandrina Cantacuzino (1876–1944), who became a prominent feminist leader after World War I, was part of this early generation of aristocratic women with the means to study in France (Cheșchebec 2006).

In the late nineteenth century, most feminists focused on women's education. Their efforts garnered more public support than the ambitious suffrage agenda of smaller factions (Bucur 2007; Mihăilescu 2002). Education-oriented feminists had radical goals, including increased public expenditure for women's education beyond the "traditional" female disciplines (e.g., music, languages, literature, home economics). They also fought for women to have access to a variety of new professions linked to the modernizing state. Thus, women passed exams not only to become teachers in girls' schools but also to practice as doctors, lawyers, architects, and engineers. Romanian women did not lag behind their German or American counterparts in this respect. Especially from the 1890s on, Romanian, Western European, and American women's struggle for educational and professional equality bore a significant number of similarities.

Sarmiza Bilcescu (1867–1935) was one of the most ambitious and, in some respects, successful feminists of the period. She challenged the interdiction against women pursuing a degree in or practicing law. A brilliant pupil, at seventeen she was the youngest and only female student admitted to law school at the Sorbonne. In 1890, she returned to Romania a celebrity, having become the French institution's first female graduate (Ciupală 2003). Despite adamant opposition from the male establishment, she put in an application to join the Ilfov county legal association. Her credentials surpassed those of most male members, making it difficult to articulate a persuasive argument barring her from practice. Yet a prolonged legal battle and public debate on women's place in the profession ensued. While her eventual victory testifies to her extraordinary professional and human capacities, the outcome disappointed Bilcescu and other feminists. Unable to attract clients (most likely because she was a woman), Bilcescu worked to help other women receive an advanced education. Not until two decades after Bilcescu's suit did another woman, Ella Negruzzi (1876–1949), successfully begin practicing as a lawyer and even then only after numerous legal battles from 1914 to 1920 (Bucur 2006a).

Entering the law profession was more than a matter of personal ambition. Feminists like Negruzzi, Bilcescu, and their contemporary Calypso Botez

(1880–1933) understood that the male ruling class used the law to exclude women from numerous areas of public and economic activity, including the vote. Their professional trajectories essentially challenged the civil code that rendered women subordinate to men (Bucur 2001b). Serious tests to this code, such as Negruzzi's, first appeared during World War I. Like other women of her time, Negruzzi realized that unless women made and adjudicated the law alongside men, the legal institutions, practices, and values of the Romanian state would remain a two-tier gender regime.

During World War I, the extreme limitations the civil code and other legislation imposed on women grew increasingly apparent. Legally, women could not manage their husbands' affairs without explicit consent (Alecsandru [1865] 2011, 65). This included selling agricultural and industrial goods. Thus, while the wife of a mobilized soldier could harvest their fields, she could not hire help or sell their crops, even those reaped from her dowry land, without her husband's written permission. The impact of these restrictions was devastating, as more than 80 percent of Romania's inhabitants dwelled in the countryside and most were illiterate.

Romania mobilized more than one million men during the war (half when it entered the conflict in 1916), approximately 13 percent of the total population, or the equivalent of the entire male population between the ages of eighteen and forty-five. Given the average size of the Romanian family at that time, around one million women and three to four million minors, or 63 percent of the population, was left in an untenable situation. When their husbands left for the army, married women had few means of income. Though wealthy women could sell some personal assets, most had far fewer resources. To sustain their families, women had to barter their limited belongings or enter into informal agreements, trading labor for food and heating supplies. Some were reduced to scavenging (Bucur 2006b).

At the onset of the war, the Romanian political class came to understand how the civil code's profound gender inequalities limited women's economic agency and started to address some of these issues through small measures. In December 1914, the parliament passed legislation that offered some economic relief to the wives of government employees, a small fraction of the population (Bucur 2000). According to the law, mobilized husbands could consent for their wives to receive a portion of their salaries or pensions. But women had to appeal in writing for such support, a problem compounded by high female illiteracy rates. The law also offered additional protections for the property rights of rural men who had been mobilized, but it made no provisions for their wives.

The 1914 law proved woefully inadequate. In September 1916, less than a month after Romania entered the war, it was modified—all rural women now gained temporary control over their husbands' property. The 1916 law, however, never came into full effect, as the government was forced to hastily evacuate

Bucharest at the beginning of December. It left hundreds of thousands of families under the Central Powers' occupation until 1918. Women whose husbands had left for the front managed many of these households. The population of Moldavia, where the government, army, and around one and a half million refugees retreated, faced additional challenges, including overcrowding and outbreaks of deadly diseases like typhoid fever. In the decades following World War I, women's aspirations were fundamentally shaped by their traumatic and at times empowering wartime experiences.

Women in Transylvania before 1918

Situated in the principality of Transylvania, Hunedoara sat on one of the easternmost extremes of the Austro-Hungarian Empire until 1919. This region had become part of the Hungarian crown in the early modern period.

Before the modern era, a landed nobility ruled Transylvania. Ethnic Hungarians (who practiced Catholicism and Protestantism) made up the bulk of this elite group, along with a smattering of German-speaking nobles and a smaller number of Romanian converts from Orthodoxy to Catholicism or Protestantism. These elites benefited from exclusive political and economic privileges underwritten by the state.[10] While ethnicity was not a category explicitly used to determine political or economic rights, the state did not provide Orthodox Christians and ethnic Romanians with tax benefits or institutional support. These groups, effectively second-class citizens, accounted for more than 50 percent of the region's population (Hitchins 1969).[11] Of the remainder of the population, Hungarians represented a little more than half (28 percent on average between 1720 and 1910) and ethnic Germans constituted the second-largest minority (about 11 percent of the population during same period). Serbs, Ukrainians, Jews, and Roma made up the rest.

Before 1867, under the Hungarian crown and later Habsburg rule, religious affiliation largely determined women's fortunes (Brie 2011; Csizmadia et al. 1979). The head of state identified as the Holy Roman emperor. The Catholic Church, the official (i.e., privileged) denomination, had significant authority in civil matters. It, rather than civil authorities, administered marriage and inheritance. Thus, legal traditions and Catholic dogma both offered benefits to and imposed limitations on women of this faith. Catholic women (generally ethnic Hungarians, though also German and occasionally Romanian), and especially members of the hereditary nobility,[12] possessed far greater personal protection in terms of social status and economic autonomy than their counterparts in Wallachia and Moldavia. For example, they enjoyed the same inheritance regime as men. Their dowry was protected as their personal property, and they had greater control over its administration than women in the principalities. Of course, the Catholic Church did not allow divorce, and thus women could not leave abusive marriages.

The state left the protection of Orthodox, Protestant, and Jewish women's civil status to their religious denomination (Brie 2011). If Protestants (mostly Hungarians and Germans) benefited from some property rights, better inheritance regimes, and even access to divorce, Orthodox (Romanian and Serbian) and Jewish women did not fare as well. Orthodox ecclesiastic traditions, similar to those in Wallachia and Moldavia, governed women's legal status and property rights. This population had no political representation and little economic and social authority. Moreover, they had fewer recourses to ecclesiastic justice than the wives of Moldavian and Wallachian boyars—a socioeconomic group absent in the region.

As a result of political (and occasionally military) struggles initiated by various nationalist movements, women's status improved over the course of the nineteenth century. After 1848, civil institutions underwent a period of secularization and a modern court system eventually homogenized the civil codes. Language/ethnicity now determined the rights of individual citizens rather than religion (Bader-Zaar 2012; Loutfi 2006). For married Hungarian, German, and assimilated Jewish women, this victory led to new rights, including even division of property at divorce, equal inheritance among daughters and sons, and the legal ability to sign contracts.

Ethnic Romanians faced more obstacles to empowerment. State institutions, like schools and banks, were explicitly and exclusively designated to serve Hungarian speakers. Thus, ethnic Romanians had to acquire fluency in this language—only then could they access education and the new professional and state organizations that offered economic and political instruments for self-representation. These Magyarization policies intensified after 1867, and more Hungarian-language schools opened in Romanian-speaking areas.[13] However, the aggressive nature of this campaign deterred Romanians from taking advantage of such tools for social and economic advancement. Nationalist ambitions to have Romanian recognized as an official language, moreover, intensified their reluctance (Hitchins 1969).

The representation of ethnic groups among different social strata in the region was strongly correlated with their education level and their degree of urbanization. More than 80 percent of ethnic Romanian women in Transylvania were illiterate before World War I (Colescu 1944). Furthermore, most lived in rural areas and were underrepresented in city settings. In short, ethnic Romanian women and men tended to be less educated and less urbanized than their Hungarian, German, and Jewish counterparts (Gusti 1938). More Romanians lived in poverty than any other ethnic group in Transylvania, save the Roma, and fewer Romanians were present among the entrepreneurial and wealthier strata.

Nationalist lines divided the feminist movements that developed in Austria-Hungary, especially after 1867 (Bader-Zaar 2012). Czech women fought for education and political rights as part of a larger Czech nationalist movement

(Havelková 1996). Hungarian feminists developed several strains of ideological self-identification, some closer to liberal ideas of citizenship (Loutfi 2006), others more akin to socialist views of workers' rights (Fábián 2007). Both groups focused exclusively on Hungarian women, even when they lived in parts of Transylvania largely populated by ethnic Romanian women who suffered the same, if not greater, forms of discrimination.

Like many contemporaries around the world, Romanian women were subject to complex forms of discrimination based on religion, class, ethnicity, and gender. Today, we would discuss their experiences in terms of intersectionality. For instance, Rózsa Schwimmer (1877–1948) became a prominent figure among international feminists and antinationalist pacifists during the interwar era. She was born in Temesvár/Timișoara, a Transylvanian city of thirty-nine thousand primarily German-speaking inhabitants, with a substantial Romanian population.[14] By the turn of the century, the population of Temesvár had grown to more than sixty thousand residents. Half identified as German speakers, while Romanians accounted for 13 percent in 1880 and 10 percent in 1900. The Hungarian-speaking population rose from 20 percent in 1880 to 32 percent in 1900. These demographic changes suggest a Hungarian-friendly environment.

Growing up, the middle-class Schwimmer identified as Jewish and Hungarian-speaking. She pursued her education in Temesvár and later Budapest. Shortly after she returned to Temesvár to take up secretarial work, her family encountered financial difficulties. Drawn to the ideals of the developing social democratic movement in Hungary, she became a feminist (Zimmerman and Major 2006). Though interested in women's rights broadly, her efforts centered on improving the economic status of working women, something she saw as a vehicle for addressing gender inequality more generally. Yet she did little to reach out to women in the same predicament outside of Hungarian-speaking communities.

Ethnic Romanian feminists strategically affiliated themselves with the nationalist movement in Transylvania (Păltineanu 2015). Romanian women's calls for the vote aligned with nationalist ambitions to gain greater representation and thus political weight in the Budapest parliament. To the Romanian-speaking taxpayers of Transylvania, political rights were the key to other forms of empowerment, such as access to state funding for Romanian language schools and economic and cultural projects. In the end, women in Austria-Hungary did not gain suffrage before the collapse of the empire during World War I.

Interwar Romania: Old Misogyny in New Bottles

Transylvania's incorporation into Greater Romania after 1919 improved conditions for the ethnic Romanian majority that lived in Hunedoara and other parts of the region. However, women as a category of citizens in this new state did not see their rights enhanced. Though promised the vote at the Alba Iulia gathering

Fig. 1.1 Peasant woman weaving, Hunedoara County, in the 1930s. Dimitrie Gusti, ed., *Enciclopedia României* (Bucharest: Imprimeria Națională, 1938), vol. 2, opposite p. 228.

on December 1, 1918, women still lacked full political rights and some lost the economic rights they had enjoyed as citizens of the Austro-Hungarian Empire. Men and women from the previously privileged Hungarian minority suffered the greatest economic and political setbacks. For example, before 1919 Hungarian women had enjoyed more property rights than their counterparts in Romania when it came to inheritance and the use of their dowries. They could also sign contracts and pursue some forms of employment after marriage—rights denied to women in the Romanian Kingdom until 1932 (Bucur 2017). While German communities in the region generally remained among the more educated and affluent groups, women from them faced similar setbacks.

While all men were granted full political rights during the interwar period, women's empowerment was limited. The 1923 constitution did not provide for women's suffrage, despite vociferous campaigns (Bucur 2001a, 2001b). Only after 1929 did married, high school–educated women (less than 10 percent of the total female population) gain the right to vote and run in municipal elections. However, educational qualifications (a high school diploma) impeded women's political advancement in a country where female education had not received sustained public interest. Women like Calypso Botez, who campaigned at the municipal level, represented a tiny fraction of the female population.

In 1932, in response to pressure from feminist groups and lawyers interested in aligning the civil code with the promises made at Alba Iulia, women gained new rights. Henceforth, all women could sign contracts as adults and control their own property, giving them greater economic independence (Bucur 2017). Yet unless both were deceased, their husbands or fathers still managed their dowries. These changes to women's legal status came, however, in the midst of an economic crisis that rendered opportunities like employment scarce. Consequently, their real impact was minimal, especially as women were not seen as primary wage earners or reliable long-term employees.

Education was one field where women made significant strides. The state did not regulate the teaching staff at private schools, and some female educators worked in these institutions. After 1918, when the government provided greater direct support for and regulation of public schools, women increasingly found employment as teachers in both public and private establishments. Still, women seldom held prestigious positions at universities or research institutes. Those who worked in postsecondary education tended to find employment at second-rate institutions. For example, the philosopher Alice Voinescu (1885–1961) trained at the Sorbonne and then Oxford. Though Voinescu's credentials surpassed those of many of her male colleagues, she never received a position at any of Romania's prestigious universities. Instead, relegated to a second-rate post at the Bucharest Conservatory, where there were no majors in philosophy, she taught history of theater and aesthetics rather than philosophy (Voinescu 1997).

The nationalist corporatist movements of the 1930s, from eugenics to fascism, took a more favorable view of some women's professions than the so-called democratic parties, including the National Liberal Party (NLP), under the condition that women's interests not extend beyond specific "female" fields.[15] The Institute for Social Assistance, established in Bucharest in 1929, received support from the eugenics movement and developed professional training programs for female social workers (Bucur 2002). The eugenicists sought to control and eliminate social problems, such as alcoholism and prostitution. They identified women as especially suited to guiding working-class individuals toward fulfilling their paternalist biopolitical vision of family values.

When King Carol II's coalition of nationalist right-wing parties established a royal dictatorship in 1938, women gained the vote in national elections. As the foundations of the multiparty parliamentary system collapsed, women's suffrage created the impression that the dictatorship enjoyed popular support. The situation was short-lived. Around the same time, the government stripped Jews of their economic, political, and civil protections and, by 1940, had transformed them into noncitizens. In June of that year, the Soviet Union seized Bessarabia from Romania. In August, northern Transylvania was ceded to Hungary for the duration of World War II. Four years of internal turmoil followed, and a large proportion of the male population was drafted into either the army or forced labor. Left to manage households, women of all ethnicities bore the brunt of the abuses leveled by troops (Romanian, Hungarian, German, or Soviet) marching across the country. Despite evidence of wrongdoing by all parties, Romanian historiography still lacks an account of these experiences as gendered developments.

Communism and Gender Equality: Ideology versus Policies

Though female suffrage was recognized after World War II, the communists seized power in 1946-47; consequently, women would not participate in free, multiparty democratic elections until after 1989. While previous regimes almost completely excluded women from parliament and government, the presence of a handful of women, including Ana Pauker, in decision-making positions seemed like progress.[16] However, the realities of the RCP's role in women's lives and women's interest in political activities were more complicated than men's, given the double burden women shouldered (Jinga 2015). By the late 1980s, RCP members comprised 23 percent of the Romanian population; however, women made up less than 27 percent of this total—a statistic consistent with other Eastern Bloc countries (Leven 1994).

This gender imbalance persisted despite high-level efforts to recruit women. For example, Nicoale Ceaușescu had aimed to bring party membership up to 35 percent by the end of the 1980s and singled out women as a target of these efforts. Yet women appeared apprehensive to join. Luciana Jinga (2015) offers important clues about women's reluctance to become members of the RCP. She points to the time demands imposed by the double workday, which limited mothers' abilities to engage in political activism. Women who did juggle familial, work, and political commitments had to rely on networks of formal and informal care and often had an exceptional spouse for support. Our analysis shows how rare and difficult such political participation was.

Postwar communist regimes in Eastern Europe created educational and professional opportunities for women, providing them with greater economic independence. Full citizenship for women in Bulgaria, Yugoslavia, Poland, Hungary, Czechoslovakia, Romania, and Albania allowed them to participate in elections. But it meant much more in terms of social benefits: The state ensured women's access to education was on par with men's. Women could henceforth enter into contracts, from marriage to property, on equal footing with men. The state guaranteed women's ability to control their property (e.g., a savings account, apartment, or car) and income, thereby protecting their economic power. The dowry, a fundamental component of women's economic relationship to men, was abolished. Of course, without private control over the means of production, property rights came to have a completely different meaning. For men, the primary property holders before 1945, this shift represented a major loss. For women, these changes brought about mixed results: some lost wealth (personally and especially through their male relatives), while others gained greater access to wages, loans, and other forms of property through the legal elimination of gender discrimination.

Unquestionably a huge gap existed between the letter of the law and its implementation. Our study delves into these issues from the perspective of women who supposedly benefited from such transformations. But first, we need to explore what these changes represented in their historical context. At the beginning of the twentieth century, the illiteracy rate among women was as high as 80 percent in parts of Transylvania (and around 92 percent in the Romanian Kingdom). The communist regime mandated obligatory primary, and later secondary, education for all children, effectively eradicating female illiteracy. This marked a radical departure from the past.

Before 1945, legal restrictions prevented women from enjoying the rights and responsibilities of full citizens. In 1954, a revised civil code took effect. It addressed issues of marriage, divorce, inheritance, paternity, and so on, following the Soviet model (Ghimpu 1967). The family code gave men and women equal legal status and eliminated the dowry.

But what sort of rights did women have? Citizens' obligations to the state—both to work and to build a proletarian-based society—largely defined their status. The regime united (or subjugated, depending on one's ideological perspective) individual interests with those of the one-party state. Marriage no longer expressed two individuals' desire to build a life together but rather their active participation in constructing socialist society. Similarly, after 1966 giving birth no longer represented a couple's decision to reproduce but the people's will (or the RCP's) to enhance the size of the working class (Biebuyck 2010). As men's and women's roles within the family became equal in the eyes of the law, they were simultaneously redefined within the collectivist ideology of the RCP.

As full citizens, women gained access to professional fields that heretofore had been predominantly, if not exclusively, male. The military was an important exception. The state required eighteen months of boot camp training from men. The small fraction of male citizens admitted to university studies undertook nine months of similar training. All men who had performed their military service became lifetime members of the reserves. Women were subject to military service as well, though it differed qualitatively and quantitatively. From 1968 on, all male and female secondary-level students had to participate in "preparing for the defense of the homeland" (*pregătire pentru apărarea patriei*), a de facto military service that included learning how to handle a gun. Women completed their service through this program, unless they enrolled at a postsecondary institution. Women who attended universities continued their service, once a week during the academic year and one month in the summer, throughout their college years. This regime ended after 1989.

Women did not have access to an officer's career in the army or the security/police forces, however. Exceptions existed, both before the communist period—such as Ecaterina Teodoriu and Smaranda Brăescu—and after, especially among athletes on military/police teams.[17] Women comprised a small fraction of the secret service forces, though the extent to which they served as officers, as opposed to informants or assets, remains unclear.[18] Women only gained open (though not complete) access to these professions after 1989, largely due to international pressure exerted on Romania as a NATO and EU candidate state. Both institutions called for the elimination of gender discrimination as a condition for accession. Today, women serve in combat positions in the military and on police forces, though they still do not enjoy equal footing with men (Rădoi 2011, 115).

After 1945, all educational institutions became coed, with no restrictions on female enrollment. There were no official gender quotas. Consequently, women dominated certain schools with a "feminized" professional profile, such as pedagogical institutes. Vocational schools with a "masculine" profile (especially in mining, heavy machinery, or oil drilling) enrolled primarily, if not exclusively, men. Women who dared cross these invisible gender lines faced obstacles at school and had difficulty being placed in jobs, something our interviews illustrate.[19]

However, women had full access to an advanced education in technical and scientific fields, and they increasingly enrolled in such programs. Romania outpaced Western European and North American countries in terms of female enrollment in engineering programs and employment for female engineers. This difference holds for other communist regime countries, such as the Soviet Union and China, where engineering reached gender parity by the end of the 1980s.

Postgraduation opportunities for professional advancement were another story, however. Even in areas deemed "feminine," from teaching to textiles, women rarely occupied management or other high-level positions. Political requirements tied to these posts were an important factor; as women made up only a small percentage of the RCP's membership, their ability to become managers in any area of public activity was disproportionately smaller than men's. In addition to political impediments to professional advancement, certain fields, like law, education, and journalism, had grown increasingly politicized. Before 1945, men had made up the majority of the workforce in these domains. As the state began to take class background into account when vetting these professionals, many "bourgeois" men found themselves barred from their occupations. Since women traditionally had limited access to these jobs, they had less to lose. Women with "unsuitable" backgrounds, however, also encountered difficulty when they sought to pursue advanced degrees and careers.[20] Furthermore, as the communist regime took control of all areas of the economy—training, production, services—it likewise assumed authority over professional certification. Thus, while women could earn a law degree and become lawyers, working as attorneys constituted an ideologically driven form of service subject to strict government supervision.

In principle, the extension of full citizenship to all state subjects meant ethnic and religious minorities would no longer receive different treatment. It also implied that minority women would enjoy greater legal protection from ethnic and gender discrimination. In reality, ethnic minorities such as the Roma remained marginalized.

The Hunedoara Region before 1945

The Hunedoara region conforms to the general observations above. The population in this region was more than 90 percent rural until the communist takeover. In 1945, the town of Hunedoara had a population of five thousand. The vast majority of residents were ethnic Romanians. Small Hungarian and German minorities also lived there, together with a small community of Jews. The town's eight churches reflected its demographics: four Orthodox churches (attended by ethnic Romanians), one Greek Catholic (also catering to ethnic Romanians), one Catholic (primarily for ethnic Hungarians), one Lutheran (with a largely ethnic German congregation), and one Baptist (ethnically mixed). In addition, there was a synagogue and a nearby Franciscan monastery, the latter also servicing primarily ethnic Hungarians (Mărginean 2015, 48).

Deva, the county capital, had a population of 13,000 in 1948, an increase of 2,500 in habitants from the 1930 census. Before 1918, this town's majority was Hungarian, as the Austro-Hungarian administration had encouraged several waves of migrants between the 1880s and 1910s. These ethnic Hungarian migrants gained exclusive rights to certain properties and became part of Deva's upper-middle classes. After 1918, the situation changed—around 50 percent of Deva's inhabitants registered as ethnic Romanians in 1920 (the ethnic Hungarian population accounted for about 42 percent of the population while Jews and Germans made up the remainder). By 1948, ethnic Romanians represented 75 percent of the total population and Hungarians 24 percent.

The region's mountainous and hilly landscape limited farmers to small plots, orchard cultivation, and animal husbandry with a focus on food products, including dairy and meat. There were some instances of large-scale agricultural production in the areas surrounding Hunedoara city. Women took an active part in this rural economy (Kligman and Verdery 2011). As schools were scarce in the countryside, however, they had few educational opportunities.

Nonetheless, by Transylvanian standards, the city of Hunedoara had an unusually high concentration of educational establishments. Among the city's schools were four primary and three secondary schools that admitted girls (Mărginean 2015, 48).[21] These educational institutions appeared after 1918, when the Romanian state absorbed the region as part of a Bucharest-based initiative to enhance the Romanian population's competitiveness in relation to other ethnic

Fig 1.2 The Hunedoara Steelworks in the 1930s. Dimitrie Gusti, ed., *Enciclopedia României* (Bucharest: Imprimeria Națională, 1938), vol. 2, opposite p. 226.

groups in Transylvania and centralize the country's educational and economic institutions. By 1945, an educated class, including women with elementary and some degree of secondary education, had begun to develop.

Coal and iron deposits were Hunedoara's most important economic assets in the late nineteenth century. The first steel plant in Hunedoara city opened in 1884. The factory belonged to an Austro-Hungarian concern that viewed this frontier land as a new El Dorado (Mateș 2012). The search for gold proved lucrative for companies that bought mining rights in the Apuseni Mountains, all of them owned and run by nonethnic Romanians. During a century of operation, the mines produced more than eight hundred tons of gold. The mining industry attracted talented and ambitious male workers from across the Austro-Hungarian Empire—from Slovakia in the north to Italy in the south—as well as local Romanians and Hungarians. The story of a migration of young men in search of riches was repeated during the communist era.

Hunedoara: A Model Region of Communist Development

At the beginning of the communist period, the Hunedoara region was overwhelmingly rural and its inhabitants mostly small landowners. Between 1949 and 1962, the processes of nationalization and collectivization transformed the rural population into pauperized agricultural laborers (Kligman and Verdery 2011). However, the Bucharest administration eventually turned Hunedoara into a model industrial economy.

As early as 1945, Secretary General Gheorghe Gheorghiu-Dej, speaking before the RCP congress, stated that factories in the Hunedoara region "will ensure the necessary steel production for the following 30 years" (Mărginean 2015, 49). He wasn't far off. Within just five years of communist rule, Hunedoara County extracted 60 percent of the nation's coal and 90 percent of its iron ore. It also put out 30–50 percent of Romania's iron-based industrial products. While Hunedoara's proportional contribution declined over the next four decades, as the communist regime diversified its industrial base, total production continued to grow. Even in 1989, Hunedoara County produced more than 30 percent of Romania's steel, 90 percent of its coal, and almost 70 percent of its iron ore (Mateș 2012).

Migration from the countryside and other parts of Romania supported this growth. Many workers came from Moldavia and Oltenia. Within one generation of communist rule, the ratio of urban to rural inhabitants reversed; by 1989, Hunedoara's rate of urbanization (77 percent) was second only to Bucharest (Mateș 2012), fueled primarily by inhabitants from other regions. Immigration from other parts of Romania grew steadily throughout the communist period, outpacing migration from Hunedoara to other regions by more than twenty-three thousand persons, generally young males (ages fourteen to twenty-four).

Deva and Hunedoara, where many of our subjects spent at least part of their lives, developed into relatively large cities over the first two decades of communist rule, requiring new services, such as hospitals, expanded school systems, and public infrastructure like roads, electricity, and running water (Mărginean 2015). The initial phases of urbanization focused primarily on housing for the influx of migrants. While several plans were proposed, by the 1950s city-planning projects came to emulate Soviet models. Hunedoara's urban development became an experiment in negotiation between local authorities and Bucharest-based ones. In the early 1960s, centralization gave way to localized decision-making. City planners' priorities more closely reflected the needs of the exploding population—a population that grew nearly tenfold in eighteen years, from seven thousand in 1948 to sixty-nine thousand in 1966. Especially from the early 1960s on, planners focused on adding hospitals, schools, and other public services.

By the 1970s, the profile of the region had changed from overwhelmingly rural to urban. In 1930, the county population was approximately 332,000 and around 12 percent lived in towns and cities, but by 1969, the region had 475,000 inhabitants and more than 69 percent of them lived in urban zones. The influx of young male workers created a gender imbalance. Among individuals ages twenty to twenty-four, a huge gender gap developed—in 1956 there were 22 percent more men than women. As women migrated for marriage, however, this statistic leveled off, and by 1966, men retained only a 2 percent majority among this age group (Mărginean 2015, 201).

Employment figures illustrate the region's urbanization. In 1968, 51.2 percent of the total labor force worked in steel production and 16.0 percent in construction, both male-dominated fields (Mărginean 2015, 197). A significant part of the workforce, by this time largely made up of women, remained in agriculture. Women who migrated to urban areas between the late 1950s and mid-1960s for marriage or education had difficulty finding full-time work in the urban economy. Some of them became housewives by default, a trajectory reflected in our interviews.

The majority of our subjects were thus participants in a very dynamic set of processes that thoroughly transformed this region. Almost all interviewees born before 1960 were born in the countryside. Though city life became an everyday reality for many of them and the lens through which they experienced modernization, most still have relatives (usually parents) in rural areas. Consequently, they have retained intimate knowledge of conditions in the countryside and the political problems rural inhabitants have faced since the beginning of communism, including issues of collectivization.

Romanian Women after Communism

The collapse of communism radically changed women's political, legal, and economic status. In our study, we identify these changes as preconditions of democratic citizenship.

After fifty-one years of royal, fascist and communist dictatorship, Romania held its first free elections on May 20, 1990. In 1991, the first fully democratic constitution with explicit full political rights for women was passed. Still, women accounted for only 3.7 percent of the elected members of parliament[22] and 2.6 percent of the elected members of local councils, despite a significantly higher percentage of women actively engaged in all political parties. This trend has persisted throughout the postcommunist period.

In 1996, with the election of a new president, Romania experienced its first power succession under peaceful, pluralist conditions. During this period (1996–99), most political parties adopted pro-Western (pro-NATO, pro-EU) platforms. Several parties, save the Social Democratic Party (SDP), began to lay the foundations of a neoliberal regime. Consequently, budgets and ideological justifications for a host of welfare services established under the communist regime, from state-funded childcare to access to subsidized housing, began to evaporate (M. Miroiu 1999). Left-wing parties (e.g., the SDP), following a precedent set by the communist regime, limited women's presence in politics to purely formal and passive roles. Center-right parties (e.g., the NLP), like their interwar precursors, ignored women's political interests and representation in politics.

During the transition period, restoring property rights became a central focus of public policy, without concern for its social cost. As properties confiscated by the communist regime started to be retroceded and state properties (e.g., factories) privatized, clear gendered trends emerged. Parliament passed laws representing the interests of a ruling male elite, paying no attention to gender discrimination. A small, mostly male, group of communist-era industrial managers and state security officials enriched themselves either by becoming clients of those who engineered the privatization process or by entering politics to appropriate state properties for personal gain (Nicolae 2010; Pasti 2006). The rest of the population, especially women, continued to live at various levels of political marginalization and poverty. Nonetheless, in our fieldwork, we did encounter several individuals of the transitional generation who represent a thin stratum of middle-class entrepreneurs.

Between 1999 and 2006, the political transformation toward liberal democracy gained speed, at least formally, through EU accession. Before 2016, this represented the most spectacular phase of democratic development. For example, despite coming in dead last, in 2003 Romania finally appeared on the Economist Intelligence Unit's list of liberal democracies (Economist Intelligence Unit 2010). In places like the Czech Republic and Bulgaria, a similar process of aligning national and EU institutions and legislation offered new forms of support for women's rights, from legislation against domestic violence and sexual harassment to providing funds for women's and gender studies programs. In Romania, this period coincided with the solidification of a neoliberal approach to social welfare; many state services (e.g., childcare, access to low-interest loans) were privatized, especially those related to caregiving needs, leaving women with even fewer means of dealing with the double burden than under communism.

This was also the moment when policies inspired by second-wave Western feminism were accepted and instituted, starting with the Beijing Platform (1995) and the *Acqui Communitaire*.[23] In 2000, Romania passed a comprehensive law against discrimination based on race, ethnicity, gender, religion, class, and sexual orientation. In 2002, the parliament passed the Law for Equal Opportunity for Women and Men. The 2003 constitution included an article on the principle of equal opportunity. The same year, the law for preventing and combating domestic violence also passed.[24] Key institutions for implementing these laws were established: the National Council for Combating Discrimination (NCCD) in 2001 and the National Agency for Equal Opportunities for Women and Men in 2004.

Over the last decade these institutions have made further inroads as County Councils for Equal Opportunity (CCEO) represent them at the regional level. Alas, with the implementation of new austerity measures starting in 2011, the NCCD lost its budgetary autonomy and the CCEOs were closed down, signaling that gender discrimination was considered a secondary, rather than a core, issue by the political leadership of the ruling parties' coalition, the NLP and the Democratic Party (DP).

Overall, there is a gap between institutions focusing on antidiscrimination, which are strong and efficient, and the institutions established to promote equal opportunities, which operate at a formal level but remain inefficient, mainly because political clientelism dictates their leadership rather than a competence-based process. Parliamentary representation continues to be overwhelming male (81 percent in 2017). Men lead the committees for equal opportunities in the senate. The senate committee has one female member. In the lower chamber, men make up 60 percent of the committee (Băluță, Iancu, and Dragolea 2007a, 2007b; M. Miroiu 2004c, 2015a, 2015c; Neaga 2013).

Contrary to the expectation of civic activists, after Romania gained EU membership (2007), the process of democratization went through a period of stagnation and even retreat. According to the Economist Intelligence Unit, in 2011 Romania no longer qualified as a liberal democracy but was identified instead as an illiberal electoral democracy (Economist Intelligence Unit 2011–15; Forbrig and Demeš 2009; M. Miroiu 2011). Our research took place during the initial period of this retreat, when citizens in Hunedoara felt less and less inclined to place their trust in political parties, the parliament, or city and local administrations (INSCOP 2015). Their eroding faith in democratic institutions stemmed from a sense that electoral promises turned out to be lies and populist campaigns brought to power governments that promoted passivity among the citizenry. However, our analysis will show that the weaknesses of Romanian illiberal democracy have not produced apathy, docility, or obedience among the women we interviewed.

Although in the 1990s the policies of privatization and marketization favored male investors, women have played a growing role in the economy as entrepreneurs (Paul 2011). As of 2016, one-third of all Romanian entrepreneurs were women, a statistic that exceeds the EU average. Women are well represented in more professions today than they were in 1989 and make up a majority of students enrolled in every level of education. The most significant forms of economic gender discrimination still concern compensation for feminized professions, as less monetary value is placed on the type of caretaking jobs that women tend to do, from medicine to education. In addition, by eliminating many forms of state support and subsidies for childcare, the neoliberal regimes of the 2000s have compounded the economic and familial challenges women face. Without a radical shift in the gender makeup of the government on the national and local level, policy change is unlikely.

Hunedoara after Communism

If Hunedoara was a dramatic example of urbanization and industrialization during the communist period, it also represents a dramatic process of deindustrialization, economic stagnation, and depopulation after 1989, especially in urban areas.

Starting in 1990, several of the largest steel plants closed and others were privatized. The total number of people employed in this sector declined from more than twenty thousand to under two hundred. Mining also suffered a tremendous blow—within two decades, more than twenty major mines closed. Since 1990, with the exception of three years, the rate of unemployment in Hunedoara County has been greater than the national average and in some years almost twice as high (20 percent in 1999, the peak year for the transition period). Unemployment has decreased over the past decade, close to the 7 percent national average (Mateș 2012). Behind these official numbers lies a complex reality. As with other regions where heavy industry dominated the economy, between 1990 and 1996 governments catered to the workers, mostly men, who lost out when plants closed and large state enterprises privatized (M. Miroiu 2004c). Many were granted early retirement with a full pension, despite official policies, and others received "compensatory" salaries though technically unemployed. For women working in lesser-favored industries (e.g., textile, leather), there were no such accommodations. As enterprises privatized and without compensatory salaries, women were fired and had to seek employment elsewhere.

The reduction of economic opportunities since 1990 strongly correlates with several social problems, especially school dropout and crime rates. According to a 2009 study, Hunedoara County had the highest crime rate in Romania, with more than 250 convicted persons/100,000 inhabitants (Mateș 2012). In these areas, men greatly outnumber women.

Since the late 1990s, when Hunedoara registered its lowest output levels and highest unemployment rates, industry has slowly begun to recover, partially through product and market diversification. Still, the region has seen a gradual decline in population. Lower birth rates account for part of this phenomenon, but migration to rural areas to practice subsistence farming and to other regions has been a significant factor (Mateș 2012; Pasti, Miroiu, and Codiță 1997). In 2011, the population of the county was 72 percent of what it had been twenty years earlier. This dramatic decline is noticeable especially in urban areas, where the population has steadily dwindled since the end of the communist period. Our respondents' experience of the transition to capitalism and democracy over the past twenty-seven years has to be placed in the context of this massive displacement of human and economic resources. Hunedoara's path from state-controlled modernization, under the communist regime, to the postcommunist collapse of the command economy and its partial recovery in a neoliberal capitalist context is extreme. Yet it is also exemplary for understanding larger processes in Eastern Europe.

Notes

1. Princes appointed by the Ottoman Porte were generally Greek-speaking elites from the Phanar District of Constantinople. Phanariot princes sought to augment their personal wealth while keeping the borders safe and maintaining their loyalty to the sultan. To accomplish this, they collaborated with local notables, most of whom were Romanian boyars, or the native nobility, though some were Armenian, Macedonian/Vlach, and Greek notables and merchants.
2. The military constituted a notable exception. Military service played an important function in men's lives, notably during periods of international turmoil.
3. Exceptions to this general picture existed. However, they involved remarkable fathers and/or extraordinary wealth. Among the boyars, some men left clearly articulated deeds that granted equal inheritances to their male and female children and ensured that their daughters could control what they had received. The ruling prince had to approve such deeds directly, which underscores just how exceptional such cases were, even among the very wealthy (Fotino 1925).
4. An important study on marriage and divorce in the eighteenth century offers a detailed portrait of the workings of marriage based on divorce cases that the authorities heard (Vintilă-Ghițulescu 2004).
5. An official term in the Romanian Principalities, denoting either the administrator of an estate, or the chief of an armed force. Some acted as an internal security force or marshal.
6. Except in rare cases of adultery with witnesses present.
7. *Îndreptarea legii* contains a chapter titled "How, When, and in What Ways Is a Man Allowed to Beat His Wife" (Rădulescu et al. 1962, 119–20).
8. Slaves were officially the property of their owners, which translated into very different gender roles for those who lived in such conditions. While men were used primarily for hard physical labor and sometimes other skilled work (caring for horses), women were used either for fieldwork or, if the owner favored a woman physically, as domestic worker and sex slave. Serfs were indentured peasants who lived on property owned by the boyars, the Orthodox Church, or the state and who owed the property owner a number of days of work (*corvoadă* in Romanian) for the "privilege" of living there and could reap the fruits of their own labor for the rest of the time.
9. In the nineteenth century, a budding community of painters with liberal sensibilities depicted Roma women. These images often appealed to the aesthetic sensibilities of lawmakers who shared the liberal and abolitionist ideas of figures like Mihail Kogălniceanu and Nicolae Bălcescu. Such paintings tell us little about the actual conditions and experiences of women in Romania. Rather, they convey the ideas and style of the painters, which one might charitably call "romantic," though "voyeuristic" is a more accurate term, given the often low-plunging necklines of women's blouses.
10. Many among the Romanian elites belonged to the Greek Catholic Church. This church developed in the Habsburg Empire as a compromise between the Orthodox and Catholic Churches. By pledging allegiance to Rome and becoming part of the centralized hierarchy of the Catholic Church, and implicitly of the Habsburg Empire, Greek Catholics retained many of the ritual aspects of Orthodoxy. The compromise allowed believers some continuity while ensuring greater political loyalty (W. Muller 1981).
11. Since the nineteenth century, Romanian and Hungarian authorities have contested the demographic statistics of this region to advance nationalist claims. Estimates from before the eighteenth century vary wildly, alternately identifying ethnic Romanian and Hungarian as the majority. However, starting in 1720, both Austrian and Hungarian statistics become more

regular and consistent. They reveal an ethnic Romania population range of 50–63 percent of the total inhabitants, with an average of 52 percent ("Megyénkénti lebontás," accessed May 6, 2018, http://varga.adatbank.transindex.ro/).

12. This group represented around 5 percent of the population in Hungary and Transylvania.

13. Magyarization refers to a set of policies imposed by the Budapest government with regard to the exclusive use of Hungarian in all government offices, from political to law enforcement, from state-funded and licensed schools to cultural institutions. The laws also applied to communities that predominantly or exclusively spoke other languages, like Romanian, German, or Serbian.

14. Technically, her birth city, Temesvár, was in the Banat rather than the principality of Transylvania, but after 1867, this region became part of the same administrative unit as Transylvania.

15. Of course, such opportunities would only be open to women whose ethnoreligious identity was considered "clean" or "pure" according to these racially exclusivist ideologies.

16. Ana Pauker became the RCP's shadow leader at the end of World War II, effectively providing direction, though she did not formally serve as secretary general. Her gender and ethnicity prevented her from assuming either the role of general secretary or prime minister. As a Jewish woman, she was aware (and made aware by leading figures in Moscow and Romania) that taking on a high-level public office would significantly diminish the RCP's legitimacy in a country where antisemitism and sexism were so prevalent (Levy 2001).

17. Steaua and Dinamo were two of the best-performing sports clubs in communist Romania. Steaua represented the armed forces and Dinamo the police. Athletes of both genders competing for these teams at national or international adult competitions had to be officers in their respective organizations.

18. There are a number of memoirs and histories of the Romanian Securitate, but none focuses on questions of gender or women's participation in this organization as professionals.

19. Malgorzata Fidelis (2010), working on women in Poland during the same period, had similar findings when she interviewed women who worked in mining.

20. What counted as "appropriate" background changed over time. Ostensibly, a bourgeois background or connections to the fascist and Nazi movements active in Romania during the interwar period and World War II were two criteria for exclusion. However, at times unofficial categories also bared on such decisions, particularly those defined as "foreigners," which sometimes included Jews, Hungarians, and Germans whose families had lived on Romanian territory for centuries. Close family links to religious denominations, especially among non-Orthodox clergy, could also mean an interdiction on access to certain professions. We offer some examples of this type of discrimination in chapter 4.

21. These were the Industrial High School for Girls, the Industrial School for Apprentices, and the Superior Technical School.

22. By comparison, the percentages of women who were elected to parliament after the collapse of the communist regimes in other countries in Eastern Europe were as follows: 8.8 in Bulgaria, 7.3 in Hungary, 9.9 in Lithuania, and 13.5 in Poland. In Yugoslavia, where the collapse followed the wars of the 1990s, the percentage was much smaller, 2.5 percent, while in the Ukraine, it was similarly low, at 3 (Matland and Montgomery 2003).

23. We identify the process of accepting antidiscriminatory and equal opportunity legislation on the part of states that sought membership in the EU as "room-service" feminism (M. Miroiu 2004c, 257).

24. However, the women's shelters that provide practical support for victims of domestic abuse are completely insufficient. For example, there is not a single shelter in Hunedoara County. Chapter 3 provides a detailed discussion of women's views of such insufficiencies.

2 Men: Working through Gender Norms at Home

WE START OUR examination of perceptions of and attitudes toward gender and citizenship by looking at how women describe their relationships with men, especially their husbands. Heteronormativity remains at the core of gender relations in Romania, and marriage with the intention to procreate is still a nearly universal expectation.[1] After 1989, in other postcommunist countries, social assumption and behaviors concerning marriage, cohabitation, and even mono-parenting underwent a transition. Before reunification, expectations in East Germany regarding marriage and reproduction closely resembled those in Romania. The state provided significant loans and other monetary rewards for young married couples and forgave large parts of these loans when they had children (Adler 1997). Following the 1990 reunification with West Germany, these incentives disappeared and the marriage rate decreased by 50 percent, as did the fertility rate.[2] In the Soviet Union, while social expectation linked to marriage remained in place, the rate of divorce significantly increased, especially after 1970, from 2.6/1000 to 3.5/1000 by 1980. Since 1991, the trend toward fewer marriages and more divorces has persisted, and one scholar has described today's numerous unmarried single-parent households (largely headed by women) as a "quiet revolution" (Utrata 2015). In contrast, Romanian women continue to marry younger and at higher rates than the EU average (the fourth-highest rate in the EU), including other postcommunist member states.[3] These statistics were fully borne out in our fieldwork, as all of our interviewees spoke about the expectation and/or experience of marriage as an uncontested norm.

Over the last two decades, quantitative studies indicate important changes in the Romanian population's views on marital relations. In 2000, 92.0 percent of men and 91.0 percent of women identified men as the rightful "head of the household," while 71.0 percent of men and 79.0 percent of women agreed that women were the "household managers" (Open Society Foundation 2000, 30).[4] Seven years later, only 49.7 percent of men and 33.7 percent of women still believed that men should be the head of the household.

To discuss the evolution of gender roles in the home with our interviewees, we focused on the following questions: How do women understand the ideal man and ideal woman? How do they describe their marital life? Who makes the important decisions? Who administers the family finances? Who takes care of the daily chores? Who takes the kids to school and who makes sure they do their homework? Who takes care of the elderly in their family?

Though fathers, sons, coworkers, politicians, and lovers made appearances, husbands were the central male figures in the narratives these women shared. Respondents spoke freely about what they thought men should be like—describing personal and moral traits as well as behaviors. Whether normative or descriptive, the household gender roles our respondents presented are significant in helping us understand how women situate themselves as citizens at the nexus between the public and private spheres, drawing our attention to the porous relationship between the two. How our respondents spoke about their roles as subjects, agents, partners, and bearers of responsibility and authority in the family allows us to fully appreciate how they negotiate their participation in the polis and in social networks beyond the home.

When women discussed their personal aspirations, their narratives intertwined their familial and professional or, more broadly, public roles. They rarely spoke of themselves independently of their relationships with others (Mackenzie and Stoljar 1999; Tannen 2001), especially in marriage. Men appeared in almost every scene they described; sometimes mentioned by name and sometimes simply as part of a "we" in the background. Though they never referenced "gender" as a concept, our respondents articulated a broad understanding of gender norms and offered specific interpretations, or rather instantiations, of gender roles. Partnership was at the center of both their normative and descriptive interjections.

Overall, their comments on men acknowledged a status/power differential: that women still somewhat depended on money and other resources provided by their husbands and fathers. Frustration and at times resentment, rather than gratitude, best characterize their attitudes. While a handful described their marriages as successful partnerships, many interviewees depicted them as tense or frayed. Very few invoked the word *love* to describe their relationships with their husbands or even fathers. Their closest allies in the family tended to be other women—mothers, daughters, and grandmothers.

Our findings suggest that a profound shift in how women understood and shaped gender roles took place in Romania during the communist period. Before the 1940s, women saw themselves as subservient to men in their marital relations, but by 2010, they had come to expect partnership and appreciation for their role in building and maintaining the household, including completing chores and home improvements, supervising their children's education, and planning vacations. Yet only respondents from the transition generation appear to see both economic and familial gender equality as an integral part of their expectations.

Partnership and Decision-Making in the Family

We asked every respondent about household decision-making. Their definitions of what constituted an important decision varied, though not much. Our interviewees largely focused on: (1) financial matters, including who administers the family income generally and the purchase of significant items (measured only partially in terms of cost—the complexity or core function of a purchase sometimes counts more); and (2) children, especially opportunities and choices concerning their education. These very priorities are evidence of gendered elements in what matters in a marriage.

As women spoke about the significant decisions made in their relationships, they used at times rich and at others stark terms. But they always decisively characterized them as part of the shared responsibility and power in a marriage—a partnership:

> That is not a family where each person keeps their money separately.... When we do something, we do it together. (A.G., seventy-four)

> [In our family] we work through trust. We do everything for the home and for our needs ... in our decisions we always listen to each other. (D.M., fifty-six)

> Q: What do you think is the secret of a successful marriage?
>
> A: There is no recipe for it. First of all, the secret is that the two partners need to understand each other, discuss any problem.... So long as you solve your problems together ... as a partner ... and are willing to concede a little bit of your personality. (L.J., thirty-eight)

In such portrayals we see trust—listening and compromising are invoked—as keys to a good relationship. Men and women presumably both play an active and equivalent role in nurturing these qualities. These same characteristics also appeared in our interviewees' descriptions of good citizenship and especially political leadership.

A few women, mainly from rural areas, did speak about themselves as subordinate to their husbands. Their comments recalled old clichés about how "the woman always follows the man" but also reflected the larger sociological landscape of labor migration and unequal gender opportunities for work that we described in chapter 1: "I got married and my husband worked in the factory, so I followed him" (A.G., seventy-four). Such statements were rare, however. Most respondents, regardless of generational or educational difference, saw themselves as partners in home making.

Across generations, women spoke with conviction and in detail about working with their husbands to tackle a range of household chores:

> Q: Who did the housework in your family?
>
> A: At the beginning only me, but after a while both of us. A long time ago men, you know, didn't do anything, but now they are more involved....

> The times changed and men now work in the home. Not only in my family, everywhere.
>
> Q: What about childcare?
>
> A: When he [her son] was little, me; after that, together. (C.B., seventy-eight)

This respondent was born a decade and a half before the communist takeover, when domestic gender roles were clearly divided, and women acted as the primary caretakers of children and the home. The way she described changing gender dynamics—as something that began to look more and more like a partnership over time—can be thought of as the most positive possible interpretation of how male-female relations have evolved in Romania since World War II.

Yet the details revealed in many of our other interviews point to a significant gap between expectations and desires of partnership and the reality of daily life. The language women used is symptomatic of this disconnect. For example, they talked about men helping, implying that women naturally assume homemaking responsibilities, while men simply assist. Despite this, our interviewees noted that men and women collaborate and share marital responsibilities more often now than in the past, a change they viewed as progress.

Women born during the first two decades of communism more clearly articulated the concept of partnership and viewed it as the norm. For example, M.T. (fifty-six) spoke about her relationship with her husband:

> A: First of all my husband helped a lot, because if he hadn't, I had no mother, no mother-in-law; [I would have had] nobody.... We completed each other. When he was free, he'd take care of our girl, and when I was, I would.
>
> Q: In your family, how did you divide housekeeping chores?
>
> A: Dividing is not the important thing, when a need arises and he has time, he does it, and me also.... When he was completing his university degree, we were married and our daughter was little, and he would play mother instead of me and play with her or finish up my chores, and I would work on his final paper. It was a difficult project that included lots of appendices with drawings, and because I was good at that, I did the sketches he needed, because we didn't have photocopying then.... So I helped him as best as I could, we helped each other.

This story brings both the potential and the limits of partnership into focus. M.T. identified household chores as *her* responsibility, not as a shared duty, and described her double burden—work and homemaking—as a matter of fact. Additionally, M.T. willingly, even gladly, worked on her husband's school project. While she helped with his assignment, he "played the mother." In the story, M.T. supported her husband's professional/educational goals without taking pride or ownership in the final product. She used the language of assistance, trading her skills in drawing for his in parenting. She was thankful her husband stepped in while she assisted with his homework. However, she considered his actions exceptional rather than as part of the normal course of his daily responsibilities. Implicitly, as Diana Neaga (2013) remarks, M.T. sees parenting not as a yin-yang relationship with her spouse but as an activity defined by mothering. This is not to deny the warmth of this familial setting. Yet it is not a partnership of equals.

On occasion, women, especially among the transition generation, compared their relationships with their husbands to those of their mothers and fathers. They were critical of their mothers, describing them as unassertive wives who replicated their own powerlessness by insisting on their daughters' obedience. M.S. (forty-eight) castigated her mother for being a "slave" to her father:

> When I met my husband I can't say I fell for him. But I liked how he treated me. [On a camping trip with friends] we were taking turns in the kitchen. When I started cooking, he came immediately and took a knife and made a tool for crushing the garlic and then cleaned the vegetables next to me.... I saw him as very interested and was surprised that there were such men who helped women, because my father never did that. My mom claimed that men have no business in the kitchen, and made such a huge mistake.... I never believed that a woman is the servant of her husband, which is how my mom saw it. After I got married, I was home on maternity leave: "Oh, M., your husband is home.... Leave the diapers alone and go heat up the food, your man is home." I said: "What, is he handicapped or something; he can't manage by himself?" I can't agree with the principle that one spouse is the other's fool.

This working-class woman, a second-generation city dweller, traces a clear generational shift in Romania under communism, as she came of age in the 1960s and 1970s: a first generation of rural migrants continued to accept traditional gender roles as they had existed in the countryside while their daughters' generation departed from their view. In M.S.'s case, other parts of the interview suggest that, like many of her contemporaries, marital partnership remains more of an aspiration than a reality.

Her story illustrates how the influential and sometimes tense relationships between mothers and daughters shape familial gender norms. In many interviews, women indicated they spent a great deal more time in the company of other women than other men and mostly among female family members. In the narrative above, our interlocutor expressed her frustrations with the norms her mother had tried to inculcate in her and the self-conscious distance she placed between those norms and her own aspirations.

At a different point in the conversation, she also rejected her father's performance of masculinity: "I said: 'Dad... you were never a farmer, you fled from your village when you were nineteen because you didn't like to cut the hay, and now, when you're old, you want to get into agriculture?'... 'My ancestors struggled to buy each piece of this land, and these officials don't want to give it back!' In the end, he came to my views, but he was still mad at me when I pointed this out." Still, her father insisted on retiring to the countryside. During the remainder of their lives M.S.'s parents worked hard without much to show for it. M.S. saw her father as stubborn and thought his decision was particularly deleterious for her mother's health. She also resented his choice as a burden she and her family had to bear, as they spent their vacation time "playing" farmer alongside her parents instead of relaxing.

New opportunities and responsibilities outside the home—as students, citizens, and workers—often changed how women thought about their roles as wives. M.S. built her view of partnership in part by observing other women and men at school and work. Thus, a rejection of the norms her parents accepted and the observations she made outside her home informed M.S.'s understanding of gender roles. Sitting in her kitchen, she recalled several times when she refused to perpetuate the gender inequality she witnessed in her parents' home. Like many of her contemporaries, her efforts were often frustrated, but she worked through these issues with some success.

Women tend to do more household chores. They also tend to describe themselves as the primary financial decision-makers in the family, a finding echoed in national quantitative studies (Open Society Foundation 2000, 30). Some simply stated that they controlled the fiscal management of the home. While their husbands made essential economic contributions to the household, they were not home enough to make decisions on a daily basis or even in a crisis. Consequently, women generally managed the funds both spouses generated. In an exclusively cash economy, this was not a small or illusory form of authority.[5] Wives literally controlled the purse strings of their families, because they were the ones who purchased everything, from food to electricity, books to vacations. They discussed their role unapologetically: "Me, me. My husband left it all in my care; that is how it was from the beginning with us" (A.N., fifty-three).

Another respondent described her authority in household management in great detail:

A: The household work, I was mostly in charge of, since my husband, being a driver, couldn't help me—he would leave in the morning and come late at night. He couldn't really help; what he helped with was shopping for big items, but for the daily needs, I shopped.

Q: Who made the decisions regarding money, the home, kids' schooling?

A: I divvied up the money and made a list of what we needed and consulted with him . . . he never said no: "If you think it is good, do it; I won't get involved, since I'm not home anyway," and with the kids' education it was also me because he came home late, and by then the kids were in bed . . . and the kids also got used to me and didn't have the courage to tell their dad what they needed. (D.L., sixty-three)

A different interview discussed the wife's control of the family's finances as a matter of necessity. She suggested her husband was not a dependable manager/spender, partly due to excessive drinking:

Q: In your family, who decides about money, the home, education, the kids?

A: They say that man is the pillar of the home, but the woman is the one who directs things. And I say that, in my opinion, the woman is the one who creates the home environment... because if the husband comes home tired, a little drunk, and you jump at him... then you are doing harm. You need to leave him alone and talk to him later.... In our family I involved him in all that was possible. I alone put aside money, 'cause he was the kind of personality, he gave everywhere, so I put aside money and when we wanted to buy something, I would say: "Look, we need to buy this." And he would say: "But we surely don't have money." And I would say: "Don't worry, I borrowed some," but I was actually borrowing from myself. I always took care of that.

Q: How did you do it, you would take his salary and...?

A: I took the salary and paid all our bills. With whatever was left, I would buy what was needed. (E.M., seventy)

In this narrative, the husband's drinking or largesse made him unreliable, while his wife was a more rational decision-maker and thriftier spender. Rather than fully engage him as a partner, she relied on white lies to accomplish her goals in the home. When she noted, "I involved him," she situated herself as the primary decision-maker and her husband as a secondary player. In such examples partnership means joint-involvement, not equality, as each spouse holds a different position of power (men as bread winners) or authority (women as primary decision makers where spending is concerned).

Especially in agricultural societies, researchers have often unearthed similar stories in which women assume authority out of necessity. For instance, comparative studies of the behavior of male and female heads of household in sub-Saharan Africa found that women tend to be significantly better stewards of the family resources, especially in poor areas. They use funds more efficiently and save more, and they are more likely than men to invest those savings into either their children's education or household improvements. By contrast, men tend to spend more familial funds on personal nonproductive expenses, such as various forms of entertainment (Nussbaum 2001; Blackden and Bhanu 1999). Our interlocutors suggested similarly gendered differences regarding the management of familial funds.

In all our interviews, women described taking on greater decision-making roles because they primarily shouldered responsibility for the home and children. They also had a flexible view of their own trajectories in life and were willing to place their marriages, household duties, and children above professional obligations and ambitions. In this regard, Romanian women are very much like women around the world.

Many interlocutors inadvertently contradicted their claims about equal partnership when questioned in-depth about specific responsibilities like parenting.

When they described who went to meet teachers, learned about schools, and participated in other educational activities, hardly anyone talked about sharing these tasks with their husbands. Sometimes, the dad would represent the family at meetings with the teachers and principal, school outings, or sports events or help with homework. More often, however, the mother assumed responsibility for these tasks:

> Q: How do you participate in your child's schooling and solving school problems?
>
> A: Well, I don't really participate, I don't have time. I go every time there is a meeting with the parents, I make time, and other than that I communicate, well we both communicate, my daughter and I. She tells me what her problems are, I try to answer, and if I can't manage I consult with my husband; and if there is a serious problem we go to school.
>
> Q: Your husband, does he go to school to the parent meetings?
>
> A: Not so much. My husband is part of the leadership team in the factory . . . so he goes to work at eight and never has an exact time for returning from work, and he works a lot, he's gone a lot of the time, many meetings out of town, so it is obvious I am the one directly implicated. Emotionally, mentally, he is with us, but physically I am there all the time. (L.J., thirty-eight)

The respondent uses the statement that "emotionally" her husband supports her and their child to attempt to balance her answer. However, this family's reality, like many others, is that mothers are children's primary caretakers, while their fathers remain in the background.

This woman, who has a full-time job, contradicts herself in other ways as well. She starts by saying she has no time to participate in her child's schooling. Yet she concludes her answer by noting, "I am there all the time." The interviewee works through the question as she responds, reflecting on her own role as a parent. She confronts her husband's absence in this part of their child's life. She seems somewhat embarrassed and feels the need to offer an explanation. Her account points to women's flexibility in prioritizing marriage, parenting, and work, a flexibility that none of our interlocutors attributed to their husbands or other men. This quality reemerged in interviewees' discussions of politics.

When women sought to promote their own professional or civic ambitions, they could almost never count on their husbands for the kind of support they were expected to show their spouses. We heard no examples of supportive behavior by a man—on the contrary. B.F. (thirty-eight), about the same age as the respondent above, was a doctor, politician, wife, and mother. She was divorced and clearly stated that the marriage failed because of his unwillingness to take on a supportive, secondary role in the home. Her example suggests the limits of gender parity in Romanian households. Women assume a double burden. When they wish to shift part of their domestic responsibilities to their husbands (as L.J. describes), they encounter complete and unwavering resistance.

A 1970s study by a team of sociologists in Romania arrived at similar conclusions about authority and decision-making in the household (Elliott and Moskoff 1983). The study found that women and men were on equal footing when it came to decisions about important issues. At the same time, women shouldered far more homemaking responsibilities. The authors attributed this paradoxical situation to urbanization and the new educational and work opportunities women had during the early decades of communism.

The tension between the desire for partnership and the realities of marital relations is crucial for framing other aspects of these women's lives as citizens. Some women present this tension as something they are aware of, which shapes how they make other choices in their life—from the professional to the political. Others contradict themselves as they try to reconcile this disconnect. Overall, they appear to make choices aimed at alleviating their double burden, choices that clearly impact the type of citizenship they can or have time to assume.

Silences and Caretaking

What our interlocutors left out when they narrated how they and their husbands approached decision-making and household responsibilities says as much about gender norms as what they discussed.

First, in our interviews, respondents talked about caring for their elderly parents and their husbands'. In most societies, women have played the primary role in caring for the old since premodern times. This is still very much the case in Romania, in both urban and especially rural areas. The state never developed institutionalized forms of eldercare and few private facilities exist. Older people, especially those with medical aliments, often end up spending a good deal of time in hospitals. Though it often involves major financial expenses, radical rearrangements of living spaces, and a significant time commitment, none of our respondents, including those who work in healthcare, linked eldercare to marital decision-making. This might imply that women feel this sort of familial obligation is nonnegotiable.

It further suggests that, although Romanian society has moved toward a nuclear model of the family since the communist takeover, traditional norms concerning multigenerational kinship and gender still govern relations between adult children and their parents. In rare cases, respondents noted that their husbands took care of their parents. More often, however, women assumed responsibility not only for their own parents but also their in-laws. They presented this as an unquestioned gender norm:

Q: Who took care of the elderly or ill?

A: Well, mostly the woman, 'cause the man is a man, he might come to wash an old person, but the woman still keeps everything in the home. (D.L., sixty-three)

Like many others, this interviewee essentialized men ("the man is a man") and presented eldercare as a task they do not engage in.

A few acknowledged assistance from in-laws: "My father, me and my brother took care of him, of course with some help from my husband and my sister-in-law" (M.V., forty-five). However, examples of husbands or brothers helping with eldercare were scarce: "I took care of those ailing, who else? I took care of my mom, an aunt, my husband—I took care of all of them" (M.B., seventy-eight). Across generations, responses like this were typical.

These findings suggest that the gender norms regarding eldercare did not alter much over the course of the twentieth century. However, the larger socioeconomic context has changed dramatically, from increasing physical distance from one's parents to the new time-consuming work and family responsibilities that women have assumed. What constitutes caretaking has also changed. For example, visits to the doctor or the hospital were quite infrequent before 1945.

How do women balance eldercare with housekeeping, paid work, parenting, and partnership in marriage? From the stories our respondents offered, it seems that they assume this role less explicitly than those associated with paid work or their children's education. Their responses point to a significant shift in kinship relations, which before the twentieth century were more explicitly based on a set of multigenerational obligations both men and women had toward parents, in-laws, aunts and uncles, siblings, and grandparents (Bolovan et al. 2009). This shift has significant implications for how women understand citizenship and politics. When we turned to questions about public services and community needs, moreover, nearly all of our respondents identified eldercare as an urgent concern that has not yet been considered seriously by policy makers. We discuss this further in the chapter on communities.

The second important absence in our discussion of familial decision-making concerned professional choices. During the communist period, the state was the largest employer in Romania. This limited professional opportunities and, consequently, as most of our interviewees began wage work during this period, restricted their career choices. Though individuals could select various fields of study at all educational levels, structural and institutional constraints dictated employment possibilities, especially for those seeking to work in specific professional settings.[6] Thus, respondents from especially the oldest two generations spoke about their work history as something they had negotiated, without reference to their spouses. They also did not mention their husbands consulting with them on their decisions concerning employment.

This absence is rather remarkable, especially since work-related choices dictated many aspects of a couple's life together, including where they lived, the extent of their economic resources, and how much time they spent together. The communist regime's state-economy produced gendered structures that profoundly impacted the daily lives of many couples. In the interviews, respondents spoke about assuming various collective responsibilities (e.g., homemaking, taking care of crops), because daily commutes or long hours took their husbands away from home for significant periods of time. Other interviewees described following their husbands from rural to urban areas so their spouses could find work. In many of their stories, respondents were not consulted in such decision-making processes but had to live with their consequences. These decisions shaped women's expectations about their own lives.

Such choices had a long-term impact on women. Some respondents complained that they lacked sufficient retirement income in old age. They noted the structural dependency pension policies had created over the last seventy years. Elderly women, they explained, receive larger pensions as their husbands' "survivors" than from their own employment. As young women, they might not have considered the long-term consequences of work-related decisions, including relocation. However, today the respondents themselves note the gendered realities of economic policies that privilege men as breadwinners and women as secondary earners. We return to this topic in greater length in chapter 4.

The third silence in our interviews pertained to political engagement. Our participants displayed different levels of participation in political activities, such as membership in political organizations or attendance to political events. When they spoke about their decision to get involved with political organizations or which organizations they elected to support, our interviewees never referenced talking these choices over with their husbands. One respondent had served in an elected political position. She bitterly recounted her husband's unwillingness to support her political work and the eventual breakup of their marriage:

> Q: How did you manage to combine your professional life with your family life?
>
> A: Pretty well, up to a point. . . . I can't claim I was fully understood, and to be honest, last year I got divorced. . . . At this point it is just me and my kid and I want to say that I feel at peace, I can focus on all my responsibilities . . . [before, he] reproached me with things like: why do I leave in the morning and return at night. (B.F., thirty-eight)

While her husband had not encouraged her, she did not mention soliciting his input when she elected to pursue a career in politics. This example dramatizes how our respondents did not seem to consider political participation as part of the familial decision-making process or partnership. These were individual choices rather than decisions reached through conversation with their partners.

Domestic Violence and Divorce

On the rare occasions our respondents talked about domestic violence, they generally did so in the third person: "In my office, I have seen situations with beaten women, women who had suffered various forms of aggression—verbal, physical, everything. . . . I tried my best to demonstrate to them that these men are not the only ones on this earth; that they need to live their lives, and it is not worth spending it with someone who beats or abuses you verbally" (B.F., thirty-eight). Others spoke vaguely about women they knew. If such references hinted at their own experience, the inference was unclear. Though several interviewees implied domestic violence was a concern, few shared details.

A small number of women spoke freely about physical and psychological abuse in their marital relations: three were divorced, while one still lived with her husband at the time of the interview. These women described good relationships gone bad—marriages where they had hoped to forge a partnership but met with too many obstacles. Alcohol was often an important contributing factor in their husbands' abusive patterns:

> One night he came home so drunk that instead of helping me put everything in place, he broke all the dishes. And so many other things. . . . I remember that my daughter was six then. . . . He had these outbursts, drinking made him crazy. But he wasn't a bad man. Now he regrets, he regrets a great deal. When I decided to postpone the divorce for one year, I said to him that if he continues to drink, I will start the action. He said he regrets a lot all that he did and I didn't deserve that and it will never happen again, that he won't drink anymore and will become the best husband in the world. . . . This came too late, to wait nineteen, twenty years for this to happen. You look behind and twenty years have passed, and many women say, "I am staying for the child." (L.P., forty-eight)

This sadly unexceptional example presents the typical cycle of violence in an abusive relationship (Walker 1987). In this case, the respondent refused to leave her husband for years because she believed he depended on her. While she did not expressly convey a sense of insecurity or fear, she described her husband "going mad" under the influence of alcohol inside their crammed apartment. Initially, concern for her daughter delayed her decision to divorce. Later, she tried to develop a greater sense of autonomy: "Both when I decided to file for divorce and when I decided to postpone I discussed this of course with my daughter. And she said, 'Mom, don't you feel pity for him? Don't you see that if he doesn't stay with you, he will be lost? Look at how he looks; he is still my dad.' I made a wrong choice then, because the time comes when you need to look out for yourself; it is simply no longer worth to think about the others, your loved ones" (L.P., forty-eight). In other words, her child, who grew up in an abusive household, encouraged her to stay. Her daughter rationalized her father's behavior by identifying him as weak and in need of care. In this story, the daughter took her mother's strength for granted as she had "pulled everyone along with [her]" for years. In the end, however, the mother left, though she did not divorce the father.

The rate of divorce in Romania is one of the lowest in Europe (5.3 percent) (Eurostat 2015).[7] Are Romanian couples happier than other Europeans and, consequently, less likely to divorce? Are women more skilled at forging viable partnerships with their husbands? Are they more tolerant of abuse and inequality? Do they accept sacrifice more readily? While we do not have definitive answers, our data allow us to speculate that satisfaction may not be a primary reason for marital stability. The narratives we heard lacked effusive talk of marital love. Women rarely spoke of their husbands as the most important people in their lives. More likely, a pragmatic view of marriage as a contract, social norm, and necessary partnership prevents Romanian women from divorcing.

Until 2011, when the media and politicians began to pay attention to sexual and especially domestic violence, the extent of this type of abuse was unknown and often misrepresented (Molocea 2015; Vlad 2015). The communist regime had not confronted this issue as a social problem. Before 2003, there was no legislation, police-training, or state institutions that addressed domestic abuse. Women often felt they could not escape abusive relationships, though the thin walls of urban apartments and the shared courtyards of village communities made evidence easy enough to gather.

After Romania began its course toward EU membership, the legislative context changed drastically. In 2014, the penal code was amended, allowing judges to extend the sentence of those who physically abused a family member by 25 percent. The abuser may serve up to seven years in prison and prosecutors can press charges without an explicit request from the victim. While in principle this article (article 199, paragraph 1) covers all familial relationships, it is aimed at the violence women suffer at their husbands' hands.[8] In 2014, over nine thousand cases of domestic violence were reported, though these were only a fraction of the total.

There are estimates that as many as 75–80 percent of all women in Romania are victims of some form of domestic abuse. A more reliable 2014 study places the percentage at 22 (self-reported).[9] After Romania ratified the Istanbul Convention in May 2016, legal definitions of domestic abuse changed (Council of Europe 2011). Women can now report psychological and economic as well as physical and sexual violence. However, signatories, including Romania, have yet to revise national laws so as to hold law enforcement agencies accountable for implementation of the convention. Our interviews suggest less change on the ground, as none of our respondents displayed much faith in law enforcement's ability to intervene in cases of domestic abuse.

Unable to count on legal recourse until very recently, interviewees who had lived most of their married lives under the communist regime tended to accept or even blame themselves for their husbands' abuse. A recent national survey suggests this attitude remains widespread: 30.9 percent of respondents agreed that "women deserve to be beaten," another 8.1 percent thought it a virtue to beat one's wife, and 6.4 percent felt that wife beating was a form of love.[10] In short, almost half of those surveyed did not see domestic violence as a social problem, an infringement of basic human rights, or a crime (INSCOP 2013).

The Ideal Man: Honesty, Hard Work, and Respect for Others

To encourage respondents to reflect on gender norms, we asked them to describe ideal masculine and feminine qualities. Later, we asked the same questions about public—political, civic, professional—roles. We also asked about their aspirations for women in their community. In their responses, many interviewees spoke at length about gender norms. Though direct references to politics and citizenship were rare, responses about ideal qualities in men and women mirrored comments respondents made later about political life. These similarities between the ideal man and woman, and later the ideal politician, reflect the overall ethical foundations of these women's ideas about citizenship. We return to these issues in the chapters on politics.

Among the communist generation, respondents explicitly rejected clichés such as masculine strength and feminine beauty. For most of these women, honesty, understanding, and kindness were desirable traits in men and women:

> Q: What should be the main qualities of a person?
>
> A: To be honest and kind . . . not intelligence, because there are people who are not very intelligent or educated, but are honest and good and do good deeds.
>
> Q: What about women in particular?
>
> A: Same, don't imagine I would say beauty, beauty is good but not essential. . . . If you don't have tolerance toward others you are always unhappy, you're never a whole person.
>
> Q: What about men?
>
> A: Same, same. I don't believe men have to be macho, like you say now. If he is not kind, loving, honest, everything is fake, and this doesn't last. (E.B., seventy-seven)
>
> A: A man should help his wife, get along, and not go around other places. Their money should be kept together. (A.G., seventy-four)

While this generation did not consciously differentiate along gender lines, gendered notions appeared in their descriptions. For instance, comments like a "man should help his wife" might suggest that women require assistance, which men are expected to provide. However, it might also imply that women occupy a central position of authority in the home. Regardless of the interpretation, the respondent did not state that husbands and wives should help one another, indicating reciprocity was not part of her definition of partnership in marriage.

The respondents' discussion of honesty provided a gendered point of contrast. While no respondents described women as dishonest, several offered specific examples of male dishonesty. In the response above, the interviewee used the phrase "not [to] go around other places" as a euphemism for adultery. If honesty specifically concerns cheating, our respondents implied men were the actors that deviated from this norm. Another interviewee noted: "A man needs to find his function and job, to be honest, understanding, and a good example. . . . He shouldn't bring discord to his community and behave outside social norms" (D.D., eighty-four). Her comment indicates that she had experienced tension caused by a man's unwillingness to follow social customs, perhaps also linked to adultery. No respondent shared anecdotes where women had to be reminded of social expectations. When our interviewees later discussed politicians, who are overwhelmingly men, the theme of honesty reemerged. Our respondents' lack of trust in elected officials echoed reservations they had about their own marital relations.

We had a larger sample of women from the transition generation and thus a greater diversity of answers. Some polarized gender norms were more evident. For example, several women stressed female beauty and male physical strength as ideals. But others spoke ironically about these clichés:

Q: What qualities does a woman need to have?
A: [Smiles] To look good, be beautiful, and have nothing in her cerebellum; that is the ideal woman today, right? [Smiles] (E.A., fifty-three)

More than half of the respondents in this group emphasized shared, not gender-polarized, attributes. When asked to identify specific differences, they failed to fully articulate answers.

When they did identify different traits for men and women, descriptions of the ideal man varied far less than those of the ideal woman. They often portrayed the ideal man as a responsible, hardworking breadwinner—"He needs to be understanding, hardworking, and responsible because he is the head of the family" (E.M., fifty-five)—and as a protective, paternal figure: "A man needs to be protective of his wife, if he is to be the pillar of the home, then he should show that" (D.M., fifty-six). Such descriptions present a binary view of gender roles, one inextricably linked to marriage.

A number of the characteristics these women focused on coincided with traits they considered essential for public office and leadership. They wanted honesty and loyalty in the home, and integrity and transparency in public life. They often felt male politicians and civic leaders lacked these qualities. Likewise, admiration for the hardworking, protective husband closely corresponded to an appreciation of good stewardship (*gospodărire*) of public goods—another trait they found in short supply among contemporary leaders. Finally, they considered a kind and loving disposition desirable in men as husbands and political leaders: "A man needs to be a good husband, hardworking, to love all these things, to combine kindness with love and humanness" (D.M., fifty-six).

Though they saw respect for others as an important attribute in men and women, our respondents felt that men often lacked this capacity in both family and public life. Several interviews referenced President Traian Băsescu[11] to illustrate this point: "A leader of Romania should be a decent man who needs to know how to address people publicly, so as not to offend people, because we didn't elect him to offend us; he needs to respect us and to command respect from us . . . if he stands up to ministers and the members of parliament, he needs to do so not by yelling at them and with elementary school language—that is not a leader of Romania" (D.L., sixty-three).

While respect featured broadly in the answers in terms of both home and politics, other characteristics, like intelligence, appeared only essential to public leadership, not to roles in the private sphere. Though a number of respondents felt empathy, or an aptitude for appreciating the point of view of others, was a useful leadership skill, only one interviewee identified it as a masculine ideal. Several respondents also remarked that men are less patient than women and believed this explained male political leaders' inability to see projects through: "I don't know if men have so much patience" (E.M., seventy). Overall, these women found that real men often fell short of their stated ideal qualities.

The Ideal Woman: From Care of Others to Care of Self

The transition generation offered the most varied, and contradictory, descriptions of femininity and masculinity. Among the characteristics they valued were spiritual faith, loyalty, respect for others, the ability to listen and compromise (or simply give in on occasion), patience, a solid work ethic, honesty, and empathy. Taken one by one, the attributes of the ideal woman aligned more closely with the qualities they looked for in political leadership than the attributes of the ideal man, even though our interlocutors did not make this connection. At the same time, like the model white housewife of 1950s America, a few respondents felt that above all women had a mandate to present themselves and their home as pleasing and beautiful (Friedan [1963] 2001).

They often invoked attributes linked to mothering and homemaking: "A woman needs to be a good mother, wife, and worker"; "She needs to be well put together, smart . . . have beautiful children, raise them well, be a good wife and faithful mother"; "Women need to be more sensitive, to have a maternal instinct"; "[She needs] to be a good mother and housekeeper"; and "[She needs] to like beauty, cleanliness, even if she doesn't have enough money . . . but to like cleanliness. And to not ignore her family, even if she has a job." The feminine gender norms that permeate these responses are inextricably tied to women's domestic roles. This same generation consistently linked men's identity to the family as well. However, they did not use specific domestic activities and responsibilities to describe male characteristics. For instance, none of them spoke of a "paternal instinct," only a maternal one. Women's responsibilities concerned things like household cleanliness while men's were discussed in financial terms.

Respondents painted a far more complex picture of women's multiple public and private roles than men's—so complex that we had to wonder how anyone could meet all the expectations they described. These are expectations that women themselves seem to embrace or at least accept. One respondent offered a faith-based explanation: "A woman, I think, can work twenty hours a day; that is how God created her. A man could not assume so many duties; they only like power and power over others" (D.L., fifty-five). A woman needed to "keep to her job, to do anything that is asked of her" (S.W., fifty-three). Other interviewees also spoke about women's strength, though they felt women should use their wherewithal to gain greater independence: "Women need to be strong, and not allow themselves to be dominated by men" (M.V., fifty-five).

This generation of women had to confront both the responsibilities placed on them as the primary caretakers of the home, as well as the public and professional obligations generated by greater educational and work opportunities. As the responses below demonstrate, they worked through these various pressures in a somewhat contradictory, even embattled manner:

> A man—I don't know—should be protective toward his wife and if he is to be the pillar of the home, then he should show it. I mean, I don't think it is normal this financial stuff, for women to have this care as well. . . . A man should think, when he establishes a family, "Can I keep this family?" . . . Women should be more sensitive, to have this maternal instinct. . . . It is not right, no matter what, for us not to be equal to men. No, it is not possible. I am a feminist, too, you know. I don't like this differentiation. Why men can and women can't? Why is woman deemed lesser than man? If a woman makes a mistake, she is stigmatized, and men can do as they please nonstop. (E.M., seventy)

This woman came of age early in the communist period. Her views on gender norms were traditional, especially in relation to the private sphere. Yet her identification as a feminist was rare among our respondents. As she spoke, she moved from a description to a critique of gendered social norms. However, she stopped short of rethinking her own view of men as breadwinners and "pillars of the home." Her contradictory statement points to women's vulnerability in the household and how social stigma and traditional values continue to shape gender inequalities within families.

Women from the transition generation discussed these issues quite differently. To some extent, they expressed opinions similar to their mothers', accepting women's double burden as a norm and identifying parenting and homemaking as essentially female responsibilities. At the same time, they more frequently linked male traits to specific domestic activities: "[He should] be a loving husband, a good father, do his job, at work behave respectfully, and the same at home—help his wife, help his child, bring money home" (M.P., fifty).

This generation of respondents also articulated a desire for men to treat women with greater respect. They wanted men to become "more understanding [toward women], and more involved in the home" (S.C., forty-four); to listen more to women (B.F., thirty-eight); and to be more honest and sincere (M.V., fifty-five). Unlike their mothers, these respondents refused to simply reconcile their desires with social expectations. They repeatedly identified differences between actual and ideal gender relations and valued a wide range of traits in men, including a sense of humor (L.J., thirty-eight) and tenderness (A.).

When they discussed feminine ideals, these women's comments diverged even more radically from their mothers'. First, they emphasized strength: "A woman can do anything she sets her head to," (M.S., forty-eight). And: "First of all, [women] are strong, much stronger than [men]; all of this 'men are stronger physically' is actually nature fooling us. Women are strong because they give birth, they know how to take care of their children under any circumstances, they know how do something from start to finish (C.P., forty-eight)." They also placed greater stress on the concept of dignity: "Women need to keep their dignity in any situation" (M.S., forty-eight); "[women should] strive to overcome their limits and never lose their dignity" (C.P., forty-eight).

These answers were peppered with comments about a female imperative to please others, act kindly, and make sacrifices and to be meek, physically pleasing, and coquettish. Yet, they discussed these characteristics in a particular context, one in which assertive women also value intelligence and independence. This context included equal partnerships with men: "The two partners [in marriage] need to be understanding and forgiving of each other, each giving a little" (A., forty-two). Whereas most among the older generation expressed vague hopes for marital equality, these respondents discussed mutual household responsibilities in concrete terms.

Even as some focused on women's care for others, a significantly larger number of women from the transition generation than the communist generation focused on self-care. While every generation we interviewed expressed a strong sense interrelational identity, this generation also emphasized taking time for themselves, taking care of themselves, and valuing pleasure for its own sake: "[Women] should find time at least once a week to enjoy some personal pleasure and not be always at someone else's beck and call—whatever their husband or family wants. . . . If she wants to read a book, she should read a book; she needs to protect her private life. If she wants to see a movie, or to go out with a girlfriend, or to do some voluntary work. . . . Because at some point, if everything you are revolves around your family, it turns you stupid" (L.M., fifty). Unlike older women, this respondent talked explicitly about her right to private, independent interests and activities. She explained that she nurtured her "private" self through contact and comraderie with other women. She dealt with the pressures of her daily life by finding sources of enjoyment and satisfactions beyond her marriage. This respondent, and others of her generation, are the first to articulate a right to routine moments of enjoyment, pleasure, and leisure.

The transition generation also directly linked gender norms to public action and politics. They presented a clear picture of how values and specific familial gender roles reflect and are reflected in the civic space. For them, citizenship and civic leadership are gendered:

> Q: What are the ideal qualities in a woman?
>
> A: A woman has many qualities, but she is not visible enough; her qualities are not taken into account sufficiently. Women are good managers, excellent mothers, and could be a good leader, a good prime-minister. . . . There should be more faith in women's ablities, something we don't really have. (M.V., fifty-five)

Women of this generation connect good management of the home and parenting to leadership qualities in politics. They think of themselves and their actions—familial, professional, civic—as inherently linked to citizenship. Moreover, they speak in a straightforward, unproblematic tone about women's ability to serve as political leaders.

Toward the Future: Reality TV and Citizenship

We had a much smaller sample of women who matured in the 1990s. Consequently, it is difficult to gauge how representative their statements are. Still, they presented fairly consistent views. Though their responses shared features with older generations, they also point to significant changes that have important implications for their views on citizenship and civic leadership.

Five of the eighteen respondents in this group identified physical attractiveness and social pleasantness as ideal female characteristics, and several defined them as the essence of femininity. One respondent referred directly to desirability: "[A woman] might be very intelligent, but if she isn't also beautiful, she develops a complex. . . . So I think all women should be beautiful and desirable" (M.M., thirty-five). Intelligence had secondary importance, if it was invoked at all by these respondents. None of the older generations emphasized physical beauty to this extent.

One interviewee offered clues about this shift. She repeatedly and enthusiastically referenced the host of a TV reality/game show as her role model: "You know, I would like to be like Gabriela [Cristea] from *Noră pentru mama* [Daughter-in-law for mom]. She is beautiful. . . . She has such a way of talking, if you are surrounded by people from high society you can talk differently, at my age not yet. . . . I would like to be like her, to be a TV hostess" (A.M., twenty-nine). A.M.'s role model was only five years older than she was. She described wanting to emmulate her idol's sophistication and accomplishments. A.M. admired Cristea's professional success, apparent ability to accommodate others, and appearance. The reference to a TV star suggests a new set of influences that actively shape Romanian women's ideas about gender and gender norms. Such role models have potentially deleterious implications for the very notion of engaged citizenship and gender equality, because of the polarized types of gender roles predominantly represented in these reality TV shows.

In the mid-1980s, Romanian TV offered two hours of broadcasting each weekday and had slightly longer scheduling on weekends. The only live shows were sports events (generally soccer matches) and Ceaușescu's interminable speeches. All other programs were carefully monitored and staged by the regime's ideologues. Consequently, people did not pay much attention to televsion. The older women we interviewed made mostly negative comments about TV programing. We can infer that older generations looked elsewhere for role models—real figures in their lives or books, for example—rather than to television.

The explosion of television broadcasting and arrival of cable companies in Romania shortly after 1989 transformed how Romanians communicate and what they think politics and citizenship should look like (Roman 2003). Therefore, it is not particularly suprising to see television's influnce in A.M.'s response (she was fourteen when the new era of mass media began). Women on TV are often young and weight obsessed. Moreover, their looks, lifestyles, and ablities are disconnected from social relaties. As A.M.'s comments show, TV reduces women's gender identity to their physical appearance and sexual desirability.

In other words, A.M. and her contemporaries may understand gender norms differently. Their conception of the ideal woman has more to do with commercialized images of physical attributes than with the kinds of moral and civic engagement older women found desirable:

> A: A woman needs to find other occupations, not politics. I see it differently, that a woman needs to stay somewhere else, not together with all these men . . . because no, I don't think she has anything to gain by that.
>
> Q: So what qualities should a woman have?
>
> A: A woman needs to always be nice, sweet, polite, delicate, sociable, elegant; to dress well, clean; to have feminine qualities.
>
> Q: Tell me please, what do you think is the secret of a good marriage?
>
> A: For her to do what he says, to let him decide, to always show him that she cares, not to bother him too much with questions, to do her job as a mother, to take care of the home, and to respect him. (R.L., twenty-eight)

This view of marriage is at odds with that of older generations. Partnership is not invoked as a goal. Instead, obedience and subservience are the keys to a good marriage. Men appear to have no responsibilities in the home, a space where women cater to their needs.

Some of our youngest respondents did provide more encouraging responses, indicating that perhaps the post-1989 landscape will be transformed anew.

Several described women as strong or felt that women should cultivate their strength: "[The women of Hunedoara] need to become stronger, more decisive about what they want from life" (D.P., thirty-one). Though apolitical, this response at least stresses assertiveness. Another respondent claimed that women are stronger than men and can do any job a man does, including serving in the military (I.G., twenty-five). Finally, one respondent stated that "women are more involved than men. . . . They know how to get by, they know how to . . . fight, where to go, where to ask; aside from that, a man is there just for [show]" (I.B., thirty-four). Like older women, this interviewee linked her remarks to women's potential for civic participation. She also drew a connection between the qualities she zeroed in on and women's role as caretakers in the home ("they know how to get by"). Her comments offer hope for change through a continuing intergenerational dialogue on gender inequality.

The communist regime's policies exacerbated the double burden placed on Romanian women. Since 1989, the disappearance of many government social services, including affordable childcare and changes in the nature of work (see the chapter on work) have presented women with new challenges. Women still assume the lion's share of household and parenting responsibilties, and women have themselves preserved and replicated a number of traditional gender roles.

Yet not all of them quietly accept Romania's patriarchical society. Women who grew up in the 1960s and '70s, for instance, often believe that their husbands treat them unfairly. In response, they are more likely to think of their own needs as individuals. Nonetheless, traditional gender norms remain thoroughly entrenched in Romania. We connect this social conservatism to women's ethical approach to community relations and to politics in subsequent chapters.

Notes

1. An LGBTQI movement has become visible since 1990, but alternative sexualities remain taboo and marginalized, especially in rural areas and average cities like those represented in our study. A recent blog exemplifies the sorts of attitudes this population faces every day; see Sereniti, "Cum e sa fii gay în România?" *Sereniti*, June 15, 2016, http://www.sereniti.ro/cum-e-sa-fii-gay-romania/.

2. Between 1990 and 1994, the marriage rate went from 7.9/1000 to 3.4/1000, well below the EU average. Birth rates went from 12.0/1000 to 5.1/1000 (Adler 1997, 40).

3. In 2011, Romania had a marriage rate of 61.1 percent. The EU average was 53.3 percent (only Malta and Cyprus at 64.6 and Greece at 62.4 had higher rates). In Romania, 21.5 percent of citizens were unmarried, proportionally fewer than all but one postcommunist member state, and well below the EU average (28.1 percent); 4.1 percent of the population (one-fifth of those who are not married) declared living in consensual unions, whereas overall in the EU the rate was 9.0 percent (Eurostat 2015).

4. *"Stâlpul casei"* (men) and *"stăpâna casei"* (women) were the Romanian terms used in the study.

5. Before 1990, Romanians had access to savings accounts through their workplace and the CEC (*Casa de Economii și Consemnațiuni,* House for Savings and Holdings). People also took out loans through the same institutions, and monthly payments were deducted directly from their wages. There were no personal checking accounts, credit cards, or large individual loans.

6. More on this in the chapter on work.

7. In 2011, the EU average was 7.4 percent. Romania had a lower divorce rate than all but one of the postcommunist countries, Croatia (4.7 percent).

8. Separate provisions in the law deal with child abuse.

9. The first figure comes from a 2012 newspaper report: Cristina Lica, "Soții bătăuși ținuți la distanță și evacuați," *Evenimentul Zilei,* February 16, 2012, http://www.evz.ro/sotii-batausi-tinuti-la-distanta-si-evacuati-966614.html. The second comes from the Fundamental Rights Agency of the EU, Violence against Women, March 5, 2014, http://fra.europa.eu/sites/default/files/fra-media-memo-violence-against-women_ro.pdf. We take the methodology and integrity of the statistics reported from the EU as being more reliable and therefore use its finding of 22 percent.

10. If we break down these percentages by gender, women supported these positions 2.5–6.0 percent less than men.

11. Traian Băsescu was president of Romania between 2004 and 2014.

3 Children: The Most Beautiful Accomplishment of My Life

ACROSS GENERATIONAL, EDUCATIONAL, religious, and ethnic lines, bearing a child and becoming a parent are core components of Romanian women's identities. Children occupied a place of pride in our respondents' stories as they described their achievements and concerns. Children also consume a great deal of their mothers' time and energy both at home and in public spaces including schools, hospitals, stores, and offices. Furthermore, they are central to their mothers' political interests. In this chapter, we explore how this close correlation between mothering and femininity impacts women as citizens and how mothers see their role in shaping future citizens.

Our respondents' portrayal of childbearing and childrearing is at odds with much of the scholarship on birthing under Nicolae Ceaușescu's regime (1967–89) (Băban 1996; Doboș, Jinga, and Soare 2010; Jinga and Soare 2011; Kligman 1998). This period, characterized by radical pronatalist policies, coincided with at least part of most interviewees' reproductive years. While women had to confront a variety of often painful issues concerning their sex lives and reproductive capacities, they almost never described raising children as anything other than a point of pride and a source of satisfaction. When they complained, they commented on difficulties securing goods or services or a want of spousal support in parenting. Their complex relationships with reproduction and children played an important role in how women then understood and continue to understand state obligations to them as female citizens.

We used the quantitative findings in *Gen, interese politice, și inserție europeană* to help us frame our own work (CNCSIS 2006–8). This study highlighted differences between perceptions and practices: "Who should teach a child how to become a good parent, spouse, friend, citizen, neighbor?" versus who actually taught individuals about these relationships. Depending on the social role in question, 58–88 percent of respondents believed that family members, specifically parents, should be charged with children's civic education. Many of those surveyed also felt schools had a role to play in shaping future citizens (24 percent). Government and religious authorities barely registered at 3 percent and 2 percent, respectively (CNCSIS 2006–8, 58).

When asked about their own experiences, respondents could identify their mothers, fathers, family more generally, school, church, the media, or government as the people or entities that taught them about social relationships. Of the respondents, 55–62 percent cited the family in general, and 6–14 percent specifically listed their mothers as the main source of their civic education. Only 1–2 percent identified their fathers. And 15 percent of respondents stated that they had learned to become better citizens at school (CNCSIS 2006–8, 58).

The study highlights how ideas about citizenship—normatively and in practice—are largely shaped in the home. Our interviews largely corroborate these findings. We asked respondents: How did having a child change your life? Who spends/spent the most time with your child at home? What are the values you've tried to teach your child? Are those values the same or do they differ from your parents'? Who else imparted moral and civic values to your children? Would/did you encourage your child to enter politics? Mothers played a crucial role in their answers. Our interviewees' own mothers had instilled familial and civic values in them, and as mothers, they passed their values down to their children.

The Most Beautiful Experience of My Life

When asked "what was the most beautiful event of your life?" and "what event or person changed your life more than anything else?" our respondents frequently invoked their children:

> The most beautiful experience was to have children. The kids and grandkids, this is what I care most about. (A.N., fifty-three)
>
> Q: Is there a person who changed your life?
> A: I think my son. Because he made me find this angle of being a mother, the need to protect someone. (S.C., forty-four)

This was the most consistent intergenerational response to any question we asked. It also cut across all the social variables we considered. A few respondents mentioned God and faith, and one talked about her husband. No one remarked on falling in love. After children, women most frequently discussed work and professional accomplishments (we address this in the next chapter). Thus, children and childcare are at the core of women's identities and sense of satisfaction.

Over the twentieth century, legislation and behaviors concerning reproduction underwent a series of dramatic changes. These shifts help explain Romanian women's attitudes toward children and childcare. In the interwar period, as Romania recovered the massive casualties of World War I (war losses were proportionally among the highest in Europe, resulting in a gender imbalance in the 1920s), the birth rate remained the highest on the continent (35.9/1000); 93.8 percent of those births took place in rural areas, where the birth rate held constant until the end of the century (Bucur 2002, 207). At the same time, in Europe only Hungary had a higher infant mortality rate during the same period. In Romania, 17.4/1000 infants did not survive. This statistic improved from the 1930s on. However, the confluence of these demographic trends meant that while Romanian women gave birth more often than other Europeans, the population grew slowly in comparison to the rest of the continent. This history had important long-term consequences for women's behavior and gender norms.

Following World War II, the Romanian population declined again, especially among men of reproductive age and particularly among the ethnic groups that Ion Antonescu's fascist regime targeted (Jews and Roma). However, the birth rate resumed a strong pace, peaking in 1949 (27.6/1000), followed by a decline in the 1950s and an all-time low in 1964 (14.6/1000) (Popa 2016). Three communist-era modernization policies shaped these trends. First, the regime mobilized all adults as workers. Women gained access to education and paid employment, leading them to delay marriage and reproduction. Second, the number of births decreased with legal access to abortion, which was decriminalized between 1957 and 1967. One scholar estimates that during this period, 80 percent of pregnancies ended in abortion (Kligman 1998). Finally, as women moved out of the countryside and into the city for education and work, they had limited childcare resources. In its first two decades, the communist regime, like others in Europe, was slow to develop institutionalized forms of childcare (Fidelis 2010; Ghodsee 2015; Haney 2002). As new city dwellers, women lost the intergenerational support system female family members had provided in the countryside. Though some women did send their very young children back to their native village, most could not count on grandmothers and other relatives for childcare. In short, without adequate state services to offset the burdens of full-time work and parenting, women had tremendous difficulty balancing their roles as mothers and productive laborers.

After 1966, abortion was recriminalized and birth rates briefly spiked (27.0/1000 in 1967–68). They quickly began to decline again, and in 1983, the rate was only 14.3/1000. Thus, despite the state's draconian pronatalist policies, women did what was in their best interest rather than what the regime dictated. These statistics are unsurprising given the outcomes of both pro- and antinatalist policies that democratic and authoritarian regimes around the world have pursued since World War II (Solinger and Nakachi 2016).[1] Women rarely decided to have a second child, and most of our respondents who gave birth in the 1967–89 period had only one. Yet all our interviewees, including the youngest ones, spoke effusively about the experience of motherhood. Their statements point to the continued centrality of motherhood in the lives of Romanian women.[2]

Women also experienced frustrations during pregnancy and especially in connection with parenting small children. As we discussed in the previous chapter, women continue to be children's main or only caretaker, as their husbands rarely assume a primary role and seldom devote as much time to parenting. Moreover, while before 1989 childcare institutions were scarce and of poor quality, even fewer exist today. Though private childcare is increasingly available, it is often prohibitively expensive and not well regulated. In addition, the cost of living and expenses associated with children's education have increased. Parents who hope to groom their children for the EU job market feel this financial pressure especially. Finally, many women now work abroad for extended periods. The climate of economic uncertainty created by the confluences of post-1989 neoliberal domestic policies and the EU markets have fostered women's distrust of the government's ability to help them as mothers: "At one point I thought money was everything. But it's not. Now my family is in the first place. . . . We need money to live. But the most important is the child. When you become a mother everything changes. . . . In the last few years since I had my child, I can say I feel fulfilled. If I wasn't living in Romania, I would be very happy." Our respondent, M.M., a thirty-four-year-old who takes pride in her work, which took her to Spain for several years, easily parsed her self-identification as a mother and her frustration at living in a country where she feels no support for her professional aspirations. Women often cited this lack of support in their decision not to have a second child.

The Cycle of Childrearing: Grandmothers, Mothers, and Children

Our respondents frequently commented on the roles mothers and grandmothers played in their lives. They discussed how women transmitted gender norms to one another: "This was how we were raised—the ones that have to stay home and raise the children, wash clothes, cook, and to leave men to their own devices because they are brighter, and so forth. At least that is how our grandmothers and mothers were raised and that is probably how this idea of self-limitation [*plafonare*] continued" (L.J., thirty-eight). While not all respondents were as critical of women's role in reproducing gender norms, they viewed mothers and grandmothers as far more influential figures than fathers. A few respondents explicitly mentioned their fathers as positive role models, but they presented such examples as exceptions or exceptional. In short, women did not see fathers, husbands, or sons as prominent agents that shaped children's gender roles in the home.

The women who grew up under communism tended to have a more critical view of their own mothers and mothers-in-law. They situated themselves in contrast to them: "My husband's mother was a homemaker and I had the impression she remained marginal because of that" (A., forty-two). At the same time, these women depended on help from their mothers, grandmothers, and mothers-in-law to raise their own children. Despite the communist regime's much-touted social services that purportedly gave women the support they needed to work, virtually all of our respondents had difficulty balancing childcare and employment. Some managed to secure prolonged, partial-paid or unpaid leave from work to take care of preschool children while their husbands worked.[3] Most, however, returned to their jobs after a brief three-and-a-half-month maternity leave (lower than some postcommunist neighbors, like the Czech Republic, though generous by contemporary US standards). On collective farms, however, female agricultural workers essentially received no leave at all.

Working mothers had two options: institutionalized childcare (from toddlers up to school age), where available, or support from older female relatives, generally their own mothers and grandmothers. A few respondents felt crèches were useful institutions. Most women who used state facilities like this migrated to Hunedoara from other regions and could not depend on familial networks. The majority of our interviewees found communist-era facilities for early childhood education inconvenient, low quality, and insufficiently available. Childcare was and remains largely a private affair, and most of our respondents relied on their extended family for help. State support exists mainly in the form of maternity leave, and most working parents with children ages two to six have limited options (Păunescu 2012; Ștefan 2006).[4]

Thus, it is not surprising that women accept and reproduce traditional gender roles in the family. Women from the transition generation had few options for childcare when they entered the workforce in the late 1960s and early 1970s. They often left their kids with their mothers:

Q: How did you mange with the kids, raising them when they were little?

A: I was lucky with my mom, we lived together with her; I did whatever was necessary and the rest she finished. (M.V., fifty-three)

For those from the democracy generation, the situation was similar: "I am lucky. I have my mom; she lives close, so during the work week, when the kids go to school, they go straight to her house" (M.S., forty-one).

Since the communist period, the school day in Romania has been much shorter for K–12 students than in the United States. Children attend school in the morning (K–8), 8:00 a.m. to noon or 1:00 p.m., or in the afternoon (especially high school children).[5] Children who are sixteen and younger generally spend the morning at school and return home three to four hours before the business day ends. For parents who work in industries with two or three shifts, schedules can be even more problematic, as reliable before- and afterschool care is difficult to find. This creates a real problem for women, who make up 47 percent of the total workforce.

When older women help with their grandchildren, they often have to rearrange their own professional schedules, since the grandmothers described in our study still work themselves. Women from the transition generation married

Fig. 3.1 Young pioneers in Hunedoara during the 1960s. Personal collection of Mihaela Miroiu.

fairly young (generally in their early twenties) and had children by their midtwenties. In 1989, for example, over 40 percent of children were born to mothers ages twenty to twenty-four.[6] A 1977 law set women's retirement age at fifty-seven (early retirement, for health or other reasons, was possible at fifty-five) (Marea Adunare Națională 1977). Consequently, a two-year-old child born to a twenty-five-year-old woman would likely have both a working mother and grandmother.

In some families, older women worked shorter or more flexible hours or retired early: "When [my daughter] got to school, my mother-in-law retired and [my daughter] went with her for a while" (S.M., fifty-six). Grandmothers who worked in the service industry occasionally brought their grandchildren to work with them. This was part of our own experience of childhood as well. For example, Maria Bucur (b. 1968) went to work with her grandmother between ages three and six. Her parents had time-consuming jobs as engineers at a factory outside of Bucharest. During the day, she played in the backroom or in the front of the store where her grandmother worked. Neither she nor the adults around her thought of this as unusual. Mihaela Miroiu's (b. 1955) grandmother raised her in the countryside until she began school in the town where her parents lived. Parents who had children in the 1950s, usually the first in their families to migrate to cities, often sent their children back home while they worked or pursued an education.

While flexible or shorter hours allowed women more time for childcare, this arrangement had economic repercussions. Since they worked fewer years, women's pensions were often smaller than their husbands' (Băluță 2006; Pasti 2003). The types of employment that allowed for flexible schedules, moreover, such as service-industry work, were often not well paid. Though the state nominally recognized caretaking, especially maternal responsibilities, in employment regulations, the labor of caretaking remained unpaid (Marea Adunare Națională 1972). In other words, the state stopped short of recognizing caretaking as work essential to the proletarian common good (Doboș, Jinga, and Soare 2010; Jinga and Soare 2011). Today, caretaking remains largely unpaid and undervalued (Dragolea 2007; Harsany 1995).[7]

Avoid Conflict: Passing Values on to the Next Generation

What does childrearing consist of and how has the female-dominated environment shaped gender roles? When they discussed their own parenting, our respondents initially focused on logistical and material issues: putting food on the table, making sure children did their homework, taking them to school, and so on: "I would take her to kindergarten in the morning; then my husband and I would pick her up at 3:00 p.m. And when she went to school, my mother-in-law was already retired and would take her to school for a while, in second and third grade. And with parent teacher conferences, whoever was free. Maybe mostly me, being a mother I was the one who did this" (S.M., sixty-five).

Similarly, when asked about cultural or religious traditions, our respondents often spoke about rituals rather than values:

> [We learned] from my parents. . . . My mother was a strong believer, and that is how she raised us as well. So on Sunday, we had to go to church, and that is how we learned. And for Easter—on Easter we would go to the midnight Mass. We would wake up; mom would stay up till the morning to do work around the house—we were three kids, and she had to get things done, she had a large household . . . she would let us sleep and then she would color the eggs. And it was beautiful, she would make us new clothes for Easter. (S.M., sixty-five)

In this example, our respondent did not comment on the spiritual message of Easter—sacrifice, rebirth, love. Rather, she reminisced about dying eggs, getting new clothes, and her mother sprucing up the house.

Our respondents seldom volunteered general comments on how their values, faith, or beliefs informed their parenting. But once we targeted these issues, we heard specific stories about mothers and grandmothers passing down ideas about good and evil, respect, love, fear, and faith in God: "My mother suffered a lot, but she always prayed for us, because there were seven of us siblings and three of us went astray. . . . I am ashamed of that, of the fact that the [gift] I received from my mother when I was little I didn't pass it down to my children. Those times were such that you could blame it on the regime, but you could have educated your child in this spirit [of faith in God], but there was too much complacency and laziness, we were complacent" (E.M., sixty). E.M.'s comments suggest two important aspects of childrearing that have potential social and civic consequences. First, her mother had clearly made an effort to give E.M. a religious education. In this case, E.M.'s mother had been a Protestant. While she did not specify her mother's denomination, we can speculate that her mother was either a Baptist or Seventh-Day Adventist. Both churches had a larger following in the Hunedoara region than other Protestant denominations. Though neither was illegal, the state discriminated against their followers from the late 1940s on. It would have required a great deal of effort for E.M. to carry on her mother's beliefs and practices (Stan and Turcescu 2007). Furthermore, E.M. married a religiously active Orthodox Christian. She explained that she hid her own beliefs and raised her children in her husband's church. However, she taught her sons only the rituals, not the moral substance or creed of Orthodoxy. Her response aligns with the findings of a nationwide study that found men and women placed little importance on religion in their children's education as future members of a community (CNCSIS 2006–8).

E.M. seemed to understand (and accept) women's normative role as their children's moral educators. She confessed to feeling guilty for having failed—perhaps as a mother, perhaps as a Christian—to pass on her mother's beliefs. By reflecting back on her mother's role as a spiritual model for her children as a "gift" she did not honor, E.M. defined herself as also failing in this regard. She made it clear that the regime's atheistic nature was not reason enough to have moved away from such spiritual guidance and instead confessed to complacency—spiritual and moral—as a mother. Her attitude corresponds to the large findings of the study we quoted earlier (CNCSIS 2006–8, 58).

Few other women spoke so directly about the relationship between gender norms and their children's moral instruction. Still, some examples indicate that mothers were expected to provide such moral models to their children. Men were absent from these stories: "My children were always the most important thing. I never liked to see someone in the street hitting a child. I never hit my children; they always simply followed my words. I talked to them so much that my throat would hurt sometimes. Or I found some other way to show I was angry with them, and then they tried to do something to please me" (E.M., sixty). As in this example, our respondents were generally averse to confrontation and taught these values to their children. This attitude has important implications for violence and civility more broadly (Neaga 2013).

Women also highlighted the negative impact of spousal abuse on their children. Both the women who left and those who remained in violent relationships felt domestic abuse was traumatic for their children. They often attempted to hide such behavior from their sons and daughters, as they did not want their children to replicate it later in life.

However, for some of our respondents, avoiding physical confrontation with a spouse became equated with evading all forms of confrontation, spilling into parenting. The respondent quoted in the previous excerpt also told us, "My husband would jump sometime to hit them, but I always said to my boys—if you want to fight, do it when I am not around." Her first statement about rational problem solving and negotiation imparts an important moral lesson in line with principles of democratic citizenship. Her second statement, however, is more troublesome, as it identifies only what is visible as meaningful. The respondent is more intent on circumventing the problem than confronting it, and she implies men are unavoidably violent.

The media echoes this respondent's attitude. For example, in 2000, an early issue of Romanian *Playboy* included an article titled "How to Beat Your Wife without Leaving Traces" (Playboy 2000). Though the publishers characterized this piece as humor, several human rights and feminist groups publicly protested. *Playboy* later apologized. However, similar materials circulate online, on television, and in other media outlets normalizing domestic violence.[8]

As Romania vied for EU membership, the Law for Preventing and Combating Domestic Violence (Law 217/2003) was passed. This law was an important structural adjustment, especially given social attitudes concerning women and violence. For example, the nationwide study *Barometrul de gen* (Open Society Foundation 2000) reported that while 53 percent of female respondents recognized that women were subject to domestic violence, only 17 percent of men surveyed did.

Over the last decade, anti–domestic violence protests have taken place. However, attendees are mostly activists involved with feminist organizations in Romania's two largest cities—Bucharest and Cluj (Vlad and Fabian 2015). While they have had some political impact, these protests have not attracted a wider cross section of women. And the problem of modeling gender roles through domestic abuse had not been a focus of sustained public concern. Our respondents' remarks remind us of women's complicity as mothers in normalizing domestic violence despite its negative impact on perpetrators and, especially, victims.

The broader issue here concerns women's understanding of citizenship, rights, and obligations. Our respondent sees male violence as a fact of life—one that is gendered in her description. As a mother, she tried to curb her sons' innate tendencies by modeling nonviolent behavior and verbal negotiation as a means of conflict resolution. However, she also shied away from intervening when the conflict did not directly involve her. She restricted her moral authority as a mother to her immediate relationship with each child. Her unwillingness to exercise her authority in the broader family network coupled with her injunction to "avoid physical confrontation if I am not present" is a potentially harmful lesson in civic rights and responsibilities.

The theme of avoiding conflict appeared in multiple interviews. One respondent, for example, spoke about the workplace:

> I always told [my daughter] to know her place in her interactions with everyone, and with her boss. Regardless of the boss's education, he occupies the decision-making position and you need to respect him as you were taught. Even if the boss is not doing a good job. . . . [My daughter] says, you taught me to keep quiet and wait for time to solve these problems. I always had the idea that people need to be respected in their place of authority, regardless. Because you can't educate your boss, if you explain to him what he did wrong, you are opening the door to discussions. And this is wrong, you are insulting your boss. (M.B., fifty-eight)

Like other women we interviewed, this respondent taught her daughter to "know her place." The interviewee did not think critically about power relations—whether expressed in gender norms or institutional settings—but accepted them as a given. Her mandate "to respect" implies an acceptation of power differences and negates an attempt to alter social or professional norms. Moreover, this mother urged her daughter to avoid conflict. When she warned her not to "open the door to discussion," she further discounted the value of her daughter's ability to negotiate a challenging situation. The only tool she offered for conflict resolution was patience, or to "keep quiet and wait for time to solve these problems."

We can only speculate on the implications of this lesson for broader civic and political issues. The respondent, displeased with all candidates, did not participate in the last election. While she had an interest in civic organizations, she was not involved in any. When asked if she would encourage her daughter to participate in politics, she stated: "I don't know, her family is too united and too beautiful. . . . It is a pity to leave your child just for the sake of your own ambition."

Yet not all respondents reported passive acceptance of power relations and some encouraged their children to be active: "My parents were my support system, as much as they were able. It was their kindness, their serenity, their altruism, their thoughtful balancing. They passed on to me all of the things they had not been able to fully accomplish during my childhood by modeling these values. I go to vote because I educated [my son] that this is the highest form of civic action; you can't [be a citizen] without doing this" (C.P., forty-eight). Born at the height of communist rule, this woman spoke about the relationship between parenting, moral values, and civic duties and rights very differently than her older neighbor. Though both were raised in a rural setting and were the first in their families to move to the city and attend high school, they learned very dissimilar lessons from their parents that they, in turn, passed down to their own children. The younger respondent saw the altruism and serenity her parents modeled as a foundation for civic involvement and action.

Is this difference generational or simply personal? Probably both. C.P. had an abusive, unhappy marriage. She left her husband in order to raise her son in a less violent, more nurturing environment. This act, in a society where divorce is frowned on, demonstrated exceptional strength. C.P. came of age in the mid-1970s, when the communist regime briefly relaxed its cultural and social policies. In 1990, she was twenty-eight, young enough to imagine a new life and new norms for herself.

In contrast, our slightly older respondent M.B. matured in the mid-1960s, around the time Ceaușescu came to power. She described missing the orderly existence of that period. For her, a well-positioned, hardworking employee, the post-1989 transition was a disaster: "When democracy arrived, [it was] like a dog unleashed. Unfortunately, after twenty years, we are still in the midst of this madness" (M.B., fifty-eight). During the communist period, M.B. enjoyed professional satisfaction and economic empowerment. A hierarchical work environment structured her experiences, one she contrasts with the post-1989 chaos. By assuming the values she imparted to her daughter—obedience, quiet patience, and hard work—she moved through the ranks and achieved a position of some authority. Her attitude is not unique, and large-scale studies, like *Barometerul de gen*, have reported similar findings (Open Society Foundation 2000; Vlăsceanu, Neculau, and Miroiu 2002).

Raising Citizens

Mothers' reflections about themselves as moral agents are often linked to specific understandings of citizenship. We asked our respondents if they would encourage their children to become involved in politics, and their answers varied widely. Occasionally, women cited that this was a decision adult children had to come to on their own. Some mothers even rejected the notion that as parents, they had a role to play in their children's civic involvement. Though in other parts of the interview some women signaled that politics constituted a male realm, their responses never delegated an advice-giving role to fathers. Below is a sample of the variety of responses, which ranged from enthusiastic (a few) to skeptical (more) to a clear but conditional rejection of politics as currently too nasty and lacking any concern for the common good (the most):

Q: Would you encourage your daughter to become active in politics?

A: Yes, absolutely, absolutely. But I don't see her being all that interested. At one point she seemed to want to. She flirted with the idea, but then she had her son and she abandoned this idea. But it would have suited her. She was always a leader and in school, always the president of her class. I would have liked to see her become more involved. (I.R., sixty-five)

A: I don't know. . . . If I knew she would have support . . . to get involved and do a good job you need to leave something behind. And it is a pity to leave your child behind. (M.B., fifty-eight)

A: No, I think the struggle is too great and the fighting and the backbiting and—no, no, under no circumstances. (S.C., forty-four)

I.R.'s comments tell us not only about her relationship with her daughter but also about her views on political leadership broadly. According to her, leaders are not born but made, and their skills are honed early on in public settings like schools. Leaders should be ambitious, hardworking, and driven. They need these capacities to succeed within the existing institutional structures. Her response suggests that parents and educators need to work together to shape younger generations of citizens. In the last section of this chapter, we pause to analyze how our respondents see the relationship between home and various public institutions in the transmission of civic values (M. Miroiu 2004a).

Civic Education: Home, School, Church, State, and the Media

Our respondents spoke about the importance of institutions in shaping and reinforcing their children's values. They marked a clear shift between the communist and postcommunist periods. Respondents sometimes described the relationship between parents, educators, and religious officials as collaborative and symbiotic and at other times as disconnected or even at odds with each other. There was no clear consensus on this issue.

To begin with, respondents had dramatically different views on the experience of raising a child during the communist period. Some spoke about the pronatalist policies as particularly traumatic for women. While a number of respondents cited the lack of freedom of information as inimical to childrearing, others viewed it positively, as it had safeguarded their children from access to the sorts of lewd and pornographic material that became widely available after 1989:

> It wasn't easy back then, but still, we had better education; now I don't really agree—I am saying from my own experience and looking at those around me—I don't agree with this television, which has gone overboard with this freedom to show on different channels . . . this lewdness [*destrăbălarea asta*]. (E.O., sixty-eight)

> It was good that there weren't so many TV shows, you didn't waste so much time in front of the television set. (M.B., thirty-four)

Women across several generations remarked on the negative impact of the mass media. In one sense, their views are not necessarily specific to Romania; parents, politicians, and commentators have voiced similar criticisms globally (Brădeanu and Dragomir 2002; Grünberg 2005). Yet their critiques are often linked to their memories of a specific regime and to the sentiment that these are new problems. The legacies of the communist period are mixed in their comments—they do not necessarily see some control over information in a negative light but instead as a tool for shaping children's behavior. Fewer distractions meant children could be trusted to do their homework and did not watch inappropriate shows when unsupervised. Significantly, these attitudes are gendered. A 2006 Open Society Foundation study found that women tend to see television as a negative influence on children, while men do not (Comșa, Sandu, Toth, M. Voicu, and O. Voicu 2006).

Our respondents did not offer further reflection on censorship and freedom of information. They did not consider television's impact in the context of conflicting school and work schedules. Nor did they juxtapose the communist regime's censorship of mass media with its other policies concerning working parents and childcare.

Respondents had a positive view of education under communism. Interviewees who compared schooling before and after 1989 unanimously felt instruction was more serious and more thorough in the past:[9] "Back then, school was very thorough.... Our teachers were dedicated to their profession, so they knew their job well and inspired us and passed to us their knowledge, so I think we learned more and the teachers were more dedicated, provided greater guidance than now" (I.P., 43). This respondent attended school at the height of Ceaușescu's personality cult (Tudosoiu 2010). She began elementary school in 1974 and high school in 1982. When she was a student, the curriculum was not only subject to censorship but specifically developed to further the regime's ideological goals. Nonetheless, she spoke positively about her education, the quality of the teachers, and the skills she learned in school.

Is this blind nostalgia or sober analysis? Comparative research does not offer a definitive conclusion (A. Miroiu 1998; Vlăsceanu, Neculau, and Miroiu 2002). The massification of secondary (1950s) and postsecondary education (late 1990s) negatively impacted the quality of instruction around the world. During the communist period, restricted access to information meant that individuals had few or no alternative avenues for learning. The state, moreover, was the only entity that employed teachers (something no longer the case since 1990), and limited work opportunities may have encouraged their dedication.

In the respondents' narratives, education has less to do with civic values and more to do with content and technical skills. Teachers appear as role models of professional dedication rather than as examples of public engagement as citizens. Still, some interviewees provided nuanced descriptions of teachers as role models: "The truth is that those who went to school during the [communist period] are people better prepared [for life]—both professionally and in their general education. From the point of view of individual freedoms, it was zero. But what was good, I repeat, was education, culture in the arts, as much as one had access. From my point of view, education and culture play a major role in shaping a person" (C.P., forty-nine).

For this respondent, as for most others, the school was not a site where parents and teachers came together to educate children. In the interviews, mothers rarely talked about involvement with school activities. While they attended parent-teacher conferences or school events, they rarely communicated directly with the school administration except when disciplinary problems arose: "I attend the teacher meetings with the parents, and then when there are problems that the girls can't talk about at school . . . I went to ask, to clarify the situation, to deal with some lies and rumors" (M.G., forty-one).

Once they started school, mothers entrusted their children to the institution during the day and only asserted parental authority when they returned home in the evening. Mothers counted on teachers to (1) impart general and specific knowledge, (2) teach skills, and (3) instill discipline. On all three counts, our respondents were critical of teachers' performance since 1989: "Democracy was not promoted and understood by those who were supposed to do it in school, from the youngest to the oldest. So democracy was poorly understood here, everyone took it like it suited them. Back under communism there was discipline and respect. . . . Now there is no respect (M.T., fifty-six). In this response and others, mothers complained that a civic education linking freedoms to responsibilities was absent from the school curriculum. Many respondents felt children needed to learn to respect their elders, institutions, and established social values and norms and thought that after 1989, Romanian schools failed to offer this type of instruction.

A small number of respondents spoke about religious institutions as a space that shaped children's values. Even those women who identified as believers and regularly attended services during the communist period or since, however, rarely emphasized the importance of the church:

> A: I respect religious traditions because that is how I was raised and I like it.
>
> Q: Who taught you?
>
> A: My parents. . . . They were, well, my mother was a very pious woman and that is how she taught us to be. (S.M., sixty-five)
>
> The child needs to be taken to church from an early age. . . . We took Alex to church since he was little, and that is good, because now he is sixteen and I don't have to tell him Sunday morning and drag him out of bed: "Today it is Sunday, get ready for church." So I say this is good—faith is a good thing; it helps him. (M.P., forty-one)

Overall, respondents identified the mother as the person who introduced religion in the home, maintained traditions, enforced church attendance, and reinforced a link between religious faith, social morals, and ethical standards of acceptable behavior. The values they stressed included respect for others, fear of God, kindness, and nonviolent interactions. These were also values our respondents identified as ideal qualities in a political leader, and the chapter on politics discusses this parallel and its relation to gender norms.

Women play a primary role in shaping their children's values and modeling gender roles. Mothers and grandmothers are the most significant presence during early childhood. They model both positive and negative behaviors and norms. The women we interviewed seem to particularly value respect for authority and nonconfrontational attitudes. Moreover, younger women's attitude to gender roles appears to be largely shaped by accepting or rejecting their mothers' and grandmothers' behavior. Women are the principal stewards of religious beliefs and traditions, which have also played an active role in reinforcing traditional gender norms and moral values. In the home, grandmothers and mothers tend to represent both religious and social authority. Considering Romania underwent a prolonged period of forced secularization, the continuity of religious faith and values is remarkable.

Our interviews reminded us of the communist regime's tremendous influence on women's ability to manage their own time as well as their capacity for making choices about marriage and parenting. How our respondents understood and reacted to these constraints is central to their self-conception as citizens and their relationship to the state. It also reminds us of the porous line that separates the public and private spheres.

Notes

1. The historical literature has paid only scant attention to women's perspectives on their resistance to these kinds of government policies (Bucur 2008b).
2. For an in-depth discussion of birthing experiences among Romanian women who grew up under communism, including the generation who became mothers after 1989, see Miroiu and Dragomir (2010).
3. Access to many public services and social benefits under communism were secured through personal connections and bribery. Some women used these means to get medical certificates prolonging their leave from work.
4. On paternity leave policy, see Monitorul Oficial (1999). Only about 5 percent of fathers use it, predominantly among those on the verge of unemployment (Păunescu 2012).
5. Evening classes are often for adults pursuing high school degrees while working and usually start at 5:00 p.m.
6. The percentage decreased by 2010 to 24.4 percent, while twenty-five- to twenty-nine-year-olds had more children (25.0 percent), as did thirty- to thirty-four-year-olds (Institutul Național de Statistică 2012).
7. This phenomenon has led to a brain drain in caretaking professions, with skilled nurses migrating to Western Europe and North America, as well as sometimes the Middle East, for domestic/caretaking employment.
8. "Breaking the Silence" is a recent project (a partnership between a group of NGOs and the Ministry for European Funds) that provides women information about relevant legislation, support centers, confidential counseling online and via telephone, and access to recent studies on domestic violence (accessed August 27, 2017, http://www.violentaimpotrivafemeilor.ro).

9. No reliable comparative international statistics that include countries like Romania were produced before 1989. For the postcommunist period, in 2012 Romania scored in the bottom third of the PISA (Programme for International Student Assessment) international rankings—well below most other EU countries (Zanoschi and Deteşan 2012). A 2012 article in *The Economist* highlighted that a tiny percentage of students perform well above the global average, while the vast majority perform below European expectations. That article, and many since, linked PISA scores to state funding. On average less than 3 percent of the state budget goes to education whereas the average in the EU is 5 percent (Economist 2012).

4 Work and Personal Satisfaction

In 1930, 52 percent of Romanian women were considered economically active, making up 43 percent of the country's working population (Gusti 1938).[1] In 2013, 56 percent of Romanian women were reported to be economically active, again accounting for 43 percent of the working population (Institutul Național de Statistică 2013). While these statistics imply stability, behind them is a story not of continuity but rather of radical legal, political, and social change (Bucur 2017).

In 1930, more than 80 percent of the population (and an even larger proportion of women) lived in the countryside, whereas today 46 percent do. In the 1930s, the vast majority of working women were engaged in agriculture: women represented 51 percent of the active population in this sector, or more than half the productive population of villages (Gusti 1938). In total, 87 percent of economically active women worked in agriculture. Furthermore, women were excluded from many professions. Today, women work in all economic sectors. Yet despite strict laws against gender discrimination, Romanian women, and their European counterparts more generally, still earn less than men for the same work (European Institute for Gender Equality 2015). At 9.0 percent, Romania's pay differential is well below the EU average (16.4 percent). However, other forms of economic inequality persist, such as wage compression and lower pensions (European Commission 2015).

This chapter focuses on the ways in which work shaped our interlocutors' identities. It examines their understanding of the relationship between pre- and postcommunist political and structural changes and their economic empowerment. To get at the gendered aspects of these issues, we asked a range of questions: When did you start to work? How did you pick your profession? Are there jobs you think only women or men are qualified to have? What sorts of relationships do you have with your coworkers? What, if any, difficulties did you encounter in your professional development? If you were independently wealthy, would you continue to work? Women's successes and frustrations at work impacted their views of politics and citizenship in relation to gender norms, notably their opinions on policies meant to foster job creation and prevent workplace discrimination and government corruption. We will further address these connections to politics and citizenship in the final part of our study.

Work as Core Activity

Our interviewees in the Hunedoara region expect to work outside the home. They feel that those around them share the same expectations. Almost all of our respondents had difficulty picturing a life without employment. When we asked, "Would you stop working if you were financially independent?" nearly all our interlocutors, regardless of age or education, responded with a resounding no. Some, moreover, were baffled: "I don't understand the question. Of course I would work; women have always worked."

When asked to explain why work matters to them, our respondents stated:

> A: I couldn't stay home, for instance. . . . Because a woman should serve as an example for what work needs to be, to be correct, to share her expertise with others.
>
> Q: What would we have to gain if we followed such a model in the workplace?
>
> A: Personal satisfaction. When I put my head on the pillow at night, I think: Have I done anything wrong [today]? Have I given any good advice [today]? (D.L., sixty-three)

> When you go to work, it is different; you have someone to talk with, [and] you can develop relationships. When you are at home, you only know routine work . . . you lose your ability to communicate with others; you aren't able to judge things properly. First of all, [a woman needs to] leave home, to change her environment; she shouldn't stay in that same environment, which slowly but surely dumbs you down. Looking back, all my girlfriends who were very rich and quit their jobs became very dissatisfied eventually. (L.M., fifty)

Across generational and socioeconomic lines, our respondents noted that work had more than an economic function; it was part of being a complete person. Work allowed women to find new communities, develop their talents and skills, exercise their curiosity, and make a difference in the world. Our respondents equated staying at home with narrow-mindedness and dullness. At the same time, not one of these working women, overwhelmingly mothers, thought work lessened their ability to be good parents. Some even contrasted their experiences with those of their own mothers', who had not engaged in paid work. They noted that their mothers had grown dull and remained dependent on their husbands (M.S., forty-eight).

Work and the Double Burden: A Communist Legacy

The relationship between the double burden and women's identities as citizens is complex. During the communist period, the political leadership took women's social and economic contributions for granted and structurally undervalued both their wages and caretaking work. In 1966, the National Council of Women raised concerns over the challenges women faced in fulfilling their duty as female citizens, which included a mandate to be productive workers and mothers. This group tied its concerns to the regime's pronatalist policies. The party leadership quieted these critiques and continued its anti-abortion program unabated (Popa 2016). Despite equality on paper, women earned less than men and had fewer opportunities to enter better-paid, male-dominated professions or advance their careers (Jinga 2015). Living under a state that legislated this kind of duplicity, the views women developed often signaled their resignation to the double burden: "I think a woman can work twenty hours out of twenty-four.... I don't think a man can take on so many responsibilities" (D.L., fifty-five).

The regime did create unprecedented work opportunities and support programs for women—including paid maternity leave; conveniently located, low-cost childcare; and access to services and products that facilitated household chores, such as washing machines and affordable dry cleaning (Massino 2007; Smith 2014). Though our respondents acknowledged the availability of these goods and services, they never directly linked them to the communist regime. They viewed these items as hard-earned benefits that rendered their double burden more manageable, not as special enhancements.

Despite these advancements, the 1972 work code introduced new forms of legal gender inequality between men and women as categories of workers: "(Chapter 1, Article 14): Woman is insured broad possibilities for self-fulfillment in conditions of *full social equality with man*, benefitting equal wages and special protection for equal work. Woman is guaranteed the right to occupy any position or place of employment, commensurate with her training, in order to contribute to the growth of material production and spiritual creativity, *ensuring for her all necessary means for raising and educating children*" (Marea Adunare Națională 1972; emphasis added).[2] Thus, though the regime claimed to operate according to the principle of gender equality, the work code gave women sole responsibility for raising and educating children. This law needs to be understood in the context of the communist regime's post-1966 pronatalist policies. The state wanted women to have more children and used such measures to advance this goal. In doing so, rather than furthering Marxist notions of equality, the state reaffirmed traditional gender roles (Engels 1902).[3] It encapsulates the paradox of women's "emancipation" under communism as the work code forced Romanian women to identify with state paternalism in order to take advantage of equal rights in the workplace. While some women may have sought to use the law to their advantage with regard to new employment opportunities, it let men off the hook for household responsibilities.[4]

As a number of interviewees reminded us, taking less well-paid jobs and time off work to care for infants had real long-term consequences. For example, women routinely ended up with smaller pensions than men. Thus, the demands of a lifetime of unpaid work performed at home often directly translated into diminished economic power after retirement. Though our interviewees were aware of and frustrated by this, they rarely explicitly linked this problem to a form of gender inequality the communist regime had institutionalized.

Our few childless interviewees had generally taken on unpaid caretaking duties for elderly relatives and others. Consequently, they too had to contend with a double burden. In rare cases husbands provided significant support with household chores. Nonetheless, nearly all of our respondents discussed at length the combined pressures of home and work, something scholars have identified as a specific condition of twentieth-century women's lives (Ghodsee 2004; Einhorn 1993; Elliott and Moskoff 1983, Păunescu 2012):

> I would come from work, and I say it again, I still wonder how I managed to do all these things around the house. I came from work, I would prepare whatever was necessary for dinner, or I would prep things ahead of going to work, so they would be there, ready. The household chores were: washing, cleaning, and you would do all this and I never went out. (D.D., eighty-four)

> I had to do all the housework after work.... Then came the kids. I had to take them to kindergarten, pick them up from there, go to work, come back. A lot changed. Now you had to work all the time; you couldn't say, "I have a bit of free time now to read." I only got some time to read at 10:00 p.m., 11:00 p.m., or midnight, when I finished housework; after that I would start to read a book or something else. (D.L., sixty-three)

In general, respondents identified older female family members (mothers, mothers-in-law, or grandmothers) as their unique source of assistance. Their stories revealed the feminization of responsibilities for parenting, household chores, and field work—usually on small plots of land people managed to keep during the communist period. One generation tended to transmit these norms to the next at an early age:

> My girl helps with cleaning and various other housework [*treburi gospodărești*], and with cooking.... My husband cooks when he is in the mood for it, but no so much in general. (A., forty-two)

> My mother helped for a while when I gave birth to my son; she took my little girl and kept her for a few days, but after that I was alone. (D.L., sixty-three)

Have women done enough to challenge gender norms related to caretaking? Some of our interviewees characterized male participation in household chores as unwelcome interference and described passing on this sort of thinking to their children (E.M., sixty-four). And others, lacking support from their husbands, clearly felt forced to put up with this situation. In short, the persistence of women's double burden does not stem from a want of self-awareness or a lack of desire for more equitable domestic roles. Rather, women have to contend with a powerful set of cultural norms that reproduce and entrench their roles (Elliott and

Moskoff 1983). The communist state, moreover, institutionalized these norms through legislation.

As they discussed daily life, our respondents remarked that women tend to have far less free time than men. A recent study confirms their assessment. It shows that, in 2015, on average women dedicate twenty-six hours a week to unpaid housework, whereas men spend about nine hours (European Commission 2017). In other words, men have seventeen more hours of free time a week, or more than two hours a day. It follows that women have less time to prepare for professional advancement, pursue personal or civic interests, or develop connections to communities beyond their immediate work environment.

At the same time, our interlocutors' discussion of their skills, professional goals, and personal preferences revealed that their double burden had rendered them more flexible, efficient, and thoughtful. It also trained them to multitask. Yet with no time to spare, immediate demands always trumped working toward long-term professional goals. Many interviewees, regardless of their education level or profession, felt caught between a rock and a hard place:

Q: Are you satisfied with your place of work?

A: Yes. I had some opportunities to get promoted, but I turned them down because of my family responsibilities, taking care of my grandmother, and then of my mother.... I turned down those opportunities and stayed here, where I fulfilled my obligations as a manager and judge. (D.L., fifty-five)[5]

Romanian women have met the opportunities and challenges of the twentieth century by becoming problem solvers, constantly putting out fires at work or home, and consummate time managers, squeezing the most out of every available second. This is how women have achieved significant success in fields once closed to them, like engineering and law. Yet employers, spouses, and politicians continue to undervalue their achievements and their double workday.

Professional Choice: Work as Vocation

The communist regime's removal of gender limitations from all fields, including the army and police, constituted an important systemic change. Until 1945, most professional organizations, like law, had strict gender restrictions that prevented women from sitting for licensure exams. Thus, while women could train in universities and other education institutions, and might even outperform their male colleagues, sexist practices curbed their ability to advance professionally (Văcărescu 2014).

Under the communist regime, women's horizons radically altered, as did their understanding of their economic value as workers. They became appreciated through their professional development and came to value themselves partly through their professional choices. Few of our interlocutors credited parents or teachers with shaping their professional goals. Instead, they focused on how their work experiences shaped their identities as women and citizens. Their responses indicate that women's views of public gender roles have dramatically changed over the course of the twentieth century.

The first generation of respondents, who had largely grown up in rural areas, often in poor to dire conditions, had the narrowest professional horizons. In 1945, less than 20 percent of all women worked in paid employment that was not agriculture and the percentage was even lower in employment that necessitated specialized or professional training. For these women, the educational and employment possibilities that they gained access to in the 1940s and 1950s represented a radical departure from the past, leaving a life of agricultural toil behind to become teachers or radiologists:

> I chose my workplace because. . . . I liked very much to help. But how did I decide? When I was a kid, and as an adolescent, I wanted to become a judge or a teacher of geography or history. But the thing is, when I was little, I also fantasized about becoming a nun. . . . I said that if I had been a boy, I could have gone to seminary school and become a priest. And from all that, I ended up working in public health. And all of it because of an American movie. There were the fights between the Americans and the Japanese, and I saw what hospital work looked like. So I decided to go to school for that. (D.D., eighty-four)

Though she grew up at a time when women could not become judges or members of the clergy, this respondent imagined a career that bore no resemblance to her mother's or grandmother's life. While she never lived out her childhood dreams, she nonetheless saw her profession as a vocation and indicated she would pick it again if given the chance to start over. She spoke of her professional choices with pride and satisfaction, as something that defined her as a person.

Women of the transition generation spoke in even bolder terms about their professional aspirations and the careers they built. While these women were sometimes guided by childhood dreams, their choices were also anchored in the new economy, now open to women in all fields:

> Initially I wanted to become an English language teacher. I loved foreign languages and had already started studying English. . . . I was set on it until a friend of mine from school took me to her dad's office, meaning at the hospital. He was chief of one of the sections and had an imposing office . . . the man himself, in his white coat, and as a person, impressed me a great deal. Plus I had seen movies. . . . So I veered toward medicine, without knowing too much about it, or having someone in my family in that profession. . . . After three years of interning, you were supposed to remain there like a family doctor. . . . But when I finished, there was an exam for specializations, so I chose the best one, TB. . . . That is how I started my specialization. (M.F., fifty-two)

Thus, this respondent picked her career after being exposed to a new work environment. An absence of overt restrictions on women's professional choices also factored into her decision. And retrospectively, she viewed this choice as a fateful one that shaped her life overall and opened opportunities and challenges she greatly enjoyed.

Structural Obstacles against Gender Economic Equality

Educational opportunities multiplied in tandem with the growth and diversification of the Romanian economy. As the urban population of Hunedoara County increased from around 50,000 in 1948 to more than 350,000 in 1970, the number of jobs in every industry and service field rose exponentially. At the same time, however, realizing professional goals also became more challenging. M.F., the responded quoted above, highlighted new considerations women had to take into account when selecting careers in the 1970s.

First, university admissions became more competitive. As more women and men earned high school diplomas, applicant pools grew. In addition, a new class of party apparatchiks—individuals who had risen through the ranks of the RCP during the first generation of communist rule—used their connections get their children admitted to institutions of higher education. Several respondents recounted how frustrated they felt when they failed to get into universities on the first or sometimes even second attempt. They often chalked this up to a lack of personal connections (C.P., forty-eight). Furthermore, since more men than women became members of and held leadership positions in the RCP, women could influence college admission processes primarily through their fathers and husbands.

Another issue respondents raised concerned employment assignments. Women's access to education did create many more opportunities for paid work. However, RCP-controlled committees assigned specific jobs to graduating students. They often placed men and women according to traditional gender roles: men received assignments that allowed them to become breadwinners and advance in rank, while women received posts that were more flexible, often less well paid, and permitted them to fulfill their expected obligations as mothers and wives. This practice directly contradicted the gender equality guaranteed in the work code.

Furthermore, despite grades and other standardized criteria for placement, the gendered nature of job assignments meant women had fewer possibilities for economic advancement. The makeup of these committees (e.g., a committee overwhelmingly made up of male professionals might opt for a male future colleague over a top female candidate) and a family's ability to bribe committee members also contributed to placement decisions. Here again, specific notions of what careers were "suitable" for young men and women dictated how families engaged in these widespread, though corrupt, practices. One respondent offered an illustrative example about the gendered aspects of job assignments: "I finished industrial electronics. Back then, they had assignments [*repartiții*]. . . . I was in the second graduating [high school] class in electronics in Deva. . . . And when I got the assignment to 'Victoria,' in Călan, they told me there they don't take women, because the number of men is much smaller than it should be and the number [of women] is too large for a heavy industry plant" (M.S., forty-eight). Clearly, the employers had normative views of suitable gender ratios for specific jobs ("the number of men is much smaller than it *should* be"). Similar restrictive gender biases sometimes guided parents. The same respondent mentioned several other factors, including family connections to the placement committee and parents' preferences for their children's employment. In this case, the respondent's parents refused to let her go to school far from their home and later pressured her to accept a job nearby. She believed their behavior was motivated by their idea that she would not manage by herself far away as well as a son would and that she needed to take care of them when they were old, thereby preferring a place of employment closer to their home.

Regardless of committees' specific strategies and motivations, women had a harder time getting assigned to their first choice of job. Furthermore, tradition dictated workers remain in the same place of employment for the duration of their careers. All of this, combined with the gendered inequalities inherent in job placement, raises questions about the reality of women's economic empowerment and the much-touted gender equality under state socialism.

Some respondents spoke specifically about gender inequity in the workplace. They mentioned promotion and compensation policies that aligned with a two-tier system of salaries:

> From the start, men don't value women in that environment [of professional sports], but even if you are in that environment, you have no room to advance. The bosses, how do they pick you? Maybe you are better, have connections, spy on others. . . . He has that feeling he likes you, leaving the whole issue with taking you as a lover aside, professionally. Many times I had the feeling that if I wanted to solve a problem, I had to be ten times better than a man. I don't go out with them drinking, I don't sleep with my boss, so how can I solve my problems, because all these issues are solved at these events. (L.M., fifty)

> Us women have always had a smaller salary compared to men, they [the management] would say that we didn't work as hard as they did, that was our misfortune of being women. . . . There is no equity, there wasn't any before [1989], and there isn't any now between women and men. There is always a distinction made if you are a woman; it doesn't matter that I am a woman, if I have the same skills and capacity to work like you [the man], or even more than you. (D.L., sixty-three)

Some of our respondents had stories about simply coping with the reality of gender inequity. Others told us about working around or through such difficulties to overcome economic, personal, or spatial inadequacies.

One interviewee grew up in a small village. Her family sent her to Hunedoara city for education in the 1940s. After graduating from a pedagogical school, she was assigned a position in a remote rural area. This experience taught her a hard lesson, forcing her to live without family support in a difficult environment. She had no running water and no electricity; there were no paved roads or public transportation: "I worked in two villages, each for one year, in Hunedoara County and then went to another village close to Hunedoara [city], where I worked for seven years; in fact, that is where I helped build the school. I participated in everything—collectivization . . ., helping with educating people about the collective farm. I worked in the summertime on the combine [in the fields], then extracurricular cultural work with the youth. . . . At school, I worked for a few years alone; I had to solve everything on my own, from director to manager, everything except janitor" (E.B., seventy-seven). Her overwhelming work conditions prevented this teacher from caring for her newborn, especially since she could not rely on help from her husband, who had frequent violent outbursts. She sent her daughter to live with her mother in her native village and could visit her child only when she had free time and transportation. Like many other working mothers with small children, she depended on female relatives, rather than the state, for help with childcare.

After demonstrating her problem-solving and managerial qualities, our respondent eventually found a job as an elementary school teacher in Hunedoara proper. She worked there until retirement. Another interviewee told a similar story about commuting between Hunedoara and a nearby village for years before transferring to a school in the city (E.O., sixty-four). Explicit feminist goals, like economic empowerment, did not lead these women to change jobs, though their choices resulted in increased personal and financial autonomy. Such experiences also caused women to distrust a state that discriminated against them and failed to offer them services as working mothers, despite claims to do so.

Women's Professions

We asked all our participants about gender norms and particular professions. Since one member of our research team focused on gender and the security forces, we specifically asked about the army and police. Women began joining the army on the same basis as men only in 2007. Though, on paper, both the military and the police have increasingly accepted women, in 2009 these two professions had yet to be fully gender desegregated. We hoped to use questions about these fields as a test case, allowing us to probe respondents' attitudes: Did they consider some professions to be "naturally" male?

Though some respondents expressed discomfort with women in combat, across generational lines, most viewed women's participation in the security forces positively:

Q: What is your opinion about women in the army or police?
A: Very good, because for many years it was an area where women didn't have access and it is a tough job, but still, women are able to do it. Women are

probably more understanding, more organized, more insistent, more stubborn in getting what they want. (A., forty-two)

Q: Do you think there are certain professions that are more suitable for women?

A: No, I don't think so. There are women capable of doing the exact same work as men.

Q: What about women in the police or army?

A: It's OK. There are women who receive excellent training and their place is there. And I'm not talking just about physical strength, but of intelligence. About what they know, what they can accomplish with their skills and intelligence, so why not? (M.M., thirty-five)

These respondents identified gender discrimination as wrong and celebrated women's decision to enter these professions. They rejected assumptions about physical strength or toughness as justifications for excluding women. Moreover, they noted specific female qualities, like good organizational skills, empathy, and stubbornness, as useful for careers in the police or army. Not a single respondent identified bravery or courage as a "masculine" trait that women lacked. This attitude is quite remarkable given that the media and the military use masculine language exclusively when discussing these professions.[6]

In contrast, some women felt men were less capable of taking on traditionally female jobs: "A governess . . . I don't know exactly, but there are work places that I don't think a man would like. There are few of them who are detail oriented and patient. A kindergarten teacher, for instance, seems to me unsuitable for a man" (A., forty-two). These interviewees pinpointed characteristics they thought men lacked—patience, empathy, and attention to detail. Overall, however, our respondents felt all professions had the potential to challenge and reward men and women equally.

While women's horizons have widened in terms of their own professional ambitions and those of their daughters, the caretaking components of a given career stand out among other elements of paid work that continue to attract women and offer them fulfillment. The vast scholarship on gendered skill sets points to how early childhood models and education shape an individual's sense of purpose and professional goals (Chodorow 1999; Gilligan 1983; Jeffee and Hyde 2000). And, as our chapter on children has shown, women play a role as primary caretakers at home.

Women translated their learned abilities as caretakers into specific professional skills. For many respondents this meant tending to the people and environment they worked in and helping to make their workplace into a community:

A: Right now we have a woman as leader of our [tennis] federation, and she has a great deal of respect for women.

Q: Do you feel that something has changed since she is in charge?

A: Yes, a lot has changed.

Q: In what way?

A: So, there is a warmer relationship between clubs and the federation. If you call, someone is there to answer, they talk to you, in other words, we [the clubs] are the ones that pay for their existence, not they for us, but [before] they behaved like they were the ones supporting us. (L.M., fifty)

For others, caretaking meant taking on leadership roles, delicately guiding others while exercising authority and discipline: "I liked to help. . . . I wanted to be a good example. At work I would come first and be the last to leave. For me work was, so to speak, the letter of the law. I didn't like to ignore the rules in place, and I tried to impress that upon all my female colleagues. So they would perform their professional duties as they should" (D.D., eighty-four).

Women grouped a variety of transferable skills under the umbrella of caretaking, capacities they identified as useful in professions as different as medicine and the military. These were also skills they felt the overwhelmingly male political class lacked. These capacities did not translate into raises or promotions commensurate with their efforts or accomplishments, however—an important gender disparity in Romanian society.

Women Pensioners: Poverty and Old Age

Many Romanian women see retirement as a period of stress rather than rest. Retired women provide free childcare and help working women with other household chores. Interviewees of all ages discussed this social expectation; they appeared to find this sort of unremunerated work unproblematic. Some respondents additionally addressed mental and social issues linked to retirement. Specifically, they noted that leaving work narrowed their social network and left their intellect and skills underused:

Q: How did you feel after retirement?

A: It has been stressful . . . when you go to work, it is different; you have someone to communicate with. (D.L., sixty-three)

For others, retirement meant a drastic decline in economic power. The financial implications of retirement in Romania differ significantly for men and women. Throughout the communist period and even today, women generally retire five years earlier than men.[7] Leaving work at the height of their earning potential consistently translates into smaller pensions. Moreover, these five years are often devoted to helping younger women with childcare and other unpaid housework, effectively filling a gap in societal needs that the political leadership has not addressed. This is a sore spot for our respondents, as the next chapter shows.

Thus, because women tend to live longer than men, they spend more time living off their pension and savings and are at greater risk of falling into poverty, a situation that reinforces their economic dependence on others. E.B. (seventy-seven), a former schoolteacher, could have requested a widow's pension when her husband, a former officer, passed away. At first, she refused it, but after five years of eking out an existence on her own pension, she put in a request. She received double the income from her husband's job than from her own. She felt angry and aggrieved: "But I worked thirty-eight years; I was not a housewife. I have my rights after so many years."

The Romanian government's latest statistics reveal that, on average, in every income category, women receive lower pensions than men. For those below the poverty line, the largest group, there is a 15 percent gender differential (Ministerul Muncii 2013). Despite this, some impoverished women continue to support their children and grandchildren with their meager earnings.

Moreover, because of the way collectivized agriculture operated under communism, some women who worked their entire lives receive only a minimal pension.[8] One respondent explained that, as she never filled the family quotas (quotas intended for four working adults), she did not qualify for a pension:

A: I only worked in the countryside, in the fields, the vineyard, digging corn, whatever was needed.

Q: Do you have a pension?

A: No, because I didn't fulfill the quota to get a pension. And then we moved to Hunedoara...

Q: How were these quotas?

A: There was a corn quota, a vineyard quota, not what was possible for one person—they asked you do to more than you had the strength for. And then when we moved to Hunedoara, of course I wasn't able to accumulate all the points or whatever to receive a pension.

Q: Would you have sought employment if you had the chance?

A: Of course—I would have a pension now. (A.G., seventy-four)

Poverty among elderly women is an unrecognized and unresolved crisis among policy makers. The parliament has not addressed this problem through new legislation on pensions. A recent EU report explains links between economic discrimination and postretirement female poverty but offers no concrete solutions for Romania.[9] Women recognize this crisis and have found imperfect means of coping—working in the gray market after retirement or renouncing their own pensions to request "survivor" pensions after losing a spouse. Without familial help, however, these women could not make ends meet.

The current rate of economic activity for women is 56 percent. Women represent the same percentage of active population as in 1930. The statistics are not encouraging. However, as we indicated earlier in this chapter, behind the

Fig. 4.1 The road to Sâncrai. On the left side are fields that villagers were able to retain and work individually even after collectivization. Today many of these small plots are no longer used actively for agriculture, as the mostly elderly inhabitants are not able to do the necessary work by hand. The sign uses the spelling from the communist period. Photo by Maria Bucur.

numbers lies a more nuanced story. Discrete changes have altered women's lives and their relationship to work. Once primarily rural workers, they are now mostly urban employees in a wide array of fields—a little less than 30 percent of women worked in agriculture in 2013, and a little more than 20 percent held employment in industry, while 50 percent had service jobs. The jump from agricultural to service work is a significant qualitative change in work conditions, benefits, and lifestyle. Moreover, in the 1990s, as industries that privileged male employment experienced a free fall, in places like Hunedoara women held their households together by working several jobs, caring for their depressed husbands, and protecting their children (M. Mioriu 2004c).[10]

Despite the gender income gap, women have used paid work to develop skills, networks, communities, and resources for themselves and their families. The expansion of social benefits under communism, such as maternity leave, affordable childcare, and pensions, made it possible for women to pursue ambitious, long-term professional goals. The most important legacy of communism in relation to our respondents' ethical understanding of politics stems from women's experience of self-fulfillment and empowerment that paid work offered them. They believe that benefits and power in a work setting should be measured against the contribution they bring to that common endeavor; they project the same correlation between contributions and benefits to their view of democratic politics.

At present, the most frustrating legacy of the past remains the unchallenged double burden women face. Women still have far too little time to pursue long-term career goals once they have children. The lack of public support for affordable childcare since 1989 has compounded this problem, making it nearly impossible for them to advance at work without personal sacrifice or significant help from their mothers, grandmothers, or other women in their families.

Notes

1. In Western Europe and the United States, women made up a smaller percentage of the workforce until World War II, when that conflict's disruptive economic and demographic consequences temporarily required women to go to work (Kessler-Harris 2003).

2. A similar argument has been made for the gender policies of the East German communist regime in the early 1970s (Ferree 1993).

3. No previous law had placed parenting responsibilities exclusively on women. None of the scholarship has acknowledged this as a product of the communist regime. While in practice women traditionally took care of small children, until the communist period, parental authority and the legal responsibility for minors fell largely to fathers. For instance, only men could be appointed children's legal guardians (Bucur 2017; Rădulescu et al. 1962). Eventually, the law recognized female caretakers, but only if they were economically self-sufficient, a rarity before 1932 (Alecsandru [1865] 2011). Eugenics was the only precommunist ideology that emphasized women's maternal role (Bucur 1995). Though eugenicist programs included public health and welfare programs (with important ethno-racial implications), they did not seek to alter women's citizenship or property rights as mothers.

4. Jill Massino (2007) discusses public campaigns meant to encourage men to help with homemaking. However, these campaigns unfolded largely in women's journals and were toothless and ineffective. They left women to initiate change in the home and failed to offer state-based incentives, positive or negative, for men to alter their behaviors.

5. D.L. (fifty-five) had many well-thumbed books on feminist political theory on her shelves. This provides a partial explanation for her explicit political feminism.

6. Both the media and the military uniquely reference military ranks, from soldier to general, in the masculine, even when a woman is concerned ("O femeie militar în Irak și Afganistan," *Unica*, November 30, 2009, http://www.unica.ro/femeie-militar-irak-afganistan-1994).

7. A legislative proposal, ostensibly focused on eliminating economic inequalities, seeks to raise the retirement age for women. If adopted, women would retire two years earlier than men ("Legea pensiilor 2018," accessed May 1, 2018, http://legislatiamuncii.manager.ro/a/535/legea-pensiilor-actualizata-2011.html).

8. In 2016, they received 350 lei, or $95, per month.

9. "Raport," accessed May 6, 2018, http://www.europarl.europa.eu/sides/getDoc.do?pubRef=-//EP//TEXT+REPORT+A8-2016-0153+0+DOC+XML+V0//RO.

10. The unemployment rate in Hunedoara County has declined significantly. In 2013, it was 5.8 percent for women and 6.1 percent for men (Institutul Național de Statistică 2013).

5 Communities: Beyond the Family

THIS CHAPTER FOCUSES on women's interactions with neighbors, friends, church groups, parochial communities, and other nonpolitical associations. We sought to understand how our 101 respondents define their relationships to communities where private and public concerns come together outside of state institutions and the home. In these spaces, the private loses its intimate character, becoming more explicitly public, and the public is more personalized, as participation in these relationships and groups is voluntary. From a communitarian perspective, the family and small, informal communities socialize individuals and provide a moral infrastructure that shapes their understanding of the common good (Etzioni 1995).[1] In short, such communities play a key role in forming an individual's self-conception as a citizen.

Here we focused on the following questions: How do women initiate and maintain relationships with neighbors? How do they make and keep friends? How active are they in their church community? What kinds of voluntary or informal associations do they participate in and how involved are they? To what extent are they active in civic associations?

The national-scale study *Gen: Interese politice*, coordinated by Mihaela Miroiu, offers context for our discussion. When asked, "Who best represents your interests?" respondents to this survey reported, in descending order: me, my relatives, nobody. According to the poll, the national administration, local authorities, the parliament, and trade unions had little significance. Voluntary associations appear very sparsely among the responses (CNCSIS 2006–8, 58). This is perhaps partly explained by a lack of formal organizations for civic action, especially NGOs, in small and medium-sized towns. Notably absent are those that promote social justice and thus, the rights of women and racial, ethnic, and sexual minorities. In Romania, such associations are only found in large cities (Grünberg 2008; M. Miroiu 2015b; Vlad 2015).

Our interviewees squarely placed responsibility for social justice on political institutions and preferred to engage with informal communities through charity. Moreover, even our respondents with limited means tended to think of themselves as benefactors, rather than beneficiaries, of charity. Thus, while most of our interviewees were acutely aware of social injustices, many believed their main civic obligations concerned mutual aid, the environment, and charity efforts.

Neighbors and Friends: Shared Spaces and Individual Ownership

A brief history of housing in the Hunedoara region will help clarify respondents' discussions of neighbors and their distrust of people outside the family circle. The industrialization policy the communist regime pursued during its first two decades of power led to the urbanization of the region. In the 1950–60s, people lived in shacks or overcrowded apartment buildings. Several families (usually two, though sometimes an entire floor of residents) shared a small space for cooking and washing/bathing (Mărginean 2015). Sheila Fitzpatrick (2000) has described the impact of similar living arrangements in the Soviet Union. Forced socialization and a lack of privacy meant that nothing was personalized. Communal and individual intimacy declined, whereas domestic sabotage, theft, gossip, physical aggression, and even informing for the secret police rose exponentially.

In the 1970s, the communist regime solved the housing crisis by erecting entire neighborhoods of standardized apartment complexes. Almost each family had a small apartment with basic facilities for household chores. After being forced to share space, people happily isolated themselves in their apartments. Women still cooperated informally, especially during food shortages (1979–89) (Massino 2009; Neculau 2004). However, the world beyond the apartment, from the hallway to the courtyard and from the playground to the street, became a no man's land.[2] What officially belonged to everyone became nobody's responsibility.

The state owned almost all apartment buildings. Only in the 1980s, when the regime eased restrictions and individuals acquired greater purchasing power, did private ownership become a realistic option. Women's participation in the paid economy and their access to credit played an important role in families' newfound ability to buy. Apartment owners formed housing associations to care for common areas. However, these organizations were premised not on a desire to facilitate the use of shared space but on the need to protect the interests of residents as independent property owners. As a result, relations among neighbors were often cautious. Moreover, when in the 1980s the state limited the use of electricity and hot water to two to four hours a day, sanitary, aesthetic, and ecological concerns linked to communal spaces went out the window. Homeowner associations began to pay attention to these types of concerns only after the fall of communism (Stănculescu and Berevoiescu 2004).

A Second Family: Elderly Women

Among our respondents, the majority of women from the transition and democracy generations had superficial relationships with their neighbors. In contrast, women from the communist generation have built community with neighbors, especially those around the same age.

Women from the communist generation lived in the same buildings with one another for decades. They grew old in their apartments and many are now

Fig. 5.1 Communist housing and neighborhood communities. These two women of the communist generation tend to the garden they planted in front of their apartment building. Together with their other neighbors, they have tended to the repairs needed for the building and its surroundings without support from the municipal government. Photo by Maria Bucur.

widows. They developed close relationships and routinely worked together to maintain their residences. Among our respondents was a focus group made up of eight elderly women from Hunedoara. With one exception, these women were retirees, and all but two were widows. Most of their children lived far away. Perhaps due to their familial circumstances, these women did not display the same sort of indifference to nonfamilial relations that we saw among younger women. For these interviewees, neighbors became a substitute for the family: "God gave me over the last few years ten neighbors. He gave me another family" (E.B., seventy-seven). The others nodded: "Yes, this is pretty much our day-to-day family." As neighbors became family, apartment buildings and communal gardens transformed into shared homes.

Though she deals with a different cultural context, Elinor Ostrom's research on communities accurately describes the attitude of the women we interviewed: when people communicate directly with one another, they tend to cooperate (Axelrod 1981; Hardin 1968; Ostrom 1990, 1998). Mutual commitments strengthened relationships between women from the communist generation; working together gave them a sense of community. In this case, community is linked to women's place of residence (A. Miroiu and Golopenţa 2015).

A.A. (seventy-one), retired but still active, voiced feelings of responsibility around neighborhood concerns:

> I don't understand the retirees who don't get out of their home to pull out weeds or do something, because if I do something, if another does something, it is better for all of us. You do what you know; nobody makes you do what you can't. Do a bit of digging, clear the plot.... Is there a dead flower? Cut it; throw it in the garbage bin. Is there some trash on the fence? Take it and throw it.... There is not enough initiative. People don't get involved; this is it. I can't just stay doing nothing, claiming I'm retired, can't be bothered. So what if you are retired? You do what you can! We've had enough of only negative examples.

This can-do attitude permeates these women's little community. They refuse to simply complain about housing issues. Instead, they take action and thereby encourage others to follow their example: "Those apartments were so ugly; I felt I had mud on my eyes when I was looking at them. So I said, 'Hey, let us at least fix ours.' But Mr. B. said, 'Let us go to the local council for money toward renovation.' Heh! And I told him, 'By the time they'll respond, we'll have mushrooms growing on our building' (E.B., seventy-seven). Mr. B., the only man actively involved in these women's communal affairs, exercised authority in his own way. M.M. (fifty-five) remembered that once she bought a special pair of scissors and started to clean up the fence around the common garden: "Mr. B. saw me from his window. He came and took the scissors from my hands, saying, 'This is no job for a woman!' I think he took it as a personal affront against his virility."

Generally, men direct building committees. However, as in the example above, women often play informal leadership roles and perform the required maintenance work:

> Q: You said the president of the committee is a man. Was he involved in repairing the building?
>
> A: Not at all. He just sits there talking. All the organizing fell on G., she is the heart and soul of all this, she organizes us, looks for companies, does fundraising, seeks solutions, supervises the workers. We may be nagging her, but we follow her, side by side. And this is how we managed to have the first building redone in our whole neighborhood. (E.O., sixty-four)

Once they successfully repaired their building, their example caught on, and neighbors in nearby buildings began to organize. These women saw this as an accomplishment: "When spring arrived, people from the local newspaper came. We had just planted some geraniums. They filmed our building and surroundings. And then the journalists called me and asked everything about what we did and how we did it, and I kept saying about what each of us did. And they said, you know, you are unique in town, because nowhere is it so beautiful, with the building finished and flowers in nearly every window. After a month the city council called us and gave us a diploma and a cash prize, which we used to buy flower seeds" (E.B., seventy-seven).

Some of the most active members of this group had strong, collegial relationships that stretched back to their youth. Like other first-generation city dwellers, they lived far from their families and had to build support networks among peers and colleagues. E.B. (seventy-seven), a schoolteacher, remembered colleagues who became friends. She recalled how they helped one another in times of need: "We were all poor—we didn't have much—but every two or three weeks we had a party with music, played vinyl records as one did at the time. We each brought whatever we could from home, be it sandwiches, food, a cookie, something, meatballs.... Colleagues helped each other.... Our female colleague had an event, a date or went to a wedding, and said, 'I don't have shoes. I don't have a dress,' and we each said, 'Come by my place. I have something.' And we clothed each other; it was harmony." The harmony E.B. and other participants invoked correlates to a high degree of scarcity and social homogenization among the communist generation. This was also significant for their discussion of politics under communism, a subject addressed in the following chapter.

Limited Trust: Younger Generations

In contrast, younger generations are less involved with their neighbors. While they engage in polite conversation with them, they do not actively participate in community matters, passively paying their building maintenance bills:

Q: How do you get along with neighbors? Do you go to them when you need help?

A: We are mostly at work. We seldom call on them, or they on us. We don't really participate in the problems of the building, even if called on by the owners' committee. Those who have the time sometimes help with cleaning in spring and autumn and take care of the common garden. We prefer to contribute money. (M.F., fifty-five)

M.V. (fifty-seven) greets her neighbors, but her interpersonal relationships with them end there: "We don't have the time and each goes to their families, and we have more important things to do." Even when they need help, younger generations of women prefer to ask parents or adult children (C.B., fifty).

Ruth Lister (2003), following Carol Pateman (1989), describes the "spiral isolation of women" in family life. In a perceived hostile environment, women tend to turn the home into the main, if not the sole, center of their lives, even if they have paid jobs outside the home. The pursuit of a career did not have the same meanings for women living in communism. While paid employment became a legal obligation, the home itself came to be viewed as a space of lesser outside control, where women aimed to retain greater autonomy by erecting walls of mistrust with those outside the family. Here, this is exacerbated by the absence of an intermediate community, between formal labor relations and family ties (Neaga 2013). It often manifests as a significant lack of trust toward people outside of a small circle, made up mostly of family, or vis-à-vis state institutions (Nicolae 2010). This distrust has led to a low level of voluntary association with outsiders and participation in NGOs.

Our respondents justified their distrust: "The unpleasant experiences with some [of the neighbors], which I did not expect to have. Not everybody was fair. Some remembered you helped them and some forgot. I saw what happened to others. They used to be friends, visited each other; then they fought for whatever reason and then gossip started" (D.S., forty). Other respondents mentioned an overall reluctance to get close to people: "I'm ashamed to ask. So I can't ask. I try to get help, but maybe you don't have friends, maybe you feel too lonely to have friends" (R.T., forty-two). Still, some interviewees described a reluctance to initiate relations with neighbors, but a willingness to help on request: "If they call on me and I can help them, I help them; if I needed help, then they helped with small things like carrying furniture and stuff. But no visits, no sharing everything about my life" (M.F., fifty-five). These younger women often refuse to ask neighbors for help, even in cases of domestic violence (Open Society Foundation 2000). The democracy generation had a similar attitude about neighbors. They rely almost exclusively on family for assistance, including help with childcare. They prefer privacy and, consequently, impersonal relationships with neighbors.

Professional Competition and Friendship: Transition Women

In our focus group of professional transition generation women, participants noted that, especially after 1989, changing dynamics at work had weakened their collegial relationships. Our interviewees attributed this to the development of a free market—pursuing wealth or survival in a capitalist system of competition:

> Q: You said friendships were more solid during communism. What do you think changed?
>
> A: We were equal [before]; we did not yet have this envy pushed to its limits. (O.D., fifty-five)

Many others responded similarly. L.L.G. (forty) remarked that under communism, most people worked in the same place throughout their careers, could not travel, and had few and uninteresting TV programs to watch. Consequently, people spent their free time in the company of work friends: they had time, incentive, and the disposition to build these relationships. Likewise, B.F. (thirty-eight) observed, in a relatively status- and income-homogenous society, people had greater consideration for one another and cheated less. Another participant stated that money and the new class structure weakened friendships; she felt free market success had changed some people (C.P., forty-eight).

Collegiality and friendship was important to transition generation respondents with professional backgrounds. Neighbors were less significant to them than they had been for women from their mothers' generation. They had to learn to distinguish between genuine friendships and limited, contractual trust with those who became their professional competitors, however.

Rural Women: A Dwindling Community

When collectivization began in the late 1940s, labor moved from the household to state-controlled spaces. Men and women migrated in search of employment in the steelworks near Călan and in factories and the service industry in other towns, decimating the village of Sâncrai's population. The village cooperative's workforce was therefore largely made up of women. In recent years the population has become older and more female; many are widows. The local shop/pub, frequented mostly by men, was traditionally the main space for public gatherings. Women met in each other's courtyards or at church.

In addition, the school had a *cămin cultural* (cultural hearth). Constructed in the 1920s, it hosted a variety of cultural activities and community gatherings. These events were less well attended as migration increased in the late 1950s and 1960s. By the 1980s, the cultural hearth's activities had largely ceased. However, our oldest respondents had fond memories of this space and the activities that took place there before and during the communist period. They remarked that teachers living in the village served as community leaders: "The teacher mobilized us all. Parents went to paint the walls, they all knew what to do; after they were done painting they were cleaning the windows. . . . Both the school, its garden and the cultural hearth were cared for" (V.S., eighty).

Before 1989, young people were involved in the cultural hearth's activities, organizing meetings, evening gatherings with music and dancing, concerts, and films. These events attracted people from nearby communes, particularly as the village hosted a ball (*nedeie*) at Pentecost. For a while after 1989, when industrial plants closed and people returned to the village, residents hoped to see a revival of this local institution. But that revival has not happened.

The Orthodox Church: Religious Privilege and the Weakening of Religious Communities

The weak correlation between religious beliefs and civic activism in Romania needs to be placed in a specific context. Before 1948, most people in Hunedoara belonged to the Orthodox Church. In the urban areas we focused on, there were also sizeable Greek Orthodox and smaller Catholic and Protestant (Baptist,

Seventh-Day Adventist, or Pentecostals) minorities. In Sâncrai, most people belonged to the Orthodox Church, and some were active in the Lord's Army, an evangelical Orthodox movement that began in the 1920s. A few Greek Catholics lived in the village, generally individuals who had married residents of Sâncrai; most converted to Orthodoxy, as no other religious services were available in the village. Women belonged to the community of believers but never played leadership roles in the parish administration.[3]

After 1945, the RCP used the secret police to control urban and rural religious institutions and discouraged intimate horizontal parochial communities. Traditionally, the Orthodox Church enjoyed a special relationship with the state known as *byzantine symphony*. The state and church acted and spoke with the same voice. No matter the nature of the regime, the church recognized it and prayed for its leadership (Leuștean 2009). The RCP tolerated several religions, including Orthodoxy, Catholicism, Lutheranism, Unitarianism, and Judaism, as well as the Baptist Church. Among them, Orthodoxy had a privileged status. Having established a *symphonic* agreement with the communist state, the Orthodox Church aided the government when it banned the Greek Catholic Church in 1948 (Ardelean 2011; Bănică 2007). The Orthodox Church profited, as it managed all of properties of the Greek Catholic Church between 1948 and 1989 and converted many of its parishioners.[4] Moreover, the security services recruited some Orthodox priests and used the confessional to collect information (Stan and Turcescu 2007). Trust in the church personnel subsequently diminished a great deal.

While nationally the Orthodox Church had a privileged position, in Hunedoara the explosion of the urban population presented it with challenges. As large waves of people migrated to cities, they lacked sufficient housing. Urban development plans projected new cultural and recreational spaces—cultural hearths, libraries, parks, stadiums, and pools—but did not anticipate new sites of worship (Mărginean 2015). Therefore, Hunedoara's growing and largely Orthodox population had few places to practice their religion.[5] For communist and transition generation respondents from the city, the possibility of an intimate parochial community did not really exist until after 1990, when several churches were built, including the All Saints Cathedral.

Our respondents acknowledged low church attendance during the communist period. The structural factors mentioned above partly explain this, as does the formal interdiction against RCP members' participation in church services.[6] However, during the communist period our interviewees stated that they continued to go to church more regularly than their fathers and husbands. They especially attended during holidays and for special events, like baptisms: "We celebrated all major events of our lives together: our birthdays, our children's weddings, baptisms; we did everything together, and we helped each other with these events, with baptisms, with weddings" (E.B., seventy-seven). In these cases, however, church attendance had more to do with social obligations and communities of kinship and friendship than with a spiritual community of worship or participation in Christian good works.

The Orthodox Church's involvement in charity work has been historically weak. The rise of the Lord's Army in the 1920s was a direct response to this perceived doctrinal and institutional deficiency. Some of our urban respondents, especially those from the transition and democracy generations, likewise identified this as one of the church's weaknesses:

Q: Does your church organize charity actions for the poor?

A: No, not really. A little, actually very little. We are Orthodox and very little comes from the church. The priests seldom organize us to help each other. (C.N., forty)

Q: What role do you think the church has had and should have in a community?

A: The church has an important role. It has one and will continue to do so. The social problems were neglected, at least by the Orthodox. Generally, the other churches got very involved in community life. But there are some Orthodox priests who created around themselves the desire to initiate social programs. As far as I know, around Bucharest the social activities are more and more widespread, they made homes for the elderly, ecumenical chapels in hospitals, pastoral care for the sick. Not so much happens in our area. I say it is very important, it is one of the attributes of a good Christian to do good to others and I think it is the first institution that should be a model for social activities and humanitarian help. (D.L., fifty-five)

For these urbanites, exposure to other religious denominations and traditions, especially after 1989, altered their expectations of the church and its social responsibility to confront issues such as poverty and eldercare. They have begun to see the Orthodox Church's lack of initiative as a problem.

Rural respondents who identified as Orthodox had a somewhat different position. For them, even during the communist period, the church was accessible and, along with the school, represented the focal point of informal communities. Everyone knew each other in the parish and many had close relationships. Yet our interviews revealed that even in rural areas, the church took little interest in community needs:

Q: Are the local authorities helping you?

A: Town hall gave us lots of money for the church, lots! (T.B., fifty-eight)

A: But we also gave! For Persian rugs, curtains, new chairs. (V.S., eighty)

Q: You say some of you are in the parish council. What exactly do you do?

A: We must take care of cleaning. (O.C., forty-eight)

> A: We bought little icons and prayer books from Ukraine, and we started selling. And we bought a vacuum cleaner for the church. We don't have one at home, but the church has. We bought new priestly robes and a cupboard for the priest to store them, and we bought things for the altar. (T.B., fifty-eight)
>
> Q: But are the parish council and the priest taking care of the parishioners? Does the priest tell you who is in need and how can they be helped?
>
> A: So in our village he only takes care of the church, less so of parishioners because there is really not the case . . . to help someone in such a personal manner . . . although there have been situations when it might have been better if we helped someone. But we were sort of shy; we could not get close enough. God forbid we embarrass the person or their family. Since we have this democracy thing, there is a sort of pride. Everybody hides within themselves and in their families; people are no longer those they used to be. (G.B., seventy-eight)

In other words, the priest and parish council's responsibility centered on the material care of the church rather than on the social needs of the parishioners. The priest rarely exercised Christian love through good works. While some of our rural respondents were reconciled to this reality, others turned to the Lord's Army for change.

Greek Catholics, the Lord's Army, and Protestants: Persecution and Community Support

Respondents from especially the communist and transition generations who belonged to the religious denominations the communist regime drove underground spoke at greater length about the state's impact on this aspect of their lives. For some, religious oppression led to social ostracism and encouraged deep mistrust in any form of collaboration between political and religious (i.e., the Orthodox Church) institutions:

> My father was a Greek Catholic priest and the communists crushed us. My mother was a teacher, was left with three children: two boys and me. She was kicked out of teaching in schools, and then my father did six years in jail because he did not want to quit his religion. That was in '48, when the communists came and destroyed under Stalin's tutelage everything that was about culture and religion. . . . We have recovered somehow, but we never fully recovered. Me, I was kicked out of school for a while; my brother was not allowed to go to school, and thus, they destroyed a family. Not only ours, many. After I finished high school, I came to take the college entrance exam to study pharmacy in Cluj. And because I had a bad file, they wrote after my name "pass without a place." (A.T., seventy-one)

While the communist regime guaranteed employment for every adult, over time it began to discriminate against "class enemies," those whose families or behaviors were deemed "bourgeois" or "reactionary." Before 1964, when the regime released its political prisoners, many people avoided contact with "class enemies," further ostracizing them.

Members of the Lord's Army in Sâncrai, especially local preachers,[7] were persecuted at the beginning of the communist era. Many were imprisoned, as T.B. (fifty-eight), V.S. (eighty), and G.B. (eighty-two) told us in their interviews. Following its formal disbandment, the largely female group had to meet discreetly in one another's homes. The wives of imprisoned preachers had no income to support themselves or their children. Their informal religious group stepped in to help (E.B., seventy-seven; M.M., fifty-five).

During our discussions with members of the Lord's Army, we asked if its adherents' relationships differed from those among regular Orthodox parishioners. The participants in our focus group thought so. They felt that interactions were brotherly (nonhierarchical and intimate) and members helped one another like family. When a member is ill or unemployed, others offer goods and money; they comfort each other in times of mourning and support the elderly and infirm: "We bring them water, cut their fire wood, wash them, clean for them, like between brothers or even better, because my family never helped as much as the [Lord's] Army did. But the priest from the church tells us nothing about all this" (T.B., fifty-eight). Women's efforts largely sustain this community with little help from the clergy.

Though not explicitly banned, Baptists and Seventh-Day Adventists were also subject to persecution under communism: "We, as neo-Protestants, were totally marginalized. . . . Years before, I could not enroll in the Faculty of Letters to study languages and history because I wrote 'Baptist' in the religion box. Ooooh . . . it was a pity; they did not allow me to even register for the exam. I wanted to teach Romanian. Well, I could not enroll there, so I enrolled to study medicine, where they did not ask for the file.[8] Had Ceaușescu lived, we would have ended up totally brainwashed and eating from the common bowl of soup, as he was planning to do to us" (A., forty-one). Though she successfully pursued an education and career, this respondent's experience of exclusion disillusioned her. She equated the regime's policies with oppression and impoverishment.

Like other persecuted denominations, Baptists developed tighter, more active communities of support: "I am a Baptist Christian, and so is my family. We help each other. At least once a month, on the first Sunday, we have a voluntary collection, which is then distributed to the poorest members of our church. For each holiday—Easter, Christmas, Harvest Day—we collect money. We call this action 'holiday happiness.' Everybody gives money or food, and we distribute it to the poor. We know which families are poorer or in need; there is a list with them. When you do something for others, this gives you a great satisfaction" (L.J., thirty-eight). These forms of assistance developed during the communist period. Baptists continue to practice them today.

Since being legalized 1989, other voluntary religious associations have appeared. A.T. (sixty-one), a Greek Catholic, told us about the Mariana Center, which includes a retirement home and offers cultural programs and psychological support. Female members travel together, have a book club, read and discuss newspapers, and provide peer counseling. M.V. (fifty-five), a member of a Lutheran church that developed ties to another Lutheran church in Holland, talked about this institution's activities. Under church guidance, people work in a youth ministry with a broad social scope: "While young, they must be taught how to be just, fair, hardworking, family-loving people, to be individuals you can rely on." In contrast to our Orthodox respondents, interviewees from other denominations explicitly linked their core religious beliefs to moral and social values.

Religious Differences and Interfaith Relations

Respondents did not express any sense of superiority or disregard for members of other denominations. In *Gen și cetățenie*, a study based on the same set of interviews as ours, Diana Neaga concludes that "despite Dennis Deletant's view that resentment developed between majority and minority worshipers due to envy[9] and despite the realization of the privileged position held by the Orthodox, from the interviews (but also from participatory observation during fieldwork) one comes to the conclusion that this exterior constraint also led to more trans-confessional cohesion among groups of friends" (2013, 253). Like Neaga, we did not notice tensions between different religious denominations. In the focus groups and when respondents recommended other subjects, they did not differentiate between their friends, colleagues, or neighbors on the basis of religion.

Some of our respondents even attend one another's churches, especially during important Orthodox, Greek Catholic, and Catholic holidays. They describe themselves as lucky, celebrating occasions like Easter twice—once in their church and then again in those of their spouse or friends. Religiously mixed marriages[10] were common among our interviewees and more broadly in the region. A few respondents had converted, but they linked their decision to personal disappointments with their denomination rather than to doctrinal obligations:

> What can I say to you? Me and my husband, we became Catholics, and we got married. We did this before marriage because I don't like the Orthodox rite, I don't like hypocrisy, to preach one thing and do another. I like simple things in life and in everything I do. . . . Generally, I don't lie, I don't mock other people; I tell everyone to their faces, without offending them. I like going to a priest whom I trust enough to make my confession, to tell him exactly how I feel and for him to tell me if I did good, if I did wrong, to guide me on how to live among people. (M.S.M., forty)

This respondent, born on the cusp of the transition and democracy generations, clearly does not link her religious identity to familial or social expectations. For her, the moral failures of the Orthodox Church, which she implied included priests' activities as secret police informants, led her to convert. She described Catholicism as a better fit with her own moral code of honesty and felt it offered more guidance on "how to live among people," or how to be an active member of a community.

Volunteering and NGOs

Valeriu Antonovici's (2015) conclusions in *Munca patriotică în communism: Radiografia unui ideal falsificat* (Patriotic work under communism: The X-ray of a falsified ideal) resemble our own findings. Despite the communist regime's use of the word *voluntary*,[11] individuals were forced to work for the common good. People came to associate the term *voluntary* with coerced participation in public works, like trash collection. Moreover, under communism, NGOs did not exist. These two factors go a long way toward explaining the reluctance, especially among our communist and transition generation respondents, to join associations and volunteer.[12] Younger generations, not included in our sample, are less apprehensive about these activities and understand the genuine meaning of the term and its practice (Molocea 2015; Vlad 2015).

Few of our interviewees belonged to NGOs, and none took part in organizations that sought to advance human, minority, or women's rights. This does not mean that our respondents do not informally organize for different purposes, however. Yet, when they do, their aim is rarely to challenge national or local policies. The most active of our respondents were divorced or widowed single mothers, unmarried women, and married women with adult children. In other words, women with more free time. In interviews and focus groups, they identified three main areas of interest: culture, charity, and nature.

Cultural Activities

During the communist period, the Metallurgist (*Siderurgistul*) Steel Plant sponsored a cultural club in Hunedoara.[13] It continues to function as a small literary circle today. Our only interviewee who participates in it was A.S. (seventy-one), a retiree others identified as the most active among our group of elderly subjects: "We meet at the literary club; we are about fourteen people. We may bring in new people now and then. The club is called Victor Isac.[14] . . . We meet weekly on Wednesdays and prepare poems, each of us. . . . They are very talented, you know! We do this as a hobby; we don't make a career out of it. We follow the ones before us who were, unfortunately, only recognized posthumously, if I recall." The type of organization and community described here is particularly attractive to urban women. Unlike communist-era volunteer work, the informal and open literary circle involves minimal obligations and requires only a small time commitment. Meetings take place regularly, but there is no pressure to attend. Furthermore, the noncompetitive atmosphere alleviates participants' performance anxiety. If the marketization of the economy after 1989 created tensions and competitiveness among old friends, this sort of organization provided a substitute for some of those weakened relations.

The Hunyadi Castle, built in the fifteenth century, also offers activities for locals and tourists.[15] During the communist period, the castle maintained its status as a museum. However, the state neglected its renovation and did not program any activities at the site. After 2001, restoration of the castle began. Over time, it has become a center for cultural activities. For example, every July since 2011, a regional NGO, DevArt, uses it to stage its Opera Nights Festival. The predominately middle-aged audience includes many of our interviewees from the transition generation. The city organizes other activities at the castle, often in election years, that tend to attract a younger, male crowd. These include reenactments of medieval battles in the castle courtyard and medieval parades.

One of our interviewees, O.D. (fifty-five), is very engaged with cultural events in Hunedoara. She organizes book launches and musical events and encourages her friends and colleagues to attend theater performances and art exhibits.[16] She hosts artists in Hunedoara and leads cultural tours. Since the Opera Nights Festival began, she has also become a fundraiser. But O.D. does this independently of any formal association: "O. keeps the flag up in all respects, and we follow her because we like it; she takes us out of our routine, she makes life more enjoyable and interesting" (C.P., forty-eight). The pleasure these respondents associated with volunteering suggests they have moved beyond the notion of activism as coerced "patriotic" work.

Charity Work

While many of our interviewees rallied behind O.D.'s cultural initiatives, others helped D.L. (fifty-five), a retired judge, with her charitable activities:

> Immediately after I retired, I got involved in community projects with two NGOs. One is the Pensioners League, which brings together many women who want to do something for the community, as this is a city with so many retirees! There are currently 230 members. I hope that by the end, we'll have at least 500 to 600 pensioners, especially women, involved in the community's activities. We have another association, a Romanian Dutch one—it is called Adriaan van Bergen—which assists with homecare for older people with health issues, and we are about to put in a proposal for another project for assisting final-stage cancer patients in need of hospice care. We hope the project will take place over the next two years. For now, it's mostly something we think about. (D.L., fifty-five)

Volunteers who contribute to these organizations are often elderly and live in relative poverty. Yet they assist others who are even poorer or lack mobility, because these volunteers see themselves as both able and relatively better off than the beneficiaries, who do not have state assistance or familial support.[17] The organizations described by D.L. offer a mutual-assistance network that corresponds to our respondents' view of charity work. The Red Cross was the only other healthcare organization our respondents belonged to.

The interviews did not indicate that NGOs in Hunedoara have organized protests or other public manifestations.[18] The local press does not report on such organizations and activities. Thus, they remain largely invisible, and the local authorities continue to ignore the issues they address. Moreover, the municipality, churches, and local NGOs overlook serious social concerns:

> We do not have even a single charity to help the children with parents working abroad or at least to help a man who drinks, who lost control. We do not care about the poor Roma people living in those buildings near the market, virtually on top of each other, without work and without resources.[19] There are no organized activities to help the afflicted. There is indifference, that's the word that I'd use to stigmatize ourselves and the municipality. We are indifferent; we have still not trained or educated ourselves to care. We need to be more altruistic and not just within the small spaces between friends. When someone is in trouble, we get together and we try to help, but our unity does not have a form yet; it's just contingent. Everything we do is haphazard and conjectural. (C.P., forty-eight)

This harsh indictment of both official and community indifference follows our respondents' critiques of the political leadership and citizenship culture. Other interviewees expressed similar views on specific municipal and national policies.

Like most villages in Romania, Sâncrai has no formal NGOs. Family, neighbors, and religious communities, like the Lord's Army, support those in need there. Demand for assistance considerably exceeds the available resources.

Environmental Engagement

Environmental pollution impacts our quality of life in significant ways. Though the Hunedoara region was almost pristine before 1945, by 1989 industrialization had transformed it into one of the most polluted areas in Romania. The results were dire: "When I was a child and a young woman, the sky was always gray, yellow, and red. The smoke penetrated the buildings' walls, the grass, everything. Not to mention our lungs. I remember, once in '82, I think, some German engineers came to offer antipollution filters for free in exchange for the residues. What do you think was the answer? 'We're not giving away our waste for free'!" (M.M., fifty-five).

The collapse of the local heavy industry after 1989 had one immediate positive effect—the air quality significantly improved as vegetation overtook the mammoth crumbling factories.

Fig. 5.2 Hunedoara in the 1970s. In the foreground, the Hunyadi Castle can be seen. In the background, one can see the smokestacks of Hunedoara Steel Plant and the clouds of toxic air they emanated. In the original photo, the color of the smoke is reddish-orange. Copyright Vilhelm Gret, used by permission.

The communist regime's environmental policies focused on the creation of parks and forest conservation. After 1989, local authorities of the neoliberal regime cut the budget for these endeavors, occasionally privatizing land and introducing few, if any, limits on development aimed at preserving green spaces. The Roşia Montana case illustrates the government's utter lack of concern for environmental problems. The government awarded a Canadian company rights to a massive open mine without any regard for water pollution and other major environmental problems, such as deforestation. The activities of this company aimed to turn large portions of pristine mountain forests into a massive open pit and to poison the ground with cyanides. Activists, especially young people in large cities much farther away from Roşia Montana than Hunedoara, placed it at the center of their environmental agenda and eventually put a stop to the enterprise (Branea 2015). This kind of grassroots activism has not developed in Hunedoara, and inattention has had negative consequences. We will return to this issue in the last chapter.

Here, however, we want to highlight some of our respondents' environmental concerns. Their comments reveal a perception of an overwhelming public indifference, especially among retirees and the young, that translates into inactivity. For example, A.A. (seventy-one) complained that the population and authorities neglected parks and playgrounds. She felt people should join associations and volunteer, since the municipality seemed unwilling to solve environmental problems:

> There are so many retirees, especially grandparents and elders who sit all day in their homes; they have nowhere to go out, a nearby park or some backyard, although there is plenty of space and plenty of greenery. They cannot go to any vacation resort due to their financial circumstances, as retirement benefits are modest. We don't have enough playgrounds either. It would be good if the municipality or the church would be much more involved to change the lives of those in need or of these people who worked a lifetime and are left alone. But they are not. If they sit idly, then at least we should get organized and do what we did through coercion under communism.

Our respondent ironically referenced her communist-era voluntary service. Yet there was a tinge of nostalgia in her voice. In essence, she acknowledged that the postcommunist regime had failed to find better solutions to environmental problems. Her comments echoed Antonovici's (2015) findings on the decline of volunteerism since 1989.

The comments of our interviewees highlight the gendered nature of how public spaces function as gathering spots. Hunedoara is "a city with women pensioners locked in their homes and men playing cards and chess in special clubs," said E.O. (sixty). Female pensioners, many of them "full-time grandmothers," have few places where they can socialize in public. Parks and playgrounds, where they once performed voluntary service and later took their grandchildren for walks, have fallen into disrepair: "If there is nobody to push the inhabitants of this city and the mayor's office from behind with a whip, they just don't care" (M.F., fifty-five). It is the old habit, the well-known routine of the top-down initiatives, she hinted. The frustrations our respondents are experiencing as a result have given rise to a critical attitude toward the activities of the municipal elected officials, as our next chapters show.

Volunteerism is central to a civil society aimed at furthering citizens' well-being (Almond and Verba 1989; Habermas 1989; Putnam, Leonardi, and Nanetti 1994). During the communist period, the meaning of volunteerism was perverted, and today, women are still reluctant to join associations. Consequently, there is little collective action. Yet voluntary nonpolitical communities are vital for democracy. They are the loci for building social capital, trust, common values, and norms. Volunteer communities cement social bonds beyond individual friendships and family relationships.

Among the communist generation, women tended to become more active, especially in homeowner associations, once they retired and/or their children left home. They also often took on new roles in their parish community or in charitable organizations. This might be the case because mothers of small children tend to identify their own interests as secondary to family responsibilities:

"I am looking after my family and my job. It is more than enough for me" (M.G. thirty-two).

In contrast, the transition generation respondents' communities appear to be more professionally oriented. They prefer professional and cultural associations. None of them belonged to NGOs with social justice or women's rights agendas. Some, however, consider themselves feminists and sympathize with the work of such organizations in larger cities (for example, O.D., D.L., C.P.). Overall, however, with the exception of charity and religious self-help groups, across generations, our respondents did not engage in significant forms of civic activism.

This lack of civic engagement should not be viewed as a lack of care for the common good or the civic spaces these women inhabit. As the chapter on work has shown, they are overall more vested in a view based on work and results in the community of employment than in a view focusing on volunteering NGOs. With the time demands these women face every day, from full-time work to primary home- and childcare responsibilities, their ability to dedicate themselves to many other endeavors is quite limited.

Notes

1. Our discussion does not include educational establishments, since the state operates nearly 100 percent of primary and secondary schools (there are not private schools in Hunedoara) and the vast majority of institutions for higher education.

2. For economic and ideological reasons, the communist states encouraged living in apartment buildings and strongly discouraged people from building privately owned, single-family homes (Mărginean 2015).

3. We found no evidence of women in leadership positions. However, some priests' and preachers' wives (*preotese*) may have held informal roles in their parishes.

4. The state banned other denominations with smaller followings, including Jehova's Witnesses and the Lord's Army. The Orthodox Church collaborated with the state to dismantle the latter movement.

5. Only one new Orthodox church was built in Hunedoara city between 1945 and 1989, the Buituri church.

6. RCP members were supposed to be atheists. However, many only feigned this belief (Preda 2009). Furthermore, while the generations of communism and transition were subject to the regime's forced secularization policies, these efforts were largely unsuccessful as significant numbers of people returned to church after 1989.

7. Though technically part of the Orthodox Church, the Lord's Army had an informal, grassroots network of community preachers. Some, but not all, were priests. In Sâncrai, the preacher was not the priest. The local priest, moreover, served as a secret police informant (M. M., fifty-five).

8. As previously mentioned, though most professions were open to anyone, certain restrictions continued to apply to both women and men. In the humanities, arts, and especially social sciences, admission committees discriminated on the basis of class origins. The same criteria did not apply to natural science and technical disciplines, such as engineering and medicine.

9. Deletant 2006, 195.

10. There is no formal obligation for a non-Orthodox spouse to convert to Orthodoxy upon marriage. In the cases we presented above, political persecution and convenience led to conversion.

11. The terms *voluntary* and *patriotic work* were used interchangeably in official documents and the press, conflating work for the common good and nationalism. Conversely, in the regime's totalizing and polarized discourse, nonparticipation in public works was construed as potentially unpatriotic or even treasonous.

12. Though legally permitted, NGOs, including sports and fishing clubs, were tightly controlled by the regime.

13. The club had a large building that included a cinema, spaces for dancing, and rooms for artistic and scientific meetings. The steel plant financed the facility and paid trainers and other staff. When the plant closed, these activities disappeared. During our last visit in July 2016, the building was in ruins.

14. Victor Isac (1917–2003) was a writer from Hunedoara. A political prisoner during the early years of communism, he taught writing and literature at the club. After the collapse of communism, he played an active role in reviving the local branch of the National Peasant Party (NPP) ("Prison Experiences in Communist Romania," accessed May 6, 2018, http://www.pametnaroda.cz/story/isac-victor-1917-1830).

15. The first document that mentioned the Hunyadi Castle was written in 1443 ("Mențiuni documentare," accessed May 6, 2018, http://www.castelulcorvinilor.ro/mentiuni-documentare/).

16. Hunedoara city has a public art gallery, a House of Culture, and a municipal library.

17. The only public retirement home has a limited number of spots. Chronic underfunding means that the institution has to rely on private donations to stay afloat ("Centrul Social Multifuncțional pentru Persoane Vârstnice," accessed May 6, 2018, http://www.primariahd.ro/pagina/centrul-social-multifunctional-pentru-persoane-varstnice).

18. In February 2017, Mihaela Miroiu witnessed the first protest against corruption in Hunedoara. As in other Romanian cities and towns, these protests took place in a grassroots fashion in reaction to a law that was about to be passed to protect corrupt elected officials at the expense of more broadly upholding the rule of law.

19. This comment refers to the Roma ghetto we mentioned in the introduction.

6 Communism as State Patriarchy

WE BEGAN OUR project with the premise that democratic citizenship needs feminism to develop (Lister 2003; Nussbaum 2001; Phillips, 1991, 1997, 1998). Moreover, democratic citizenship assumes individuals are rational actors who understand their own interests and freely make political choices. Without respect for individual autonomy and political pluralism, democratic citizenship and feminism, in the most generic sense, are meaningless. In the one-party state, leadership was hierarchical and centralized. The RCP did not consider individuals to be rational, autonomous actors. Following the Leninist principles of the "vanguard of the proletariat," RCP leaders considered themselves the only "conscious factor" in society. They claimed to know people's interests better than citizens themselves. Every local, regional, and national enterprise and institution was set up to operate according to this principle. How individuals came to understand and relate to these communist institutions was what we sought to hear about in our interviews.

A fundamental goal of our research was to understand how our respondents conceive of and shape their relationship to politics. The communist regime described in these paragraphs marked their lives in every aspect. Women from the communist and transition generations had a prolonged experience of single-party rule that profoundly impacted their understanding of politics. Since the RCP dictated individual-state interactions, intimate family choices, professional development, and consumption, the political was personal.

The democracy generation, born after 1970, had not reached adulthood in 1989. For them, communist politics represented a context rather than a direct relationship. While a few interviewees in this group had finished high school in 1989, most were schoolchildren. Though, like all elementary school students, they participated in communist organizations, such as the pioneers, they have few memories of the period or the regime's impact on their lives. They most often discussed the economic crisis of the 1980s and the government's failure to effectively address it. However, their memories frequently drew on their parents' stories about the daily stress associated with procuring basic goods.

Keeping these differences in mind, we asked respondents the following questions: How and to what extent did politics impact their individual experiences? What was the RCP's role, and how did the party affect them? What were the pros and cons of communist-era policies, particularly in terms of gender norms and the post-1966 pronatalist policies? Did they join the RCP and did membership alter their professional or personal lives? How did they manage the economic crisis of the 1980s?

Our analysis focuses on explicit opinions respondents expressed about government policies. Previous chapters touched on many of the themes addressed here. In this chapter, we examine in greater detail how these women saw the communist regime and how they believe it shaped the public sphere and their view of citizenship.

The Party Hierarchy and Personal Autonomy

The paternalistic communist state cared for its citizens, though in a humiliating fashion. To paraphrase Fyodor Dostoyevsky, regimes of this kind "free you of the burden of freedom" in exchange for bread.[1] Consequently, our interviews revealed a number of ambiguities, as respondents sorted through the protective and oppressive aspects of communist regime policies. Our interlocutors zeroed in on the tension between too much and too little state care. None of them had experienced Western-style welfare policies, whether minimal (like the United States) or optimal (some of the Scandinavian countries), so that was never their frame of reference (McBride and Mazur 1995).

Between 1948 and 1989, the party was ubiquitous. All factories, schools, hospitals, and administrative institutions had an RCP Base Organization (*Organizație de Bază*), a nucleus of party members who worked in the establishment to manage professional activities in accordance with the party program (Partidul Comunist Român 1970). In an attempt to organize and control workplace activities undertaken by every category of employee, from manager to janitor, the RCP mandated the creation of an Organization for Democracy and Socialist Unity in each institution. These organizations had the appearance of autonomous workplace groups parallel to the RCP, yet they were entirely subordinated to the RCP through the reporting mechanisms. The local units reported to regional bodies controlled by the RCP, and the regional bodies, in turn, reported to a national organization: the Front for Democracy and Socialist Unity, established in 1968.[2] This front was itself subordinated to the RCP in terms of both personnel and financial resources. Party members in each institution elected representatives to the Bureau of the Base Organization (BOB), an organization that played an important role in the ideological training of institutional management and staff. In this regard, a limited form of bottom-up accountability existed at work.

Anecdotal evidence and our interviews suggest that personal and professional qualifications often led to BOB officials' election. For example, in hospitals, top doctors generally sat on the BOB; in factories, it was engineers with significant experience in their fields; and in schools, hardworking, well-performing teachers tended to win elections. Among potential BOB members, the RCP favored those with a talent for negotiation and conflict resolution. More women served on BOBs than at higher levels of the party structure.

Though they did not confer it, BOBs vetted employee applications for party membership. Following an initial investigation, the BOB called a vote of all party members at its institution. Applications were then forwarded to the local party office (in Hunedoara, the municipal council). The local office verified applicants' statements and presented them with a membership card. Without party membership, employees were disqualified from managerial positions, promotions, and significant salary increases. In certain politically sensitive professions, nonmembers simply could not practice. In law, for instance, they could not hold judicial or prosecutorial positions, and in education, they were barred from teaching in the social sciences and history (Jinga 2015).

During the dictatorship of the proletariat period (1948–65), "class enemies," sometimes broadly defined to include nonethnic Romanians, could not become members of the RCP. Furthermore, the regime imprisoned many individuals who had belonged to interwar-era political parties as well as middle-class professionals, small business owners, intellectuals, and priests. (Dobrincu, Tismăneanu, and Vasile 2007). Respondents from the communist generation often discussed this history: "He was an engineer. He was also a political prisoner. When the communists came back, he was a pupil and a group of pupils were waiting for the Americans who did not come. And many have hoped in this thing when the Russians had already arrived. Afterward, they formed a group of young people and somebody divulged their identity" (D.D., eighty-four). Religious minorities, like Greek Catholics, were also arrested and barred from the party (A.T., seventy-one). Later, during the nationalist-communist period (1966–89), individuals with relatives or connections abroad could not join the party. Women from the transition generation were the most affected by these policies (Neculau 2004).

To mobilize all individuals, the RCP created institutions for young children meant to transform them into "new communist men." At the age of nine, children joined the pioneers; at fourteen, the Communist Youth Union (CYU). At eighteen, they were invited or sometimes pressured to apply for RCP membership (Jinga 2015). In the 1980s, the communist regime created a kindergarten organization, the Fatherland's Falcons, to attempt politicization of four- to eight-year-olds.

Women remained a minority among party members, and even fewer held leadership positions in the regime. In 1949, the percentage of female members was only 8 percent, according to a report by Ana Pauker (Jinga 2015, 257). When Nicolae Ceaușescu came to power in 1965, that percentage had grown to 25. Over the next thirty-five years, Ceaușescu attempted to recruit women, yet in 1989, they made up only 36 percent of the party's membership (Jinga 2015, 259). Female underrepresentation in the party was common across the Eastern Bloc (Fidelis 2010).

In *Gen și reprezentare în România comunistă, 1944–1989* (Gender and representation in communist Romania), Luciana Jinga (2015) concludes that the RCP rarely listened to women members and left little room for bottom-up initiatives concerning gender issues, especially after the party removed Pauker in 1952. Raluca Maria Popa (2016) has shown that the NCW, the official women's organization, attempted to promote women's issues, especially access to safe birth control and concerns over the double workday. However, the evidence she and Jinga present reveals the female leadership's inability to meaningfully shape policy.[3] In short, aside from a few local initiatives and minor legal modifications, the RCP and the women's organizations it controlled dictated policy to women rather than engaging them as active citizens with legitimate concerns. This institutional context framed our respondents' interactions with both local and national authorities between 1945 and 1989.

Communists by Conviction? Communists by Choice?

The Bucharest leadership often reprimanded local RCP offices for low female membership in the party. Pressure to enroll more women perverted the recruitment process (Jinga 2015). Respondents often discussed how people were pressured into joining the party. D.D., an eighty-four-year-old retired nurse who moved to Canada in the 1990s, recalled:

> Q: Do you think you suffered because of communism?
>
> A: Yes. My husband was a political prisoner. I was always fearful. Even when I was coming back from work, I was looking behind to see if there was anyone following me. I wasn't even accepted in the CYU because they saw me wearing a little cross around my neck. I wasn't allowed to advance in syndicate positions or to attend special courses on postgraduate professional education. My colleagues who were part of the party were sometimes promoted, given raises. As for me, I always had the minimum salary. In the 1970s, I couldn't stay put in the same place, as I wasn't making progress at all. . . . Thus, I became member of the party, just like that, not because I wished to.

She joined the RCP not out of conviction or an interest in politics but because she realized it was necessary for professional and economic advancement. E.B., a seventy-seven-year-old retired elementary school teacher, similarly noted: "I was not able to advance. I filled out my file twice, and it was turned down because I was not a party member and I had to become one eventually."

Respondents from the transition generation also joined the RCP to minimize professional risks. While they generally received membership as a reward for good grades, a quota system governed admission (Budeancă and Olteanu 2009; Cioflâncă and Jinga 2011):

> Q: What were your reasons to enroll in the party?
>
> A: Years in a row there were no medical specialization exams. There was a time when I heard that only party members will have the right to take the

exam and I asked the mayor of the commune to allow me in the RCP. I told her, "I want to enroll in the party so I can take my specialty exam," but she said, "I am sorry, but first I need to receive two peasants to be able to receive an intellectual and the last two I made members was when I received the agronomic engineer. I do not have any places this year." (L.G. fifty-three)

This particular quota was based on class and place of residence. Though this respondent did not mention gender, under Ceaușescu it was also a factor (Jinga 2015). Here, the local female mayor privileged one quota requirement over another. Bucharest's conflicting directives occasionally enabled local authorities to make choices; these worked to the advantage of some applicants and the disadvantage of others.

D.L. (fifty-five) became a member because she wanted to pursue a law degree. She worked as a jurist in a textile factory. Because her father was an ethnic Greek, however, she never held a leadership position or worked as a magistrate under the communist regime. This was her biggest professional regret. Ethnic Hungarian women, like O.D. (fifty-five) and L.L.G. (forty), had similar stories about pragmatic membership gone unrewarded because of ethno-nationalism.

Even in rural areas, people had difficulty evading pressure to join the RCP. G.M., an eighty-three-year-old pensioner from Sâncrai, recalled how they were "nagged to become party members." She worked for the Agricultural Production Cooperative. She joined the RCP to further her daughter's education: "My daughter wanted to go to college, and for that at least one parent had to be a member of the party. My husband was sick. If he were to become a member, he had to spend more time in the factory, two hours every day for meetings, and he would have died. Then what could I do? I had to enter the party for my daughter to be able to go to the law school."

V.S., an eighty-year-old retired collective farmworker from Sâncrai and G.M.'s neighbor, got off more easily:

> A: My neighbor was in the party.... Back then, if you were not in the party, your children were not allowed in schools. But in my case, my husband was a member.
>
> Q: Your husband became a member because he was forced or because he wanted to?
>
> A: Yes. How could you want that? He didn't want to, but he had no choice.
>
> Q: But those who were members lived better than the nonmembers?
>
> A: Eeee.... To hell they did! They were all working, just like us!

Her comments remind us that pressure to join the RCP was not gender specific. Yet since women identify as their children's primary caretakers, this pressure could have gender-specific qualities. Sometimes other family-related considerations also impacted women's decision to join the party. V.D. (forty-eight) enrolled in the RCP in 1989: "My husband was about to get an important position, as a military commander in Orăștie,[4] and the condition was for me to become a member as well." Significantly, none of our interviewees described joining the party as anything other than giving in to pressure or as an opportunistic move. Nobody claimed to have signed up out of conviction.

If Communism Gives You Lemons[5]

By the 1970s, the RCP had developed a more meritocratic system for recruitment, at least in the professional sphere: "They were no longer accepting in the party all lazy, uneducated people and people who amounted to nothing; they needed capable people" (E.B., seventy-seven). This allowed women to join the party and cultivate skills they could use in entrepreneurial, civic, and political pursuits after 1989. For example, A.S. (seventy-one) stated: "In the RCP I had many positions and was elected to many committees and commissions, as I was very active. After '89, I started capitalist activities. . . . I still have my party member card; I'm not afraid of it. That was the regime and the context. What else could I have done?"

In addition to her job as an accountant, A.A. (seventy-one) had party responsibilities. The skills she honed served her well after 1989: "I was going to multiple locations and attended meetings. Most of them had to do with the production line: to work, to build, to do that, what to do. As I was working on a construction site, there was always a working plan, there were always objectives. They discussed a lot about work, professional preparation for everyone, seriousness, behavior between people, between employees. They also discussed families, not to leave them on their own, to make sure they behaved appropriately, so they would not embarrass themselves in society." Her response illustrates how the RCP paternalistically intervened in citizens' private lives.[6] A.A. was part of the BOB structure. At BOB meetings, she sometimes had to consider marital problems,[7] as spouses, even nonparty members, could lodge complaints at their husband's or wife's workplace: "We had cases when the wives of our RCP members came to complain about the abusive behavior of their husbands. As party secretary, I was running the investigation of the cases" (M.M., fifty-five).

In the examples our respondents mentioned, complaints came from the wives whose husbands beat them or spent their salary inappropriately, impoverishing their families. Sometimes the BOB took measures to address these complaints, as the anecdote above suggests. Punishment ranged from a written warning to salary garnishes or even exclusion from the RCP. In the absence of policies targeting domestic violence, BOBs gave women a space to air their grievances. When women like A.A. or M.M. sat on the BOB, accusations stood a better chance of being investigated and offenders punished.

The Best of Communism: Education

Almost all respondents from the generation of communism came from poor, rural families. This demographic barely touched on the drama that unfolded after the regime nationalized private property, annulled individual ownership rights, and took away citizens' control over their income. Many of these women were the first in their families to live in an urban area. They agreed on the benefits of communism, including free education and healthcare, job security and pensions, and affordable housing (Jinga 2015; Mărginean 2015).

After the communist takeover, industry expanded exponentially. Development required educating people and luring them away from the rural, subsistence economy. At the beginning of the communist period, 60 percent of Romanian women were illiterate (Jinga 2015, 14). The regime guaranteed seven years (as opposed to four before the communist takeover) of free, compulsory education. In the 1980s, it raised the requirement to ten years of schooling. In addition, students and parents no longer paid tuition for vocational, high school, and postsecondary education. The regime had eradicated illiteracy by the 1960s.

During the 1940s and 1950s, the children of poor workers and peasants benefited from an educational affirmative action, as the regime reserved most seats in high schools, vocational schools, and colleges for them (Jinga 2015). The children of "class enemies," conversely, competed for a small number of places, when they were allowed to compete at all. These measures permitted respondents of the communist generation to leave the countryside and earn vocational, high school, and even postsecondary degrees.

A.A., a seventy-one-year-old retired accountant, described a typical situation that many of our respondents reported:

> I was a girl from the countryside. We were six siblings. My parents were humble; they worked all their life, and from the money they made from selling cereals and animals, they bought land to give to each of us when we got married. Before communism, they could not afford to educate us in the city, as they had to pay. Once communism came, I was able to leave the house, go to school, have a scholarship, and study for a vocation in the city, like some of my brothers. Back then, the tendency was for everyone who had the opportunity and was capable of learning to go to the city and study something according to his or her capabilities. After graduation, I was able to find a job and make a living on my own.

The RCP did not have the funds to support the regime's free public services. To finance their programs, the party appropriated all private property and redistributed this wealth as it saw fit. The process pauperized peasants, artisans, and other small business owners (Kligman and Verdery 2011):

> The land was taken for the collective farm. So were the cattle, the machines—everything that existed in the household. My parents and other people's

parents were left without anything. They were barely able to raise ten chickens. They were very poor. My mother would come to me and she wouldn't have ten lei to give me to buy notebooks. She would give me five. That is what she had, as the state took all the wheat grains. They left them very little. They were barely able to live. They worked for the collective farm. My brothers who remained in the village would do the same. They all worked but made very little money. For them it was really bad. (A.A., seventy-one)

Though she was proud of her education and professional achievements as an accountant, our respondent was also aware that her success had been partly contingent on the terrible economic losses her family incurred.

Respondents unanimously valued education. Sometimes they idealized communist-era schooling: everything was better or more "real" then—the professors were more dedicated, the admission process more correct, the students more disciplined. B.F., a thirty-eight-year-old family physician, was nostalgic for the respect people with an advanced education once enjoyed. She felt they were seen as intelligent and qualified and believed that after 1989, these people's skills had been marginalized. However, B.F. overlooked how the dictatorship of the proletariat imprisoned many intellectuals and that until 1989, most party leaders did not have a higher education (Tismăneanu 2003).

While many respondents acknowledged that after 1989 there was even greater access to education, especially higher education, they felt programs offered little preparation for the labor market. This stood in contrast to the communist era: "Now it is much worse than during the communist time. It is much worse because the youth is not guaranteed jobs, is not guaranteed housing, they go to school for nothing, they get an education for nothing because, even when educated, they do not have work in their country, and if they do, they are poorly paid. Then they go crazy, leave their parents, leave their dear ones, their native places to go abroad [to be among strangers] and work for nothing. Strangers will never see them as their own" (M.B., fifty-seven). Her comments demonstrate how women from the communist generation internalized the state's approach to education. The regime allocated seats in vocational, high schools, and colleges in order to supply the centrally planned economy with a labor force. After graduation, the RCP's local leadership assigned jobs to graduates. Thus, while education was free, the central planning committee dictated access to it. The system was not designed to empower women (or anyone) per se but rather to control the flow of qualified labor into the areas it deemed necessary.

Job Security

Women had new employment opportunities under communism. Article 18 of the 1965 constitution stipulated: "Citizens have the right to work. The state will ensure the ability to perform, according to one's skills, labor in the economic, administrative, social or cultural sectors of activity, to be remunerated according to its quantity and quality. For equal work, there is equal pay" (Constituția Republicii Socialiste România 1965).

The industries in Hunedoara County, however, privileged male workers, especially between 1948 and 1956. In 1956, 39 percent of Hunedoara County's active female population were salaried workers,[8] but by 1966, the percentage had dropped to 24 (Mărginean 2015, 203). These statistics indicate the regime failed to plan for women's employment. Two industries—mining and steel—employed 65 percent of the salaried population, and men dominated both fields. Consequently, women had to compete with one another for a limited number of jobs outside these industries. Overall, given the higher percentage of women in the active workforce in the 1930s, this suggests that, despite its claims to the contrary, the communist regime did not prioritize equal economic opportunities regardless of gender.

Although they wanted to work, some of our respondents could not find employment. Others ended up having to commute on a daily or weekly basis:

> Q: How did you manage to commute to work?
>
> A: Imagine that I had to commute with a slow train in harsh conditions . . . eight hours a night, you understand? I still carry that image with me at night. . . . Yes, with workers, with. . . . I am thinking how courageous I was. Do you know what I mean? . . . . Anything could have happened to me. . . . I was hitchhiking to get to the other train that would bring me home. I would work a shift and then had to hitchhike to reach the railway station. I was riding with whoever would take me. (O.D., fifty-five)

This woman, a medical doctor, had a commute that involved unsavory, unsanitary, and sometimes unsafe conditions. While she and others lodged complaints, nobody in the regional party leadership addressed their concerns.

For C.B., a high school teacher around the same age as O.D., employment under communism meant "a lifetime routine" without significant change or new opportunities: "You know why? Because you were mainly a prisoner of a certain job and place." C.B. had been a good student with the potential to do humanities research. However, after 1974, the RCP stopped creating new positions in institutes for research and higher education. This policy was part of an effort to integrate "learning and production." Consequently, the regime created new jobs for college graduates only in villages, small towns, and newly established industrial towns—locations without universities or other research facilities. In short, the regime's claim to provide job security did not always translate into safe, sufficient, or fulfilling jobs.

Housing Benefits

The massive industrialization and urbanization that began in the 1950s dislocated a large part of the population (Mărginean 2015). The state began to construct large apartment buildings. While some people lived in rural or even urban single-family homes (many nationalized by 1948), most resided in small, standardized, somber, state-owned apartments. Only a state real estate agency existed. Respondents from the communist and transition generations learned to see this form of social control as a type of personal security:

> Q: How did you manage with the housing?
>
> A: After you got married, the state would really help you. Everyone would petition at the right moment and the company would allocate a house.[9] The state would take care of you and provide a job, a house. From this point of view it was easier, I mean, you would obtain a job more easily, and you had a certain financial stability. (A.A., 66)

Like most respondents from these two generations, her answer showed an uncritical view of the patriarchal state and reflected in part the discomfort generated by the instability of housing markets since 1989. The state would "take care" of you, like a parent looking after a child. However, she did not consider other aspects of this power relationship, for example, the standardization of home options without regard for individual preferences or needs (e.g., people with limited mobility).

Other interviewees, however, pointed out the stifling effect of communist-era housing policies:

> I remember you couldn't take a house in Hunedoara because I didn't have approval for relocation [*mutație*]. We lived six kilometers away, and it was considered a rural area. And then, with huge sacrifices and huge bribes, I bought a completely dysfunctional studio, at the edge of the city, which allowed me to obtain a working permit in the city. . . . How many compromises and charlatans you have to encounter to get such an ID! The same with my Hunedoara ID . . . a lot of hypocrisy. At all levels, there was this issue of connections, nepotism, of everything the communist regime encouraged and everything it left behind. Nothing passes fast from one day to the other. Communism said we were equal. How were we equals? How were we equals when some had everything[10] and others barely survived? It wasn't even possible to fight with the system anymore, which was so corrupt and crassly careless. Thus, did communism bring me anything good? (C.P., forty-eight)

Though she acknowledged access to cheap state housing, her rhetorical question at the end implied a "no" answer.

C.P.'s account provides an excellent example of how the communist regime used access to housing to both limit individuals' choices and reinforce its control over their movement. The regime generally distributed housing to citizens after assigning them jobs, allowing it to further police their mobility. To obtain a *mutație*, a person needed approval from the local authorities who granted it on the basis of employment, marriage to someone in the new location, or similar circumstances.

Fig. 6.1 Dilapidated communist housing. In the 1980s, the local government in Hunedoara decided to add new apartment buildings to alleviate the lack of adequate housing. They were sold to a private investor after 1990, but today they remain unfinished, a relic of unfulfilled promises. Photo by Maria Bucur.

Women like C.P., who sought employment in urban areas, negotiated their goals differently than men did. In Hunedoara, the situation grew increasingly complex in the 1970s. New types of services and jobs appeared, allowing women to find work in hospitals, food canning, and accounting. However, as C.P. mentioned, there was significant competition for these in-demand jobs. A culture of bribery and nepotism developed. Most decision-makers who assigned jobs were men, and the "supplicants" could offer a variety of bribes—money; hard-to-find goods, such as coffee or foreign perfume; or sex.[11] Our respondents did not offer any personal examples of trading sexual favors for employment in cities with better schools and access to other services.[12] However, women across Romania experienced this sort of coercion.

Marriage was another means of mobility. Until very recently, wives traditionally followed their husbands, often migrating from rural to urban areas. This was especially the case in places with a limited job market, like Hunedoara. If women wished to stay in the city—after finishing high school, for example—they often had to marry. These arrangements generated a power differential in the marriage.[13] For women who wished to move to the city, marriage was often a surer bet than employment, especially when the gender imbalance between men and women ages twenty to twenty-four surpassed 20 percent in the 1950s (Mărginean 2015, 201). The communist regime's legislation created the economic conditions for this gender imbalance and women recognized the connection between their predicament and politics.

Though our respondents did not offer many examples, some used their gender to their advantage. The transition generation, who began seeking housing in the 1980s, provided most of these anecdotes. By then, housing policies had changed. The state no longer guaranteed access even to rental units. People were allocated work after graduation from high school or college but had to find their own housing. The only exception was "social housing."[14] One respondent discussed this sort of arrangement:

> In Târgu-Jiu, we had nothing but abject poverty. We had no place to live. He [her husband] had a precarious situation so it was impossible to live with his family.... We arrived as resident physicians. We were constrained and I was pregnant, so I went to the mayor. And I went to him so many times until he told me, "Comrade, if you come one more time and I see you like this," he said, "I think you will give birth ... so I beg you not to come anymore." ... I had no options, you know. I had this strength many times in my life. And then, out of pity, because this is the right word, he gave us a studio. (O.D., fifty-five)

In extreme cases like this, women sometimes successfully used their status as mothers, appealing to the sentiments of male decision-makers. These instances only reinforced the unequal and gendered power dynamics that the communist regime allowed or even encouraged.

Most women from the transition generation, especially those with a university education, could only buy apartments. Their daughters, the democracy generation, consequently had a particular image of communist-era housing and nostalgically discussed the communist period. However, their views were generally based on secondhand information: "I have a very good opinion about Ceauşescu's time. It was much better than now. They gave you a job after graduation, a house after marriage; now you don't have anything anymore. You are taking the risk to go to college and end up a shepherd and live in a sheep cot or I don't know where" (M.D., twenty-four). As we have shown, the devil was in the details that our older respondents shared, details the democracy generation ignored. Job safety was a benefit with many hidden costs and access to housing a process mired in gendered power differences and abuses.

The Worst of Communism: Pronatalism

While our respondents expressed nostalgia for some of the benefits communism offered, they unambiguously condemned other aspects of the regime. At times, they discussed these issues in relation to gender; other times, they framed them as problems both men and women faced. Their most significant critiques concerned political control, the lack of individual rights, food shortages, and their inability to access birth control and information. Here, we address these issues in order of their impact on women's identity as gendered subjects of the communist state.

The most uniquely gendered and significant communist regime policies concerned birth control. Abortion was decriminalized in 1957 as the government prioritized its need to mobilize women in the workforce. Thus, it gave them tools to regulate pregnancies. Over the next decade, without help in managing their double burden, women opted to have fewer children.

Greater access to education also provided important positive incentives to delay reproduction, especially in the absence of available or affordable childcare services. For some women, childcare facilities were not conveniently located, while unsanitary conditions and poor food quality forced others to take their children out of daycare. For instance, grandmothers raised both authors. Mihaela Miroiu's mother did not have access to childcare, whereas Maria Bucur's mother had to cope with a child who was continuously sick when left in the daycare of a state facility.

In 1966, the Ceaușescu regime returned to a vision of women's reproductive capacities that eugenicists had promoted during the interwar period (Bucur 2002). The regime legislated a draconian pronatalist policy that utterly altered the relationship between the state and every fertile female citizen (Băban 1996; Doboș, Jinga, and Soare 2010; Jinga and Soare 2011; Kligman 1998). The RCP's all male Political Executive Committee ignored the National Women's Council's critiques of the law (Jinga and Soare 2011, 112–35; Popa 2016). The policy dictated and curtailed women's sexuality, as the law imposed significant prison sentences on women who had an illegal abortion or anyone who assisted them. Safe birth control was increasingly difficult to find. Gynecological exams became a political obligation. In short, the state assumed control over women's uteruses.

While the radical gendered implications of these laws are undisputed, few scholars have analyzed women's refusal to comply with these policies as a form of political dissent. A 2008 study, however, puts this act of dissent in a larger context, comparing it to Greek Catholics who continued to practice their religion after it was outlawed (Bucur 2008b). By engaging in illegal forms of contraception, especially abortion, women refused to accept the communist government's takeover of their reproductive capacities. For over two decades, millions of women of childbearing years placed their lives and liberty in danger, knowing the potential consequences of their behavior: lifelong sexual or medical problems, public shaming, exclusion from the RCP, and prison time.

Our respondents discussed these atrocious policies and shared their views of these measures:

Q: What do you think was worst for women during communism?

A: They forced you to have four children. Basically, you did not have the chance to live your youth, to live like husband and wife, because you always feared you would get pregnant. Many women died because they themselves interrupted their own pregnancies! The secret police would arrive, the prosecutor would arrive, and they stayed in the hospital while you were there. It did not matter that you had two more children at home, if you aborted they would imprison you. I do not miss those times. No. (D.V., sixty-nine)

A: It was horrible. It was impossible to have a normal sexual life because of fear of getting pregnant. And if you were to get pregnant, God forbid, you know. . . . I mean you do not know, because you are young. . . . You were not able to get an abortion, in case you would make it there . . . even I, as a nurse, could not . . . and we would get interrogated in detail about what we did and so on. . . . And that fear. . . . Birth control pills, if you wanted to take them, you needed to procure them from the black market in Timișoara.[15] I did not like this time. It was the same in bed: with fear, with anxiety. . . . Especially toward the end, we were scared at work as well, in case someone would come . . . fear of having an informant among patients that are curious to hear what we were talking about in the hospital. (E.C., fifty-three)

A gynecologist, A.C. (fifty-five), provided the most illuminating and detailed account of how women experienced the combined policies of coercive birthing and food shortages:

The lives of the women I was treating were bleak, full of deficiencies. If you were higher on the professional ladder, you made all kinds of deals with a store seller to get a bit of butter. It was humiliating. There were mothers who could not offer their children an orange. Not only could you not find oranges and bananas, among other things, but you could not find apples, the most common fruit grown from local trees. Women always had to find solutions to procure food for their children. I remember a comment my son made when I came home and I said proudly, "I procured a bit of butter." He asked me "Mama, don't we know how to purchase anymore? Why do you have to procure?" I think with this he said everything, and we were a family of a physician and an engineer with a single child. (A.C., fifty-five)

In the 1980s, the dearth of consumer goods and services became ubiquitous. Many basic goods were rationed: food, fuel, gas, and electricity (Olteanu, Gheonea, and Gheonea 2003). The economic crisis made raising a child increasingly difficult. Women had to assume the costs and risks of compulsory motherhood. Under this regime, they began to view pregnancy as a heavy, even an unwanted burden; it was "a problem that needed to be solved" or "a situation that you have to get rid of."

As other scholars have observed, women rarely spoke about pronatalist policies freely. Consequently, the topic was little studied in the immediate postcommunist period (Băban 1996). Gail Kingman's book, *The Politics of Duplicity: Controlling Reproduction in Ceausescu's Romania* (1998), familiarized international audiences with the drama Romanian women experienced. A decade after its publication, a new generation of scholars working in Romania continue to explore this topic (Doboş, Jinga, and Soare 2010; Jinga and Soare 2011).

Scholars are not the only ones reluctant to address this history. Only four of our respondents talked about reproductive traumas. A.C. (fifty-five), the gynecologist quoted earlier, provided the most extensive narrative of the impact pronatalist policies had on the lives of her contemporaries. She spoke primarily from professional experience:

> I do not know what the pronatalist policies meant from stories. I know what they meant from what I lived, because as physicians, we were forced to do checkups to detect pregnancies. Women from the country would be loaded up in cars after church service (this way the militia would find more women at once). They called these cars cockpits. They were a type of big van with wood benches inside. They brought them at the dispensary, and I did around sixty gynecological checkups a day. There was also a gynecologist from Hunedoara. I had to check to see if they were pregnant or not and record the pregnancies, with or without women's consent; that was the thing that seemed to me very degrading.
>
> I looked for cervix injuries, vaginitis, thus diseases, but it seemed to me degrading to force a woman to accept the checkup as if I were a cattle slaughterer. If a woman was pregnant and the pregnancy was not recorded in the first three months, the physician could be prosecuted for not recording it. And then I was recording one, two pregnancies because I knew I would discover a six- or seven-month pregnant woman who did not succeed in interrupting her pregnancy, and I would record her so that I would not be prosecuted. This happened even in hospitals. There was a woman hospitalized with amygdala, so they took advantage and brought a gynecologist as well, to check if she was pregnant. And so on. Working as a gynecologist, I saw how women tried to get rid of pregnancies, and perhaps this also disgusted me completely and made me completely hate communism.
>
> Poor women, they sought all kinds of solutions! I found a swivel in a woman's uterus, or there were some bags that had metal handles that women introduced in their uteruses to get rid of pregnancies. I witnessed many infections, many deaths that nobody says anything about. Many women died, young women who remained pregnant in impossible and diverse circumstances. There was no means to protect against pregnancy whatsoever. There were no birth control pills. There were no condoms. Many young women were so desperate.
>
> For one of these young women, I literally cried, and I will not forget her for the rest of my life. She was eighteen years old and got pregnant. Her boyfriend left her, and in anguish, she introduced a wire rod in her uterus, which she perforated and got peritonitis. I participated in her surgery, and I have had that image imprinted in my mind my entire life. I was with the department head physician when we opened up her belly. Everything was pus. Everything

had to be taken out, uterus, additions, thus that woman was at menopause at eighteen as if she were fifty years old. Even the bowels were affected. We had to perform a bowel resection, and in the moment we would try to sew the tissues, they would break under our eyes. Everything was decaying. I do not know how we managed to save her life. She had draining tubes, and through each of them pus would flow. After months of suffering, we managed to save her. For years, I wondered whether it would have been better for her to die at that moment, as she was left physically and psychologically mutilated. She never recovered. She was at menopause at eighteen years old, suffered a hard surgery, which, due to the big quantity of pus, led to complications and was left with chronic abdominal pain. Psychologically, she was destroyed, as she was already an old woman at a young age; the possibility to get married and have children was canceled by the surgery, a surgery that saved her life. If that girl had had the possibility to undertake an abortion under legal conditions, the following year after, she could have gotten pregnant; she could have married and could have had children.

It was a horrible time. Women refused to have sexual lives, and from this, family fights and abandonment resulted, as women were scared, scared of pregnancy. For a woman any sexual contact meant only panic and pain, not pleasure. It was continuous stress.[16]

To control the population at large, the communist regime presumed every fertile woman was guilty of not wanting to get pregnant. The regime did not trust women to fulfill their civic duty of compulsory motherhood. Both the letter of the law and its application clearly communicated that to reject a pregnancy was criminal. As E.C. (fifty-three), a nurse, explained: "We were scrutinized, terrorized, and even at work, we were nosed around, even by patients, who wanted to have us caught up and jailed." Thus, the collapse of communism rid women of an intimate and constant fear.

In contrast to the horrific traumas women experienced before 1989, A.C. (fifty-five) depicted the postcommunist period as a net gain for women. She primarily linked improvement to the control women regained over their reproductive lives, which she identified as a political issue: "Today there are means of contraception; there is information. Any young person is informed, unless he/she does not want to be. There are subsidized birth control pills for students, pupils, and women in difficult family situations. They are given away by the family physician if he/she completed family planning classes or by family planning centers, which are everywhere. It is extraordinary what happened after the collapse of communism, if only from this perspective." For her and other women of the communist and transition generations, the end of communism and the beginning of democratization were "a permanent celebration, regardless of the difficulty of the transition."

Scarcity and "Rights"

The beginning of the communist period pauperized some populations. Even those who had little before the takeover became poorer. However, none of our respondents spoke about this issue beyond discussions of collectivization. Instead, they tended to focus on increased economic opportunities without linking these improvements to the regime's expropriation policies.

Some generational differences emerged when respondents specifically discussed their economic well-being during the communist period. The communist generation often expressed sentiments along the lines of "everyone could manage. You could not find [things], but no one died of starvation" (T., fifty-seven). This woman grew up poor, and her statement has to be understood in terms of that background. It does not equate to a blanket endorsement of communism. Similarly, many women from the generation of transition consider the communist period in relation to other experiences, especially the post-1989 era:

> A: Although the salaries were not high, with ten lei I was buying food in the market for a week, as meat was three lei per kilo.
>
> Q: What about during democracy?
>
> A: Well ... they gave freedom, so anyone can go anywhere, whoever has money can go anywhere, whoever does not have money cannot go anyway. If one does not have money he goes stealing, as some became rich and others poor, that is what I see more of during democracy. (D.L., sixty-three)

Despite D.L.'s critique of her declining economic power after 1989, she did not have high praise for consumption under communism.

Many of her views, and those of her generational cohort, stem from the economic experiences of the 1980s. The international oil crisis and Ceaușescu's attempt to maintain his independence from foreign powers (including the Soviet Union) amplified the economic hardships Romanians faced. Ceaușescu invested heavily in nonviable industrial enterprises (some in Hunedoara) and sought to eliminate Romania's foreign debt by exporting consumer goods. Consequently, in Romania, there were massive shortages of basic consumer goods, including food, clothing, and heating supplies. As one respondent recalled: "You had to wait in line at night to get milk; to get bread and oil on a ration; to get some poor-quality chickens after six to seven hours of staying in line, small like pigeons.... You had money to no avail" (G.A., seventy-two).

Though not explicitly formulated as such, there is a gender division in how people accessed consumer goods under communism (Massino 2007). Men generally procured electricity, gas, and fuel (from wood to coal), legally or illegally. Women dealt with food. Consequently, our interviewees' answers focused primarily on food shortages. Women from the communist and transition generations had the most experience contending with these challenges. They remembered daily activities as frustrating, humiliating, and traumatizing. L.M., a forty-nine-year-old tennis coach, is one of two respondents who traveled to the West before 1989:

Q: What were you impressed by during your trips to the West?

A: I went abroad and I bought for myself soaps and chocolates, chewing gum and stuff like that; this is what I desired back then. Athletes from the West were looking down on us, at our poor gear (they had twenty [uniforms] for each competition whereas we had three that we used to hand wash daily): "Look at the poor!" We went to Italy, in Milano, and breakfast included hot chocolate: "Our chocolate is good, isn't it? You don't have it in Romania." "Of course we have it as well." What could I say? I despised those people, and you know why? We played tennis better than them, and they were looking at us with pity.

The memories of material shortages among those from the democracy generation concern their role as consumers, rather than buyers of goods: "My parents, through their jobs, not having any connections in grocery stores, fed us strictly with the food on ration, which was hard to cover the calcium and vitamins that our bodies demanded. Now this is reflected in the diseases of my generation. I myself got a bad anemia. After I had my son, I did not have teeth anymore, the teeth wasted away" (V.D., thirty-eight). When she euphemistically mentioned "connections in grocery stores," V.D. connected memories of her family's poverty and its effect on her health to the artificial scarcity created by the regime. Others of this generation made fewer, if any, political references and simply recalled scarcity and their family's efforts to secure goods. V.D., moreover, pinpointed the source of her generation's less negative recollections of the communist period: "We were optimistic because we were children."

However, there is another important connection between consumption and citizenship. Groceries that could be purchased only with ration cards were called "rights." People bought their "rights" to bread, oil, sugar, meet, eggs, or flour. Thus, the regime distorted the very notion of "rights," distancing it from the concept of rights found in the UN Declaration of Human Rights, the ideas of freedom and property or the pursuit of happiness (Gheo and Lungu 2008; M. Miroiu and Miclea 2005). Faced with these abstract rights, the communist generation often reacts with bewilderment: "The current ones give us empty words. They do not give us anything" (C.O., fifty-four).

Scarcity and Social Solidarity

Authoritarian regimes with austerity policies, such as those of the RCP, can encourage a *homo homini lupus* syndrome.[17] Conversely, they can also cement informal associations and forms of solidarity. A few of our respondents openly acknowledged manipulating their connections to secure various advantages: "During communism, I did not stand in any line. My husband worked for a cafeteria restaurant. He utilized a truck, so he had rides to Bucharest. He brought food, he brought everything. . . . I really did not lack anything when my three children where little. They really did not know what it meant to eat chicken claws and soy salami. For me, it is more difficult now" (L.C., sixty-three). Similarly, S.B. (forty-two) worked as a cook in a cafeteria: "I was working like a slave on a plantation, but I was able to support three families at that time, to get food for others and to have very good relationships with many important people, as all of them needed me. Now, there is everything, but what for, if there is not enough money?" Both women contrasted the secure economic status their privileged access to resources gave them under communism to the hardships that followed, when their artificial advantages melted away.

In larger urban centers, like Bucharest or Timișoara, the size of the population magnified the experience of scarcity as people queued for hours for basic goods (Gheo and Lungu 2008; Neculau 2004). In medium-size cities and villages, informal networks (family, friends, and neighbors) more readily supplemented the official supply chain. The neighborhood feel of smaller towns also dampened the brutal struggle for survival, as everyone shopped at the same stores and small markets, personalizing the experience of scarcity.

Our respondents contrasted the value placed on and the quality of human relationships during periods of shortage to "the selfishness and loneliness of nowadays" (L.G., fifty-three). Women from the communist and especially the transition generations responded at length to questions about passive resistance. Addressing the difficulties of securing food and other daily tasks, their stories centered on sympathetic friendships as a form of resistance in a bleak, claustrophobic, and depersonalized society. Echoing the views of the entire second focus group, O.D. (fifty-five) offered the following description:

> I was an organizer during communism, and I have continued to be one under capitalism. I would go and say "D., we don't have the means, but we'd like to party!" And D. would sell me under the table salamis, Nescafe [the group laughs], and Pepsi. I remained my entire life profoundly grateful to her, she organized us . . . she gave us a hall. You know what I mean? She would always give us a steak with fries because there was nothing else you could find in a restaurant. . . . I bought a video player that cost the price of a car . . . a huge financial effort. We gathered here, there were only two small rooms, we ate bread spread with grease and chili, because what was good needed to be saved for my son, remember? And we bought beer (the only brand on the market) with one and a half lei, yes, and we would sit on the floor watching the black-and-white TV; but I swear, secretly I saw all art movies, all the movies awarded at Cannes and the Oscars. Maybe there was also in our youth that dose of romanticism, dreams, ideals, plus another aspect: we were equal folks and besides all this we read way more. Women booksellers, shops and restaurant managers were the cleanest. This abject envy did not exist back then. Then we got lonely, we became capitalists, we became evil in our desire for wealth. (O.D., fifty-five)

Like O.D., other respondents described a decline in social solidarity after the fall of communism. Pointing to specific causes of that solidarity, such as the economic homogenization of the population, not all were nostalgic:[18] "There was solidarity against someone and against all interdictions" (D.L., fifty-five). That "someone" was the regime and its politics of scarcity. It became an object of loathing. Our respondents collaborated with those around them to keep the noxious aspects of the regime at bay, a form of solidarity that disappeared in 1989: "I had a single, eight-hour [per day], noncompetitive job; the borders were closed and temptations were few. We had two-hour propaganda broadcasting per day. What could you possibly do? Meet your friends. We did not trick each other because there was no competition. Nowadays relationships are much more pragmatic and interested" (V.D., forty-eight).

"With No Freedom, There Is No Creativity"

RCP members among our respondents acknowledged the advantages they enjoyed under communism. However, they were often very critical of the regime as well. They offered both general and specific critiques, some of which were damning.

When we asked, "What was communism good for?" E.B. (seventy-seven) and A.S. (seventy-one) responded in a lively and decisive manner:

> It was good for nothing. It ruined everything, the entire Romanian heritage. Besides ruining the economy, as rural as it was at that time, the agriculture was still functioning; now it is absolutely nothing and nothing works. In the first place, it ruined people's minds because it promoted unfortunate, lazy, uneducated, and garrulous people to top jobs in state institutions and eliminated from those jobs the educated and hardworking.... It ruined people's minds so badly that even now the majority expects the extraordinary, expects a miracle to happen. They expect to receive. Who can you receive from? Nobody gives you anything for free if you do not provide it for yourself, if you do not work your bones to make a living. Communism did not provide it for free either, as you paid the house they allocated to you, you studied and made efforts to get that job, not to mention they would send you to the end of the world, as the job distributions were mandatory. If our country is in this state today, it is also greatly due to this state formation that we had for so many years; forty-five years, it is a lot of time and many generations. (E.B, seventy-seven)

A.S. (seventy-one) specifically discussed freedom of information and expression and liberal competition:

> I do not understand those nostalgic people that miss communism. First of all, we were stagnant. All countries were developing while we were left unchanged. We were too restricted: somebody dictates, leads, and you do exactly what they say. We had two to three hours of television broadcasting, and it was all propaganda; you were not allowed to go abroad.... If you do not give people freedom, you do not have creativity! For us to be a real democracy maybe thirty or fifty years need to pass. There is chaos everywhere. But even so, it is good to allow people to be free. That is how they become creative, how they discover and create values.

Beyond official propaganda, few Romanians had direct knowledge of the West (Gheo and Lungu 2008; M. Miroiu and Miclea 2005).[19] Closed borders rendered the rest of the world a projection: "It was bad, as you had no connection with anyone. Romania had no connection with the external world" (I.P., forty-two). The secret police constantly monitored foreign visitors and Romanians could have contact with them only in controlled situations. After 1989, contact with the rest of the world was often experienced with bewilderment and anxiety instead of as a liberating encounter of discovery. One of the few respondents to recount a trip abroad, A.B. (fifty-one), described her reactions: "The first time I made the comparison was in 1987, when I went to Israel. When I came back I questioned for the first time how will we ever come out of communism. How? What will happen when we will come out? The differences were so big! I am not surprised at the stage we are in now because I know the abyss we started from and nobody took us tactfully from the beginning, as was the case for others."[20]

After working for thirty-five to forty years, women from the communist generation retired soon after 1989. The regime never delivered full gender equality—women earned less, performed significantly more hours of unremunerated labor, retired earlier, and received smaller pensions than men (Muravchik 2002; Pasti 2003; Pasti, M. Miroiu, and Codiță 1997). Today, many of these respondents barely get by and cannot count on support from their children, who also face economic hardship. Age kept most of these women from exploring new opportunities after 1989, and political parties and civic associations have failed to attract their support. Moreover, prevented for decades from exercising their will outside of private circles of family and friends, they are not initiated in the practices of grassroots political and civic activism (Antonovici 2015). Consequently, women from the generation of communism feel they have been forced to do things their whole lives. At best, they might potentially assist younger women in constructing a post-1989 society.

Women had an adaptive and pragmatic relationship with communism. Under this regime, women generally did not lose property, social/professional positions, or political rights. Rather, the communist takeover offered them access to education, work, and housing, and many women continued to find satisfaction until the introduction of the regime's pronatalist policies (1966) and the economic crisis (1979–89). Yet the dearth of information about the West, travel restrictions, and limited contact with foreigners meant women from the communist generation had little to compare their lives to (Jinga and Bosomitu 2014).

Women from the transition generation have a more ambivalent view of communism. The state offered them employment but often assigned them to undesirable locations with poor conditions. They had difficulty securing state housing. This generation consequently does not feel a debt to the communist regime. Moreover, older respondents see political involvement as a waste of time. Before

1989, they developed a pragmatic view of party membership as nothing more than a means for professional advancement. They did not question the gendered policies of the regime, except its pronatalist program. They felt the scarcity the regime created was the main source of their problems, which they confronted by developing mutual-assistance networks (Neculau 2004).

The democracy generation has vague memories of life before 1989. Thus, its members have an even more ambivalent relationship with communism. Some find the dearth of consumer choices and the restrictions on speech and movement reprehensible. Others describe the regime positively, since it took care of citizens, and draw comparisons to the present lack of job security, rising housing prices, and declining access to education.

Given the all-encompassing web of party organizations during the communist regime, our respondents thought of politics overall as hostile and oppressive. Their experiences often led them to avoid political engagement after 1989: "I had to be mad to enroll in a political party once the obligation was released. It was a frustrating waste of time in the recent past. Meetings and meetings. Many idiotic, long speeches. Give me a single reasonable motive to do that once I am a free person" (M.M., fifty-five).

In short, the communist experience taught women that: (a) politics is a top-down affair where the state generates policy and imposes it on citizens; (b) political inactivity has no effect on them; (c) civic engagement cannot impact Romania's economy; and (d) "volunteer" work is really unremunerated, systematically imposed labor (Open Society Foundation 2000). The lesson they missed was that of the social contract. Only women from the democracy generation have had the opportunity to make direct and transparent choices about their lives (e.g., job, place of residence), political representation, and liberal association in pursuit of common goals and interests.

Notes

1. This formulation appears in "The Grand Inquisitor" chapter from *The Brothers Karamazov*.
2. "Lege nr. 57 din 26 decembrie 1968 privind organizarea și functionarea consiliilor populare," accessed May 6, 2018, http://www.cdep.ro/pls/legis/legis_pck.htp_act_text?idt=27845.
3. Some Eastern European feminist scholars believe the communist regimes had feminist agendas: equal civil and political rights, access to jobs, state support for parenting (daycare, for example), and direct political representation (Daskalova 2007; Ghodsee 2015). Though we agree these policies promote greater gender equality, we do not see them as part of an intentional, explicit feminist agenda. First, the state policed and limited individual rights and personal autonomy. Next, the communist regime did not permit free association or political or civic initiatives (Fitzpatrik 2000; Neculau 2004). The Romanian state exerted tight political control over women's organizations. Consequently, the RCP did not represent women's interests.

4. A city near Hunedoara.

5. The expression "If life gives you lemons, you make lemonade" has several Romanian equivalents, including: "*Să faci din rahat bici, și să și pleznească*," or "to make a strong whip out of shit." This expression was frequently used during the communist period.

6. This makes it difficult to distinguish between the public and private spheres, a distinction at the core of many Western feminist critiques of modern politics (Okin 1987; Pateman 1988).

7. Her euphemistic reference to "appropriate behavior" might refer to either the social or gender norms the RCP promoted.

8. In Hunedoara city, it was only 20 percent, while nationally the average was 44 percent.

9. The Romanian term *casă* generally means abode, including an apartment.

10. C. P. referred to the categories privileged in the 1980s—party activists, the secret police, and employees engaged in the distribution of essential resources (e.g., food, electricity, and gas). This last group often participated in the black market.

11. The euphemistic term for trading sexual favors was *plata în natură*, or "natural payment."

12. For some concrete examples see M. Miroiu (2017).

13. The 1983 comedy *Buletin de București* (Bucharest ID) highlighted the power dynamics of such marriages. The comedy ran in an environment of increasing cultural censorship, suggesting that the regime considered this issue an unproblematic social reality. When it came out, the film was popular, implying it portrayed a familiar situation.

14. These were small apartments with minimal comfort for people living in abject poverty without family support.

15. A city several hours from Hunedoara. Since it was close to the Yugoslav border, where birth control pills and other contraceptives could be bought legally, a lively black market developed in Timișoara.

16. Florin Iepan directed a documentary on this subject, *Children of the Decree*. It was first broadcast in 2005.

17. Man is a wolf to his fellow man.

18. By law, the largest salary (a manager's) in a given workplace could not be more than five and a half times higher than the smallest salary (usually a female janitor). Housing was relatively uniform and apartment size depended on the number of family members. Privileged members of the communist nomenclature and the secret police were not subjected to the same restrictions.

19. Illegally listening to Voice of America and Radio Free Europe was an exception.

20. This is an allusion to the assistance given to Czechoslovakia, Poland, and Hungary (the Visegrád Group) by Western Europe in the early 1990s. Countries not included in this group or in the former Soviet Union did not receive substantial foreign investment for a considerable period after 1989.

7 Facing Capitalism and Building Democracy

In May 1990, Romanian women participated in free national elections in a multiparty system for the first time. This was their first opportunity to exercise their political rights as full citizens of a democracy. The introduction of market-economy institutions and the restart of Romanian capitalism also marked this moment.

In this chapter, our analysis focuses on our interviewees' responses to the questions that elicited the longest and most significant answers about this period. Specifically we look at how they responded to the following questions: How do they make sense of this brief period of democratic citizenship? How do they understand the relationship between the move to a market economy under a neoliberal regime and decline in job security? How do they view the evolution of Romanian democracy and in what ways do they participate in politics? How do women define "good governance," and what are their political priorities? What do they think about Europeanization and globalization and how does it impact them?

Interviewees were often more forthcoming in their responses to these questions than those concerning their private lives and the communist regime. It became apparent that the affairs of the polis and the exercise of democratic citizenship made up an important part of their lives. As we will show, their preference for an ethical approach to politics played at times a negative and at other times a positive role. On the one hand, they saw themselves as ill adapted to the ruthless politics of the postcommunist period. On the other hand, their comments pointed to an important role they could potentially play in consolidating democratic practices and realigning political agendas to focus on citizens' needs.

Exiting State Patriarchy

When Romanian legislators passed a new constitution after 1990, the state discarded its Marxist-Leninist foundations, which had emphasized citizen responsibilities and the state's duty to ensure basic welfare. It adopted a regime based on the rule of law and individual rights (*Constituția României* 1991; *Constituția României* 2003). Today, Romanian citizens' duties include respect for the constitution, the law, and the rights of others; loyalty to country; and active contribution to the public budget through taxes. Along with responsibilities, citizen rights are fundamental for the maintenance of a democratic constitution. There are no formal gender restrictions. In addition, a number of institutions[1] oversee antidiscrimination laws that guarantee women full access to politics.[2]

In the years following 1989, the state as a service provider and protector of citizens' rights was a novelty for Romanians. Until then, the state had been a paternalistic entity that cared for its citizens in exchange for unconditional obedience, like an authoritarian parent watching over a child:

> Put yourself in our place. You go to bed in a world in which the state controls what you do and do not do in your home, what you eat, whether and where you go on vacation, what to watch on TV, to stay out at a restaurant only until 10:00 p.m. And you wake up in another world in which the state doesn't care what you do. Well, of course the first reaction was to rejoice. That's normal. But it also scared us. The scariest part was that the state cared less and less whether everyone had a job and even less whether we had any food to put on the table. (M.M., fifty-five)

The Marxist-Leninist regime had relieved citizens of the "burden of freedom." Their sudden and complete liberation from the state was disorienting. It required learning to navigate in a world with radically different rules (M. Miroiu 1997, 1999). Our respondents described feeling confused when they discussed why the state stopped ensuring the right to work; the apparent inability or unwillingness on the part of the neoliberal state to tame savage forms of capitalism; the lack of control over carelessness, corruption, and ethical public behavior; the role of local and national elected officials, politicians, and parties; and why women made up only a tiny minority of political leaders.

Facing Neoliberal Capitalism

Economic policies under communism explicitly opposed a free market.[3] In a command economy, the logic of production is divorced from consumer demand. For instance, one respondent, D.L. (fifty-five), a jurist in a local textile factory, recounted traveling to Bucharest before 1989 with Hunedoara County's commercial inspector for a textile exhibition.[4] Every five years, this gathering showcased new goods. At the meeting, the male commercial inspector selected skirts, blouses, coats, dresses, and suits for local production and sale: "Imagine this little rotund bald guy, with a worn-out briefcase, who was slightly color blind, and with the obsession that all the comrades from the county had to dress soberly. To heck with his 'sober'! His choices were not sober, they were somber." The inspector never asked his female colleague for input on what professional women like herself would find useful or appealing. In short, demand counted for nothing in shaping choices in production.

After 1989, Romania's planned economic system collapsed. Between 1989 and 1996, capitalism primarily developed through the privatization of entrepreneurship. Before sale, the government granted employees shares of the state companies where they worked. Managers, generally men, grossly undervalued factories' worth and sold them to phantom corporations they had created and owned. On paper, private owners legally took over factories. However, the value of employee shares dropped artificially. Consequently, in the first postcommunist decade, public trust in the emerging stock market flagged (Pasti 1995, 2006). Many individuals came to see privatization, the introduction of a free market economy, and corruption as interconnected processes directed by a small group of men (Nicolae 2010).

Simultaneously, political parties emerged. Many posed as revivals of interwar organizations, notably the NPP and the NLP. Most parties had solidly nationalist platforms; some used communist-era rhetoric, marrying a nationalist agenda with anticapitalist propaganda. The National Salvation Front (NSF), a remnant of the RCP, dominated elections between 1990 and 1996. NSF politicians worked to reinforce a popular fear of foreign investment.

In 1996, when the NPP, NLP, and DP won the national election as part of the Democratic Convention (DC), a massive privatization process ensued that continued to privilege Romanian, rather than foreign, investors. Privatization had dire consequences: massive bankruptcies, skyrocketing unemployment, and a general impoverishment of the population—more than 52 percent of the population lived at (22 percent) or below (31 percent) the poverty line, as did more than 8 percent of entrepreneurs (Dinculescu and Chircă 1998, 17). The Hunedoara region was hit particularly hard.

In December 1999, the EU green-lighted Romania's accession. The political and structural situation began to improve. Changing investment policies and political leadership led to increased foreign investment, especially after 2001. The free market became a more acceptable reality. However, due to the global economic crisis that started toward the end of the decade, the results were not as spectacular as in countries where this process began earlier, especially members of the Visegrád Group.

Our research took place in 2009, after Romania had experienced several peaceful democratic elections and had become an EU member. Most people had come to accept that the state no longer orchestrated economic development or job creation. They had begun to understand their role as taxpayers. Still, we identified important differences between the ways people in rural and urban areas confronted these realities and understood their relationship to politics as citizens. Though we noted some generational differences, education level and place of residence correlated most strongly with our respondents' attitudes toward capitalism and democratic multiparty politics.

The Hardships of Capitalism: Job Uncertainty and Democratic Politics

We have seen how women identified with work as well as their varying evaluations of the state's ability to provide them with jobs. Rural communist and transition generation respondents were more attached to the idea of massive state intervention in job creation and security. Though they complained about the availability and quality of consumer goods during the late communist period, they seemed unconcerned with what they might produce, so long as jobs were available:

> Q: What do you think the state should do with the money it has?
>
> A: If I would have the state's money, you know what I would do? I would give it to the poor ... as the poor do not have ... and create jobs for everyone who can work. (B.E., eighty-two)
>
> A: The state must support all the people and give them jobs. (O.C., fifty-four)

Why should the state assume responsibility for job creation? According to the Sâncrai focus group, without job creation programs, young people "become tramps and give us troubles" or do not get married (O.C., fifty-four); they leave the country (T.B., fifty-eight); or depend on their grandparents' small pensions (V.S., eighty). In short, respondents believed massive social unrest and poverty would result. They were perfectly aware of discrepancies between the active population (four million) and pensioners (six million) and of the likely consequences of this imbalance: "Who is going to pay our pensions?" (M.G., forty-eight). In other words, how would the state be able to replenish the pension funds?

These interviewees based their expectations on guarantees made by a state that no longer existed. As it drastically reconfigured public policy, the current neoliberal regime seemed unaware of how women had come to depend on the caretaking state, especially given the double burden they had to assume most, if not all, of their lives. Our respondents equated democracy with risk taking and the appearance of transparency, both of which they appreciated. However, without first having their basic social needs met, our interviewees had little use for the new regime's promises, such as the rule of law.

As they discussed the eradication of collective farms, our rural respondents criticized both the politics of deindustrialization and agricultural privatization:

> I would like for agriculture to advance a little.... Many elders were left [in the countryside] and it is hard for them to work the land and a lot of it is left uncultivated. So, if they would strengthen agriculture a little bit it would be much better for the entire country.... It would have been good if agriculture, whether called collective or something else, if it were up to me I would give it to everyone.... To ask every person who does not have a job: "How much can you work?" "For this [amount of time]." To bring people to work, as many are without jobs, to pay them and give the people who own the lands 20 percent, 30 percent and, you know, things will work better. (S.M., sixty)

Though she did not use the term, this respondent described a cooperative farm. She felt that the state could help organize operations like this, thereby assisting both the elderly population in rural areas and unemployed youth. While nobody we interviewed spoke positively about communist-era collectivization, they imagined solutions to their economic problems that resembled pre-1989 programs and proposals.

When pushed to consider the significant decline of state resources since 1989, our rural respondents emphasized the role of private initiatives, including foreign capital investment:

Q: If the state does not have money to invest, who can create jobs?

A: Oh, forget about that! We create jobs, if not, let French and Italians come; they have money. (V.S., eighty)

At the same time, our interviewees pointed out the drawbacks of capitalism: "The employer keeps you at work and when he comes to pay you, he does not have money. You stay a month, two months, three months or maybe half a year" (T.B., fifty-seven); "They will pay employees very poorly. Employers do what they want. You do not like it? Leave. There are ten people waiting in line" (O.C., sixty); "You think a Romanian employer would pay more than an Italian one? Do you believe that? Ah! There is nowhere a bigger ineptitude than privatization in Romania." (T., fifty-seven) That our respondents, like most of the Romanian population, lacked the social and economic resources to spark radical change from a centrally planned economy to a market-based one goes a long way toward explaining their contradictory statements about the state's economic role in a free market.

The year we started our research, a quantitative study on "risks and social inequities in Romania" was published. The findings revealed how paternalistic policies, focused on assistance rather than development, impacted the population's understanding of democratic change, risks, and the political roots of social inequality. Our subjects' comments and the solutions they proposed were consistent with the suggestions offered in the quantitative report: "Successive early retirement, fraudulent retirement (especially disabled and agricultural), 'luxury retirement' from the army, police and secret services led to the growth of the number of retired from 3.5 million in 1990 to over 6 million in 2000 while the employed population decreased from 8.1 to 4.6 million, thus creating major imbalances in the welfare system and leaving many persons and families with no income, under the threshold of poverty" (Comisia prezidențială pentru analiza riscurilor sociale și demografice 2009, 2). The report concluded that "benefits for children, for the disabled, orphans, the young out of orphanages, homeless, poor families with many children or single-parent families, long-term unemployed, the HIV infected, victims of violence and trafficking, and other social segments at risk were completely ignored or only superficially protected through programs that most often were inefficient and/or unsustainable" (3). Our respondents likewise viewed long-term state assistance as currently insufficient but necessary for poor children, persons with disabilities, and the elderly. To them, short-term entitlements with strict limitations were acceptable for the unemployed.

In contrast to our rural respondents, urban interviewees more readily accepted capitalism. Some, even among our oldest respondents, had become active in the free market economy. For example, A.S. (sixty-nine) described how she supplemented her pension as a caretaker and through small-scale farming:

> You must have very broad perspectives. You have to get rid of the idea of having a secure job . . . but if you do not have it, you must create it. And I think there is no such thing as poor people, only lazy people in this world. If you really want to work you will be satisfied with whatever work you find. You do not have to ask for help. Everybody asks for help: "The state should solve this and do that . . . city hall should do this, the state that." . . . Nobody will do anything for you if you do not do it for yourself in the first place. Now, it is true that the state has its own responsibilities for the ill, for orphans or abandoned children, obviously. As my husband says: "We are paying nonworking people, that's how it is here!" And they get used to that help and no longer work.

E.B. (seventy-seven), a former schoolteacher, also vehemently opposed the entitlements the paternalistic state had to offer. She criticized the communist regime, arguing it discouraged individuals from taking responsibility of their own welfare: "The great majority expects a wonder, a miracle to be given. Who is going to give it to you? Nobody gives you anything for free, not even communism gave anything for free." She then cited the type of "patriotic work," outlined in our chapter on communities, identifying it as a policy of forced labor. Similarly, A.S. (sixty-nine), a retired nurse and an active entrepreneur, praised the ways the free market and democracy encouraged creativity: "Why did America develop? Look at the Russians, they have a bigger territory than Americans, have resources, and won the Second World War. And where are they now? Americans allowed everyone to do what they wanted, with the condition of respecting certain laws. If you pay your taxes nobody asks you anything."

C.P. (forty-eight), a transition generation woman, emphasized the virtues of competition. After reading widely about and observing the free market in action, she came to believe that "communism was worthless. It was the greatest possible stupidity." Under capitalism, people "learned to start over and over again. We are still influenced by communism—patterns do not get out of your mind—but in twenty years, at least our generation somewhat got rid of those reflexes." Yet she had her critiques of the free market as well: "The generation of my parents felt better because they were coming from abject poverty and the communist political regime gave them job security. . . . It was not this craziness of unemployment, with what is going on, which for many is dramatic."

Though they experienced it in general, our respondents did not directly address the gendered aspects of privatization. This is unsurprising, as most interviewees were not high-level managers and, thus, did not have direct access to the decision-making processes that shaped the transition. One respondent, however, offered exceptional commentary:

> Q: Why do you think no woman got rich through the process of privatizing the [steel] works?
>
> A: Women did not have the courage to do what a [male] manager or a chief accountant dared to do. A woman said to herself: What if I, as a mother, was caught? Not only am I risking my life and freedom, but also the life and development of my children. They started to get rich, not on their own efforts, but through business with the state, which they represented as well. A woman was careful, not adventurous. I think that in Romania 80 percent of those who became rich after the revolution did it not as a result of their own efforts. (M.D., forty-eight)

M.D. equated women's risk aversion to moral superiority. Yet she overlooked the larger context. Even if women had set aside ethical concerns or more readily taken risks, under communism, they seldom held the sorts of leadership positions that allowed men to profit from post-1989 privatization. Consequently, structural barriers also prevented them from thriving in the new economy, especially during the first decade (Pasti 1995, 2003).

While men and women enjoy equal property rights, Romanian capitalism, like communism before it, has a strong gender bias. The overwhelmingly male leadership that ran the communist state and its economic institutions has remained in place throughout the transition to the free market (Pasti 2003, 2006). Many of these leaders failed to invest in the capitalist economy, using the wealth they generated through the acquisition of state business to support lavish lifestyles and/or campaigns to preserve their political power at the local level.

Most women in our focus groups and interviews did not directly address the male monopoly in politics. Rather, respondents focused on corruption, occasionally citing how the male communist elite accumulated state resources by fusing politics with business. Our interviewees rarely discussed how the judicial system remained weak and generally failed to act on evidence of illegal profiteering during the first postcommunist decade.

A number of scholars have concluded that women tend to be more risk averse than men during periods of economic and political crisis. They link this phenomenon to the responsibility women feel toward their families, particularly their children. Women appear to be more open to risk during periods of stability (Brindley 2005). This context helps explain why, despite making up 36 percent of Romanian entrepreneurs (well above the EU average), businesswomen only generated 11 percent of the wealth in this sector (Paul 2016, 42). As latecomers to the process of privatization, women did not benefit from the dubious practices of the first postcommunist decade facilitated by the NSF and subsequently by the SDP.

Additionally, female entrepreneurs are often motivated by noneconomic factors. Andreea Paul's excellent analysis of women's ethical incentives closely correlates to our respondents' comments. As our chapter on work illustrates, women are largely driven by a desire to work hard and use their talents. Other incentives, in rank order, include: a desire to succeed, realize a particular dream, or secure their children's future. Feelings of courage, passion, and responsibility likewise motivate them. Women rarely cite wealth as an incentive (Paul 2016, 54). It follows then that our respondents consider public policy, politicians' actions, and their own role in political life primarily through an ethical lens.

The Birth and the Growth of Democracy: Liberty and Responsibility

The instability and social insecurity of new democracies often contribute to a generalized distrust in politics. In Romania, other factors exacerbated this phenomenon, including unfair internal competitions for office, the use of public office for personal financial gain, failed campaign promises, and the explosion of a mass media with dubious ethical standards. The Economist Intelligence Unit notes: "Levels of public trust are exceptionally low in Eastern Europe. . . . Less than 10 percent of people in this sub-region trust political parties and less than one-fifth trust their governments and their parliaments. The proportion that is satisfied with the way democracy functions in their countries fell from 40 percent in 2007 to only 33 percent in 2009" (Economist Intelligence Unit 2010, 12). At the national level, in 2016, trust in the political parties (8.3 percent), the parliament (12.6 percent), and government (22.6 percent) was even lower (INSCOP 2016).

At the same time, our respondents spoke with pride about their civic duties. They abide by the constitution and laws, pay taxes, respect the rights of others and often care for the elderly, sick, orphans, and even their own husbands. Yet the question remains, To what extent have they assumed an equal role in shaping public policies according to their views of what is needed? Does legal gender equality translate into access, allowing women to fully exercise their democratic citizenship?

Our respondents believe that a robust democracy requires moral foundations. They consider that representatives should be competent, responsible individuals with a sense of duty and ethics. Some consider women more qualified to serve as local and national leaders. The qualities they associate with political leadership closely resemble those they assigned to the ideal man and woman (see the chapter on men). Yet they also observed that in Hunedoara, men's social status and incomes have declined since 1989 (Kideckel 2008).[5] Respondents from especially among the transition generation offered an unfavorable image of men at the present:

> Q: What have men been doing after the collapse of the steelworks?
>
> A: To compensate for their professional exclusion, men did not do anything; they did not even get involved in the activities of the community. Some

have left abroad or found refuge in the countryside. Many started drinking and do not do anything. (D.L., fifty-five)

While D.L.'s narrative explicitly focused on unemployment, her broader social concerns and discussion of her own civic activities point to an implicit critique of men and their lack of concern for their community and responsibilities as citizens.

Other respondents were skeptical about men's competitiveness in a job market that included foreign investors. O.D. (fifty-five) mentioned an Italian investor who only wanted to hire women, believing they were far more responsible: "Were it not for the women of this country, Romania would become a wasteland of crosses with male names on them, because without you [women], none of them could survive more than a month." Her friend C.P. (forty-eight) added: "Since we proved that in times of crisis, women work more and come to the forefront, gain and are capable, can carry the daily burdens and be involved in the activities of the community, I say that it is high time for men to slow down their ambitions to be the only [political] leaders."

During our conversation with urban women of the communist generation, E.O. (sixty-seven), who saw politics as a game, posited that men participated in politics because it let them focus on abstract responsibilities and avoid concrete ones. In the same spirit, A.A. (seventy-one) added: "The man likes to go out, not to stay at home and take care of little things around the house. And then, to escape, men like to have managerial jobs to seem that they are doing something."

Across generations, respondents felt professional accomplishments, achieved through one's own talents, were the most significant qualification for public office. M.C. (sixty), for instance, connected the notion of nonproductive capitalism to "fake" democracy thusly: "In so many years, instead of learning how to produce, we learned how to sell. Today, in a democracy, as back then, instead of learning how to behave, we claim other rights. What right do I have to claim if I do not produce anything, if I do not do anything, but I must be given?" This interviewee, like others, linked citizenship, rights, and liberties to the cultivation of a strong work ethic and overall "real" democracy to an authentic concern with ethics and a sense of responsibility on the part of both the leadership and average citizens. As this chapter shows, our respondents consider that a democracy reduced to the ritual of periodic elections is not authentically democratic. Instead, they wish to see a functional democracy, in which politicians represent the interest of the citizens and follow up on their electoral promises and, in turn, citizens contribute as active taxpayers and entrepreneurs. In short, they have embraced a contractarian ethical perspective of politics.

Our respondents connected "real" (i.e., consolidated) democracy to ethics in public life, something they believed Romanian politics lacked. When we asked, "What is deficient in Romanian democracy?" they described a chaotic public sphere. Linking freedom to responsibility and rights to duties, in each focus group and in many of the interviews, women described an absence of restraint or sense of responsibility in present-day politics. They felt only a stable rule of law could alter the situation:

> Q: Why do you say that our democracy is not real?
>
> A: Everyone should respect the law; that is what holds everyone together in a real democracy. Why can one country be civilized and ours is in this stage that makes you truly embarrassed to say that you are Romanian? (L.L.G., forty)
>
> A: Democracy means the rule of law, a state in which justice dominates in any law, any decision, and in their compliance, things which do not happen here. That is why people are disappointed. Our political system protects nonvalues and this is bad. There is no meritocratic selection, there is nepotism, there is a mafia; it is anything but democracy. (E.B., seventy-seven)

The respondents felt that after 1989, many people attempted to maximize their wealth while others struggled to survive. They believed interpersonal relations were altered as a consequence. Though only superficially ingrained through propaganda, the communist regime had encouraged the altruistic substitution of self-interest with self-sacrifice (M. Miroiu 1997). This moral code has continued to have some resonance: "We became lonely. We became Westerners and capitalists; we are full of spite in our rush for wealth. We only follow our interests, we betray each other, and we are audacious" (O.D., fifty-five).

These changes impacted many friendships; honest relationships have grown increasingly rare, especially for those who acquired money and status:

> Q: Do you think people are more selfish?
>
> A: Nobody does anything anymore without a reward. People are no longer as good or kind. Everybody seems stressed out, nervous. They do not have the strength to work with one another, as they barely solve their own issues. The richer one gets, the worse, more selfish, and greedier one becomes. (A.A., forty-two)
>
> A: Unfortunately, these years after the revolution brought forth all our misery, everything possibly bad, all the values in which we believed collapsed; and power, money, and political relations were revealed. (M.D., forty-eight)

Our interviewees connected selfishness and dishonesty to political corruption. They largely addressed corruption in its most extreme forms—notably the use of state institutions for personal gain, often through the preferential awarding of government contracts, a predictable phenomenon given how national goods were privatized. While these practices continue to exist today, people have become less tolerant of them. Our interviewees have come to equate corruption with the undermining of the common good: "I am truly ashamed! I believe that democracy and the rule of law are possible in this country, if political classes get tired of stealing. I do not know when. Maybe during my grandchildren's lives they will not have anything to steal anymore. I think that only future generations will solve this issue, but not in the next ten to fifteen years. I am resigned" (L.L.G., forty).

Other respondents provided concrete examples of corruption on the local level: sidewalks unnecessarily repaired (sometimes three times a year), allowing a company "belonging to whom it should" (A.A., forty-two) to profit, or a city program to import Hungarian birch trees rather than harvesting them from the surrounding forests (M.B., fifty-one). Discussing the issue of corruption, D.L. (fifty-five) adopted a philosophical tone: "It is possible that power in itself can corrupt in a context where you have control over other people. But I was a leader as well and did not change. It has to do with your human abilities, with the human inside you." While her remarks did not include gendered distinctions, she offered no examples of honest male political leadership—an absence that stood in contrast to her positive portrayal of female leaders and suggests she felt gender norms shape an individual's approach to political power and responsibility.

Our respondents expressed a general lack of trust in political institutions and elected officials, including political parties, the parliament, and national and local administrations and councils. National surveys reveal similar findings: public trust has eroded as political campaigns have grown more populist, governments more corrupt and nonresponsive to electoral promises, the media more biased, and NGOs, intended as independent observers, weaker (Forbrig and Demeš 2009; M. Miroiu 2011; Nicolae 2010; Vlăsceanu and Hâncean 2014).[6]

In many ways our respondents' distrust of the political system stems from their ethical view of politics. Since 1989, political campaigns, including those of pro-Western reformist parties, have courted voters with populist, often unrealistic promises. When politicians fail to make good on campaign commitments, public trust fractures. To counteract the "dirty hands" or, more precisely, "spotted hands" phenomenon Romanian politicians have had to justify their actions (Walzer 1974). As Romanian's transition from authoritarianism to democracy and from a planned to a market economy has been a largely top-down affair involving a host of international interests like the International Monetary Fund (IMF), the World Bank, NATO, and the EU (Karl 2005; Krastev 2009), many politicians blamed externally imposed reforms for their inability to follow through on campaign promises. (Preda 2002, 2009).

Nonetheless, mistrust remains, as our conversation with the focus group in Sâncrai illustrated. These mostly retired women with limited education provided us with an ironic and humorous demonstration of the value of campaign promises: One participant, V.S., left our meeting. She later returned to show us "what we gained from politics thus far." Slightly hunched at eighty years old, she walked back sporting an SDP scarf and a Greater Romania Party cap; in one hand, she clutched a Democratic Liberal Party (DLP) pen ("which doesn't even work") and in the other a plastic NLP bucket ("at least that was useful"). The discussion became lively:

> Politicians see us only during their campaigns, ladies! (T.)
>
> Then they also come with their trumpets. . . . [She laughs.] From their cars with music, they give us presents, they install water pipes, they install gas pipes, they install everything. [The group laughs.] After elections they do not know our names anymore. (M.B., seventy-two)
>
> They bring us a plastic bucket. [She laughs.] (V.S., eighty)
>
> And a pen, like for blind people. (O.C., fifty-four)
>
> They gave her two pens and only one to me, which does not even work. (M.G., eighty-three)
>
> Or an empty sack with the name of their party on it. (M.E., seventy)
>
> Things like this to fool the people. (O.C., fifty-four)

While they have become accustomed to politicians' attempts to sway their votes with insignificant pension increases and useless campaign paraphernalia, as well as a real lack of choice in local elections, Sâncrai's women have not given up on democracy. As Amartya Sen writes: "There is very little evidence that poor people, given the choice, prefer to reject democracy" (1999, 13). But more has to be done. As one respondent, M.F. (fifty-five), noted, Romanian politicians lack a clear understanding of the electorate's problems and needs. She argued that only after analyzing the issues facing the population could politicians successfully play their part and make honest campaign pledges.

In our interviewees' view, the routine failure on the part of politicians to make good on campaign promises has transformed politics into a dishonest game—one where winning requires politicians' stances to alter as power shifts. In other words, political activity "is not for people with principles" and party doctrines and platforms only exist on paper (A.B., fifty-two). Politicians tell stories, but only stories. If we believe them, "we are getting drunk on cold water" (A.A., forty-two). Another woman added that, if the politicians' lies were not enough, "[the] media manipulates [the public] miserably" (C.P., forty-eight).

This mistrust in politicians and parties discourages women from getting involved with politics and sometimes even from voting:

> Q: Have you ever thought to run for a public office?
>
> A: I have never thought of it—I cannot act like this; you must be duplicitous. You promise something, but do something else. Once I say something, I cannot compromise too much. Everything I have accomplished is based on my work. I have no reason to fawn, to be a sycophant. And for these things you must be a cad. I cannot be like that. (D.M., forty-eight)

At times, it seemed almost as if celebrated ethicists and political theorists had inspired our respondents' views. Some of their arguments about the importance of following through on campaign pledges appeared to be straight out of Immanuel Kant's deontologist view in *Groundwork of the Metaphysics of Morals* or his *Critique of Practical Reason*. Others offered opinions similar to that in Alasdair MacIntyre's virtue ethics *After Virtue* (1981). The next section focuses on solutions our respondents proposed, many of them bearing a striking resemblance to Joan Tronto's *Moral Boundaries. A Political Argument for an Ethic of Care* (1993) and *Caring Democracy: Markets, Equality and Justice* (2013).

Governance: Problems and Solutions

Our interviewees' experiences dissuaded them from seeing electoral politics as a space to discuss their interests, concerns, or potential solutions to problems. They view elections as manipulative populism, not as an exercise in political pragmatism (Gherghina and Mișcoiu 2010). Moreover, our respondents felt they were taught that their role is to solve the problems of others, not create them.

Given this context, what does good governance mean for these women? How would they handle the local budget if they had the power? Our interviewees consistently answered these questions with detailed, thoughtful responses. For them, good governance was, above all, a venture that both politicians and citizens participated in: politicians ought to uphold their promises and tend to their responsibilities, while citizens should actively participate in the identification of public problems and solutions.

During the focus groups and interviews, respondents frequently discussed moral and physical cleanliness (and, by extension, dirt as a chronic problem). They contended that, if politicians had clean souls then the environment, citizens' homes, and city streets would be clean (E.M., forty-nine). For some respondents, law and order could bring about cleanliness through punishment: "People repeatedly commit the same error because our society does not punish them," or "those who err rarely pay for their mistakes" (L.P., forty-seven; M.D., forty-eight; O.C., fifty-four). Many favored fines to maintain order: "It is only when people's finances are affected that they start to get better" (M.B., forty-two). However, this requires the authorities to enforce the law: "If you, as a local policeman see someone who littered a pack of cigarettes, or ate a banana and tossed the peel on a fence, and do not fine them, then nothing changes. There are many who can improve these badly behaving people, but nobody gets involved" (A.A., forty-two). They connected this problem to poorly designed welfare policies and offered their own solution to simultaneously address two public issues:

> You see someone who is on prolonged unemployment benefits, not to mention those who are on welfare, healthy, and shows up at city hall when the money is disbursed. Why is there no one at the city hall to give them work today?

A group to clean the city. Nobody really talks about work. Rights, rights, but no one to say, "Man, I would like to work on something, to get me a job." There are so many [people] in parks wasting time. And we cannot find someone to dust a carpet. No one, only money to give them for [doing] nothing. (A.A., seventy-one)

And D.L. (sixty-three) noted: "I would ask people to work, as it was during Ceaușescu's time with voluntary work, not like right now. . . . I would take all who live off social benefits to work in a neighborhood. This is what should be done with this money: you go and work eight hours a day, instead of only asking for money. . . . These people having social benefits could clean the city, and you know how? Super clean!" At the crux of their comments lay a perceived link between welfare policies and a lack of individual responsibility. Researchers working on these issues have voiced similar concerns (Preda 2009).

Without knowledge of the exact figures, our respondents identified expensive public policies with dubious beneficiaries (Nicolae 2010). In particular, communist generation women described a series of problems concerning social protection policies, including awarding an impossibly large number of "revolutionary allowances" to those who supposedly participated in the 1989 revolution, supporting men "forced" to retire from jobs in heavy industry in the early 1990s (M. Miroiu 2004c), and a largely fraudulent increase in entitlements for disabled persons, from 42,000 in 1989 to 670,000 in 2008 (Preda 2009). In addition, our respondents raised the issue of tax evasion. Very few of our interviewees reaped the benefits of any of these illegal practices. They chastised both elected politicians and the private citizens engaged in them. Former judge D.L. (fifty-five) believed that "if a coherent fiscal legislation and the control of wealth whose sources are dubious would be solved, we could bring back into the state budget a part of the funds that were removed from the public sphere through different unfair business practices."

Public Spending: Women's Priorities

Our interviews confirmed national-scale quantitative research that suggests women prioritize local public expenditures in drastically different ways than male political leaders and voters do (CNCSIS 2006–8). Many of our interviewees' critiques targeted city hall as an oversized, poorly organized, nontransparent institution: "First of all, I would make the city hall efficient. I would restructure everything; I would compress departments, hire competent people, who can have as many achievements as possible based on their competency. I would downsize the staff, because that is where we spend a lot of money. In addition, I would analyze the needs of institutions subordinate to city hall and rank them based on priority" (A.A., forty-two).

Our respondents did not feel public spending was consistent with electoral promises and believed that political considerations and connections largely determine the allocation of funds. Several women favored raising local taxes and actively seeking EU funds for projects to enhance life in Hunedoara (A.B., fifty-one; A.A., forty-two; A.A., seventy-two). There are, however, hurdles beyond local control: favoritism dictates how the national government doles out financial support and auctions state goods, which generate public wealth and are often hurriedly organized at the end of the calendar year (M.B., fifty-seven). Using the pretext that there is unspent public money that needs to be allocated to specific projects within a short period of time that wouldn't permit a public auction (or the money becomes unavailable), political leaders prioritize their own political clientele as the beneficiaries of such contracts.

Our interviewees knew where they would invest public funds if they could: in programs for children and the elderly, in healthcare and the environment, and in infrastructure and the Hunyadi Castle. For urban women, children were their uncontested first priority, a reminder of their gendered self-identification as parents.

As primary caregivers, our respondents were especially concerned with the effect of poor governance on their children's education and safety. They wanted more investment in schools and afterschool programs as well as quality kindergarten and full-day childcare centers, "so your family could go to work" (A.A., forty-two). Though this respondent did not expressly state that the issue affected women predominantly, as our chapter on children made clear, the availability of childcare impacts primarily women, as they are the parents who spend the most time with childcare related tasks.

The need for such programs has grown increasingly acute since the collapse of communism, as local and national authorities have failed to replace the state-run network of daycare centers and the considerable number of kindergartens that closed. Rural schools have also been hit, and depopulation has led to further decline in the number of schools.[7] Consequently, school transportation is a growing problem in rural areas: "There were national programs for education and smart mayors knew how to take advantage of them. There are minibuses, there are sixteen of them in our county, they are all new, but they are parked somewhere in Deva. They are not used because mayors could not find drivers. The budget for drivers was not approved" (M.B., fifty-seven). Our interviewees could only explain their elected officials' incompetence by equating it with a lack of concern for Romania's most vulnerable populations. They understood both that political mismanagement had made access to education more difficult as well as its consequences—a rising dropout rate that had reached 25 percent in 2016.[8]

Similarly, our respondents wanted to see the local administration create caretaking programs for the children of migrant workers. To deal with the economic hardships brought on by the transition, a significant number of Romanians migrated across the EU for work (Roman and Voicu 2010). Some of our respondents had participated in such work; more had family and neighbors engaged in such employment. Many of our respondents viewed migration as a growing political problem with long-term consequences. They felt policy makers failed to address this issue: "The mistake that the state made was to allow families to break apart. How? Either the mother or the father, or both of them went abroad and left their children behind. Some stayed with their grandparents, who aside from food cannot offer anything else. The state does not care about these children" (M.T., sixty).

The interviewees also insisted on the importance of state-funded healthcare as a matter of principle. They unanimously felt that the hospital and other local medical services were among the region's best-managed public goods. The mostly elderly and widowed women from rural areas we spoke with also placed a high premium on healthcare. They discussed their concerns about access to local services and money for prescription drugs: "We have something that works very well in this city. And that is because Dr. B., the director of the hospital, is amazing. He is a real manager. He knew how to attract funds. He is from here. He is not with one foot in Hunedoara and with the other in Bucharest. But what about those from rural areas and those with small pensions? What to tell them to do? To treat themselves with nothing?" (M.F., fifty-five).

Welfare for the elderly and poor constituted another significant issue. The majority of urban women thought public money should be used for nursing homes, free cafeterias for the poor (many of them elderly), and subsidized housing. D.L. (fifty-five), who spends a good deal of time volunteering in nursing homes and tending to children with migrant parents, asserted: "It is the duty of the state [to ensure the care] of enfeebled and lonely elders and children left behind by working migrant parents and not to just leave [these people dependent on] the kindness of relatives and neighbors. If you do not ensure social protection for these truly vulnerable people, what kind of social protection do you claim you offer? For who? For what? For those you offer electoral bribes to? Could children be abandoned simply because they do not vote?" Conversely, women from rural areas considered care for the elderly and the poor a familial or humanitarian issue. Consequently, they felt it fell to families and the church, rather than to the state, to solve these problems. A 2008 quantitative study revealed similar preferences for private eldercare solutions among rural populations (CNCSIS 2006–8).

Our interviewees from Hunedoara love their parks and forests and see these spaces as the responsibility of both the government and private citizens. To maintain them, they suggested solutions that would also assist with unemployment: "Rather than seeing them on the streets not doing anything, you would provide these people with meaning. It is the least you could give them to make them feel useful" (L.M., fifty). They feel that residential associations might also play a role, if mayors used contests and awards for "the most beautiful gardens" to incentivize them (E.B., seventy-seven; A.A., seventy-one; G.S., sixty-nine).

Fig. 7.1 Hunedoara in 2017. This view of the city from the hill where Hunyadi Castle stands offers a panoramic look at Hunedoara today. The smokestacks that featured prominently in figure 5.2 are gone, as is much of the metallurgical industrial landscape that dominated the city's outskirts. Photo by Maria Bucur.

All the women we interviewed complained that city hall neglected the town's streets and sidewalks. Some respondents refused to vote in local elections as long as potholes and dirt remain on their streets (E.O., sixty-three; L.M., fifty). Rural women, who often work in their homes, wanted more investment in sewer systems and gas heating.

Some respondents also discussed the possibility of revitalizing tourism in the region. They felt the Hunyadi Castle, an emblem of the city, was the area's only real tourist attraction (Mărginean 2015). "I would try with the castle. The castle is the most awesome thing in our city" (L.M., fifty). Tourism centered on the castle "could be a great source for revenue, but, since I have been living in Hunedoara, this castle kept being renovated but never finished or really improved to attract tourists" (I.R., thirty-nine).

Women as Politicians

Though our interviewees had a sophisticated understanding of political and community issues, aside from voting, very few were willing to entertain the idea of active political engagement. While overall, they saw politics as a male field, a hostile environment unwelcoming to women, their responses revealed some age- and residence-based divisions. Urban communist and transition generation women viewed women's political participation in a more positive light, especially when it came to refocusing public policies on the average citizen, conflict resolution, and reducing corruption, in the way women formulate solutions to civic problems (Paul 2011).

So why don't women want to get into politics? To some, politics is "a crazy world. I only see revenge, a continuous struggle over who should be first. Honestly, I have a bad impression about women who get involved in politics. I limit myself to cultivating beautiful things" (D.S., forty-one). C.P. (forty-eight) thought that politics is a world of "big infamy. Politics is not for my soul. I can't create an alliance, break it, bring it back. . . . I don't think it fits me." But she was open to another kind of politics, one of strong moral convictions that "would make me feel the fire inside."

Repeatedly, women told us that politics was a "waste of time" or "I would not resist hours of endless and sterile debates on a subject" (M.F., fifty-five). These statements suggest that political debates and speeches rarely touch on issues of interest or concern to these women: "Every political party wants to get the power and satisfy their own interest. If there would be a political party interested in lower classes and the welfare of society maybe I would get involved, but as long as political parties do not care about us I do not care about them either" (M.P., forty-four).

Others shared personal experiences, including stories about leaving public service after 1989:

> I worked in the financial audit at the iron and steelworks for thirty-eight years. I only fought to protect the good of the state and enterprise. I worked all the time, but respecting the law became a problem for me at work [after 1989]. Thus, I can't accept that; I defend the law and others breach it and trample on it. (A.A., seventy-one)

> The city hall's money was in my hands as I was the manager of the budget-finance office. I could not accept what the political managers asked from me. I had three options: to accept, to go crazy, or to leave. I decided to leave. (M.B., fifty-seven)

Both women alluded to pressure to participate in or turn a blind eye to illegal activities at work. More senior, elected officials (in both cases men) directly caused their resignations and led these women to distrust the words and deeds of politicians more broadly.

Some interviewees had had forays into active political participation. V.D. (thirty-eight), for example, got involved with the activities of a political party:

Through a women's organization [of the party] I had the opportunity to access some funds distributed to healthcare, thus to hospitals. I supported the girls from the gymnastics school from Deva. There were funds from different societies, companies, nonprofit, all kinds of donations. I was working with receipts and invoices. The money didn't go to the party, but where it was needed. I was buying all kinds of things: for schools, for single-parent families, for hospitals. We went to hospitals and gave to newborns everything they needed for when they go outside the hospital. We offered support to children with disabilities. Anyway, our activities covered the entire county, wherever there was a need. It was an amazing experience, and I get goose bumps even now when I recall it. As long as these activities were done in collaboration with great people, I have participated in them. But the woman I admired, who attracted all of us to get involved and who led us at the national level, was eliminated and, with that, all good actions at a local level collapsed as well. In that moment I gave up. If everything in the party is based on [personal] interests and not good deeds, why should I be there?

Others had similar experiences. C.P. (forty-eight) told us she had been involved in a party that has since dissolved. Its male leaders relegated her to doing secretarial work. And L.L.G. (forty) joined a women's organization run by the Democratic Union of Hungarians from Romania. She hoped this was a feminist organization, but had to readjust her expectations. Led by one of the party leaders' wives, the association's agenda had nothing to do with women's civic interests:

Q: What then was this women's organization doing?

A: I will summarize: while men discuss and do politics, women embroider and take care of elderly and poor voters. A purely feminist organization, right?

She quickly grew disenchanted with the organization and resigned.

E.B., the seventy-seven-year-old retired elementary school teacher, one of the first among our respondents to get involved in politics after 1989, became a member of the NPP. She also served as the president of the International Union of Free Romanians (IUFR)'s local affiliate, an NGO associated with the party. She joined for idealistic reasons: she wanted to help build a new world. She was also drawn to the IUFR's charismatic president, Ion Rațiu. Rațiu lived in exile in England during the communist period. In 1990, he ran for president on the NPP's ticket. While E.B. and others felt his election would have attracted foreign investment, Rațiu only received a small share of the vote: "I personally knew Rațiu from different contexts. We crossed part of Transylvania together when I was at the IUFR. I have never met a more tolerant, kind, and democratic person. If he were to become president of Romania, he could have attracted foreign investment, as he was very well known. Businessmen, at least English ones, would have come, as well as French, and many others. It would have been completely different." Her idyllic view of the party was short-lived for two reasons. First, she began to feel personal interests—the restitution of property after communism—and political vengeance aimed at the RCP and its membership drove the NPP's local leadership. Second, she disapproved of how the party treated women. Sent off to conduct campaigns, lobby, and pursue humanitarian work on the party's behalf, women had no decision-making power and never figured on electoral lists. Over time, E.B.'s perception of politics grew dimmer: "I went crazy when my son-in-law and daughter wanted to enter politics. I prayed to God for a miracle for them so they will not get involved. They have nothing to do there. Politics is nothing but a dirty gutter." Nonetheless, E.B. felt that if more women successfully ran for office "different flour would be ground in our mill."

We did find two stories about women's success in politics. B.F. (thirty-eight) works as a family physician and serves as president of the SDP's local organization for women. Convinced she could effectively manage public resources, she entered politics in 2001.[9] Well-known in town, she believed she brought important skills to the municipal council: "I am accustomed to reading. In my profession [as a physician], if you do not update your knowledge, you get behind. And then, having this reading "flaw," as I became part of the municipal council and because I did not know what it was about, I started reading everything on the relevant legislation. This way, even from the very first meetings I managed to make myself known; and currently, if the mayor knows I said something about a law, he knows for a fact that I am right." B.F.'s work on the city council ruffled some of her male colleagues' feathers, however:

Q: Do they consider your proposals?

A: Thus far, yes. Unfortunately, I also had some initiatives that bothered the men, and honestly, even the men from the party I am a member of, because a woman should not be smarter than them and especially [not] smarter than the president of the party.

B.F. described the barriers women in politics face thusly: "The scalpel is in the hands of the leaders, and they are men. It depends on them if a woman is placed on the list of candidates and for what position. When they need to sacrifice a candidate, they prefer a woman. Men think politics is their territory because it has been traditionally. They have no interest to change that, as men would lose their monopoly over public resources." To maintain power, men often ignore or ridicule women (Matland and Montgomery 2004; Popescu 2004, 2006).

As indicated earlier, B.F.'s political work negatively impacted her home life—her husband, who disapproved of her public aspirations, refused to support her or adequately assist with childcare. They eventually divorced. As a single mother, B.F. remained political active. She resolutely believes that women should have more faith in their own strength and ideas. She also insisted that women ought to be more willing to take risks, even when men hurl insults at them or create obstacles to their success. Furthermore, B.F. thought that it benefited men to have more women in politics since they brought to the table diplomatic skills and a balanced approach to problem solving.

L.G. (fifty-six), a physician in a mining town close to Hunedoara, had the most pragmatic and consequentialist approach to politics among our respondents. She connected the experience and skills she cultivated as a member of the RCP to her post-1989 political success. In 1992, she joined the newly formed DP. For her, politics essentially equated to public resource management: "Even though I disagreed with many things, it was necessary to make myself heard, because otherwise I would not have received help in my medical activity." The only doctor in town, she understood that without direct participation in the allocation of resources, healthcare facilities and, by extension, the taxpayers' well-being would suffer. Therefore, political participation became a necessity for her, a matter of fulfilling her Hippocratic oath. Determined and pragmatic, she was elected each time she ran for the local council:

Q: Why do you think your political involvement has been useful?

A: Being one of them helped me buy my own space for the dispensary and for this I even had the understanding of my colleagues in the opposition. In the previous meeting I succeeded to receive from city hall an important amount of money, which I want to invest in a central heating system in the dispensary.

Q: What if you would not have been involved in politics?

A: Obviously I would not have been able to do what I have just told you. Four years were enough for me to understand what it is to be uninvolved [in politics]. If you are not a member of the council, you do not have access to resources.

As a middle-aged female physician in a small community, L.G. did not feel she was subject to gender discrimination: "When you are over fifty-five, it seems that your authority is respected despite your gender. They respect me as a professional, a human, and a politician." Yet, L.G. did not aspire to a higher office. Like most of our other respondents, she viewed national politics as remote, harsh, and ultimately disconnected from people's real problems. However, in contrast to the interviewees who do no more than vote, L.G. was optimistic and pointed to specific goals: "We have not yet succeeded to bring the gas system, only to build roads. However, we will access SAPARD[10] funds and will build the gas infrastructure as well."

When respondents discussed the low level of female participation in national politics (the national parliament and administration as well as EU representation), they seemed more conscious of gender discrimination. In 2014, the World Economic Forum ranked Romania ninety-seventh globally in terms of women's political representation (when we conducted our research, the ranking was similar) (World Economic Forum 2014). The majority of our respondents blamed men for excluding women from politics: Men are misogynist and afraid of being in competition with women, "who have no place because of men who all the time do something to eliminate women" (M.C., forty-one). "Men simply do not let them" (A.A., seventy-one). "It is difficult, as men continuously lie until they believe in those lies" (M.B., thirty-four). This was not the only obstacle to women's formal political participation, and our respondents identified other gender biases. For example, they noted that women do not have as much time for party meetings, trips, or gatherings in local pubs where party leaders often get together to make decisions (L.P., forty-seven). In addition, women do not have access to the same financial resources as men, "and without money, they have no chance" (A.A., forty-two; M.B, thirty-four). Finally, female politicians are excessively sexualized and scrutinized: "The media only shows Elena Udrea's governmental activity as her butt, legs, and bags, and say she is the president's blonde [i.e., Barbie doll]. Have you seen what they did to Mona Muscă?[11] They destroyed her. They lynched her "(L.P., forty-seven).

Yet some respondents also ticketed women themselves for not participating politics: "We are guilty because we continue to believe that a woman should stay 'in their place,' that women are not capable of doing what men do" (D.M., forty-eight). In other words, D.M. and others understood that women have to challenge gender stereotypes in order to change the situation.

Respondents noted the unique qualities women bring to politics. The positive stereotypes they identified are also commonplace in the United States or the EU at large—from greater social responsibility to greater attention to detail and from conflict resolution skills to the ability to balance multiple public needs. Many of these qualities strongly correlated with how respondents understood and performed gender roles at home, at work, and in various communities.

Overall, our respondents believed that female politicians' allegiances would be to their constituents rather than to their party. One focus group that included women who were active professionally, civically, and/or politically, generated two enthusiastically received ideas, a women's party (B.F., thirty-eight) and a technocratic government consisting of women (D.L., fifty-five):[12]

> Q: Do you think that what you say is bad and wrong in Romanian politics has anything to do with the fact that women do not decide on anything important in this country?
>
> A: It has a lot to do with it. (C.P., forty-eight)
>
> A: I believe the solution is a technocratic government consisting of women. (D.L., fifty-five)
>
> Q: Why only women?

A: Because they are more responsible and I am convinced that there are expert women in any field. (D.L., fifty-five)

A: First, think about the fact that women are raised in a spirit of sacrifice; they are amazing organizers as we are the ones organizing the entire family life. We know how to manage more with fewer [resources], to share what we have among all family members, and to find solutions in situations of crisis. (O.D., fifty-five)

Beyond the National: Europeanization and Globalization

Since we conducted our interviews at the moment when Romania joined the EU, we wanted to explore how our respondents understood political processes inside the country in relation to international developments. They expressed a range of opinions, generally positive, about Europeanization and globalization, which confirmed quantitative data from the same period (2014): 60 percent of Romanians trust the EU (the second-highest rate in Europe), and Romania has the fewest euro-skeptical political parties (Eurostat 2015). The only other international actor interviewees mentioned was the IMF.

Our respondents had a pragmatic and optimistic view of Romania's participation in global political and economic structures. They described EU membership as a blessing and an important historical event:

A: If we had not entered the EU, we would have remained natural satellites of Earth. (C.P., forty-eight)

A: We have more rights. We no longer need visas; we can even travel without passports, and this is a very good thing. (S.B., forty-two)

A: They [the EU] will curb this plunder. (A.A., seventy-one)

A: I consider the EU integration beneficial, although sometimes I feel like we are not our own bosses anymore. But this is the outcome, and we cannot oppose it. I hope that with the EU accession, we will succeed in being more civilized. (B.F., thirty-eight)

In short, our interviewees described as progress even aspects of EU membership that limited national autonomy. Interestingly, they rarely discussed economic issues. Instead, they focused on the institutional, normative aspects of EU membership and the forms of political citizenship it created—from freedom to travel to curbing corruption. A.A. (forty-two) underlined EU policies concerning human rights: "Through these commissions, through directives imposed on the judicial system, through legislative changes, they managed to thwart things that blatantly and severely breached human rights."

A few, like M.B. (fifty-seven), considered EU accession beneficial but premature: "First of all, they should have educated us in terms of democracy and the rule of law and only then accept[ed] us. We should have gotten rid of these

Balkan-like things. It is good you have to account for all the money you spend from their funds, not like now when they are building a roundabout for seven million lei."

Respondents saw unequal power relations between Romania and the EU as the price of admission. They felt that becoming part of the "club" and taking part in EU governance better equipped Romanians for positive change. However, several expressed concern over some of Romania's current euro-parliamentarians' competence: "It is not acceptable to send uneducated, unprofessional and incapable people there, relatives and birdbrains" (A.M., forty-nine).

Respondents viewed other international structures, such as the IMF and multinational corporations, as well as the unequal dynamics and general governance of these organizations, more negatively. Some provided familiar arguments about the noxious consequences of neoliberalism in an era of globalization. They linked privatization, deindustrialization, and the difficulties of capitalism to external forces: "First, they brought us to bankruptcy and after that they made us live off loans so that we will do only what they want. . . . All possible jobs have been liquidated; there is a bunch of unemployed and, besides this, we no longer produce anything in agriculture. We import everything from them; eat all sorts of crap" (L.C., sixty-three).

D.C. (forty) expressed similar opinions. Focusing specifically on Romania's international loans, she argued: "We have become an outlet. . . . Was the IMF loan really needed? I do not think so. Why have they not borrowed from the population's bonds from the treasury? Romania still has money in that form. First of all, the loans should have been from there. From us. So that we, as a country, ultimately, could have tried to see what can be done. We will pay the loans all this time. Perhaps even our children will pay for these loans."

Most of our respondents couched critiques of neoliberalism in their experiences of the pre-1989 command economy (especially communist and transition generation women) and of privatization in the early 1990s, led not by the IMF, the EU, or multinational corporations but by Romanian interests. However, they felt that when international investors participated in the privatization process, they availed themselves of the corrupt system NSF and regional RCP party bosses turned investors had created (Nicolae 2010). Describing the sale of the Hunedoara Steel Works to the Indian British investor Mittal in 2004, M.D. (forty-eight) stated: "Before that . . . , the [managers] started to get rich, not on their own efforts, but through business with the state, which they represented as well." When M.D. referred to "their own efforts," she emphasized the corrupt environment facilitated by the regime, one that stifled fair competition.

In short, though some respondents seemed resigned to globalization in its neoliberal forms (e.g., "It was meant to be," "we could not do anything") and though it fell short of their hopes, most believed that many of the post-1989 changes have been good: the introduction of capitalism and competition; the instauration of democracy, even if preponderantly electoral; and the rule of law, even if it is threatened by corruption.

Our interviewees articulated clear and critical positions on Romanian politics since 1989. They expressed hope and demonstrated thoughtful engagement. These women have come to see themselves as citizens with the right to free expression and association. They avail themselves of these rights when directly participating in politics and actively seeking out information from diverse media sources.[13]

Importantly, our respondents expressed their opinions as citizens with full voting rights under a pluralist political regime with free and fair elections, a historic first for Romanian women. They believe that those in power should represent women's interests and unabashedly critique elected officials' failure to do so. Our interviewees feel they fulfill their part of the social contract in many ways: by working, often more than men; respecting the law and the rights of others; paying taxes; volunteering in their communities; voting even when political parties exclude, marginalize, or ghettoize them; and actively participating in politics.[14]

At first glance, our respondents' ethical evaluation of political behavior might seem naive. After a more in-depth analysis, however, it becomes clear that their insistence on ethical critiques stems from their desire for democracy and a stronger rule of law. Our respondents have internalized democratic values and attitudes. None conveyed extremist opinions or questioned the virtues of democratic pluralism.

Generally, the disappointment women feel derives from neoliberal capitalism's slow and ruthless entry into the region and a lack of concern for social welfare. They are frustrated by abandoned electoral promises, how the male political elite sets budget priorities, and government inefficiency. Likewise, they feel that parties do a poor job of selecting politicians. Though our interviewees often thought that women were prepared to lead, organize, and administer, they felt sidelined in a patriarchal state. However, EU membership has made them optimistic about a more open and just society, especially for their children (M. Miroiu 2015b).

Notes

1. Consiliul Național pentru Combaterea Discriminării (CNCD), Agenția Națională pentru Egalitate de Șanse între Femei și Bărbați (ANES), and Comisiile pentru Egalitate de Șanse la nivelul Senatului și Camerei Deputaților.

2. "Ordonanța privind prevenirea și sancționarea tuturor formelor de discriminare," 2000, accessed May 1, 2018, http://www.mmuncii.ro/pub/imagemanager/images/file/Legislatie/ORDONANTE-DE-GUVERN/OG137-2000.pdf; *Legea nr. 202/2002 privind egalitatea de*

şanse între femei şi bărbaţi, accessed August 27, 2017, http://www.dreptonline.ro/legislatie/legea_egalitatii_sanse_femei.php.

3. Under state socialism, welfare programs are not a corrective to an unruly capitalist system. Thus, a fundamental distinction can be made between state socialist regimes and social democratic policies in other countries meant to address income inequality (Popescu 2006).

4. A position the communist regime created to direct industrial and commercial production. The appointee served as a local link to the central authorities.

5. Men received compensatory salaries for losing jobs and early retirement benefits (Pasti 2003).

6. While in 2016 this trend remained intact, trust in the institution fighting corruption was nonetheless very high (INSCOP, *Încrederea în instituţii*, 2016, accessed August 27, 2017, http://www.inscop.ro/aprilie-2016-increderea-in-institutii/).

7. Romania's fertility rate has remained below 2 percent since the 1990s.

8. "Program educaţional pentru reducerea abandonului şcolar," accessed August 27, 2017, https://www.portalinvatamant.ro/articole/scoala-mea-87/program-educational-pentru-reducerea-abandonului-scolar-6526.html.

9. In 2016, she was one of only two women elected to the municipal council.

10. A special EU fund for candidate states.

11. Mona Muscă was a prominent NLP member. The media scrutinized her purported ties to the secret police before 1989. Though a formal connection between Muscă and the secret police existed, the media could not prove that she provided consequential or harmful information. The same outlets failed to go after male public figures who undisputedly informed and sometimes even lied to the secret police (M. Miroiu 2013).

12. In late 2015, the Romanian president appointed an interim administration with more female members than any previous government. Minister of Justice Raluca Prună and Minister of the Environment Cristina Paşca Palmer are both self-described technocrats. During their yearlong tenure, they demonstrated unfailing integrity in a volatile political environment.

13. Though media outlets have political allegiances, varying perspectives and much information is available.

14. Some of their views on women's multiple abilities bear a strong resemblance to ideas theorized by Martha Nussbaum (2001).

Conclusion

Seven Years Later

In the spring of 2016, Mihaela Miroiu helped organize a training session in Hunedoara targeting women, irrespective of political affiliation, interested in running in local elections the following June. A large number of women attended, most between the ages of thirty-five and forty-five, though transition generation women were also represented (including several of our interviewees). Their desire to make a difference in politics was palpable. Many had become well versed in feminist political discourse and understood why, despite their efforts, they had hit the proverbial glass ceiling. After two intense days of training, participants could describe gender-specific conditions that led to their marginalization as potential candidates.

In June 2016, the political parties active in Hunedoara generated electoral lists, and once again, they sidelined women. Across the ideological spectrum, party leaders ranked candidates without consideration of their merits or integrity. Moreover, the results demonstrated a clear gender bias. The county council's leadership is all male, and only seven of its twenty-nine members are women.[1] At the city level, of the twenty-one elected council members in Hunedoara the number of women dropped from four to two (one participated in our interviews).[2] Of Hunedoara County's sixty-nine mayors, only two are women (both work in rural areas).[3] In Sâncrai, one man has served as mayor for twenty-six years.

Why is it that in spite of their obvious interest in direct participation in politics, women in Hunedoara County remain almost invisible in elected office? Mihaela Miroiu tried to find out the answer from the most successful local businesswoman, who has also been someone keen on participating in local politics. C.H. (fifty-six) is part of the transition generation and has demonstrated great lucidity and pragmatism in engaging with the needs of the local population, both as employees and as voters. She explained the context in which she decided to become actively involved in both thusly: After 2009, migration among the young labor force to other EU countries spiked. Foreign investment in Romania increased, together with local entrepreneurial activities. While Hunedoara has not seen spectacular growth, the local economy steadily improved and started to come out of its two-decade slump.

C.H., who served in the Romanian Parliament, made important contributions to turning around this trend.[4] For the past five years, she has been involved in local politics, and over the past four years, she has also been active at the national level. As a businesswoman, she created five hundred new jobs since 2009. Political parties initially courted her as a parliamentary candidate. However, during his 2016 reelection bid, Hunedoara's mayor asked C.H. to refrain from publicly endorsing or campaigning for him despite continuing to count on her financial support. The tenor of electoral politics had grown more populist, and the mayor and his opponents opted to appeal to the electorate's frustrations rather than build on the economic successes entrepreneurial women like C.H. had created. C.H.'s business acumen and vocal role in national politics turned her into a perceived political liability.

In a conversation with Mihaela Miroiu, she criticized the local party leadership and the media for casting her activities in a negative light: "When I ran for parliament in 2012, people saw me as the great new hope in terms of generating more jobs. I succeeded in doing so and also in attracting investors who also generated more jobs. The supply of jobs came to exceed the local demand by 120 places." But the media, "which shifts with every passing whim of the local parties, managed to turn local opinion against me, and to make me out as a greedy rich woman whose ambitions are endless and who doesn't know her place. They often hinted that it would be best if I just got out of politics. No male politician, regardless of how corrupt, drunk, irresponsible, or inefficient, had to endure [such demeaning and unfair media scrutiny]."[5] In November 2016, the media attacks put her in great peril of losing the election. But having weathered these sorts of nasty public accusations before, she handled the negative media with calm and flair, a virtue that seems more and more necessary in a politically hostile climate (Slote 1983). Most other women politicians do not yet possess this tough training and the skills that come with it. The absence of such "tough skin" training has remained an electoral handicap for female voters as well, as chapter 7 shows.

C.H. represents a fairly typical case for the climate and opposition women face when they dare compete in political contests on their own rather than remaining obedient to the will of the local party boss. Her story confirms the continuing widespread trend on the part of most men, as well as some women, to deny women full acceptance and authority in the public space, whether the authority is political or even intellectual.

The gender disparities in Hunedoara concerning the definition and exercise of democratic citizenship, the development of public policies, and the distribution of resources mirror national trends. EIGE identified Romania as the EU's least gender-equal country in 2015 (EIGE 2015). Its criteria included women's access to (a) financial resources (Romania at 21.1 versus the 58.0 EU average); (b) political power (19.2 versus 49.8); and (c) time for civic activities (17.4 versus 37.6). In short, Romania fell below half of the EU average in each category. Our research also pointed to the pivotal roles money, power, and free time play in the consolidation of democratic citizenship. Romanian women's participation in the paid workforce and their access to education and healthcare more closely resembles the EU average, and our chapters on work and politics under communism show the important gains made between 1945 and 1989.

During the communist period, women experienced a half century of formal equality under the law. They also made up 30 percent of elected officials. How did an even harsher political patriarchy develop after 1989? The numbers are puzzling: Immediately after the fall of communism (1990), female elected officials represented 3.7 percent of parliament, reaching a high of 11.0 percent in 2008 before declining. Since then, women have made up 6.5 percent of parliamentarians at most.

Though many of our respondents belonged to the RCP, they view political activity as foreign, a contradiction that points to the superficial nature of women's political access under communism. Until 1990, women's political participation was not intended to further their interests but largely served as window dressing (Jinga 2015). As our respondents repeatedly suggested, political engagement under communism was yet another chore for them. This does not mean, however, that our interviewees are not drawn to the idea of greater political participation. Yet, with negligible exceptions (see C.H.'s case), they believe politics is devoid of ethics and feel powerless to change this. Without a fundamental shift toward a more ethical approach to politics, women remain reluctant to participate.

An Ethical Citizenship of Care

As the chapter on communities showed, religion often frames our respondents' relationships with communities outside the family. Only one interviewee, M.F. (fifty-five), identified as an atheist; religious institutions and communities play important roles in most of our respondents' lives, especially in rural areas. In other words, the communist regime's policy of forced secularization failed (Preda 2009). With religiosity on the rise in Romania, sociologists have observed a parallel increase in concern for social problems (Katarzyna 2013). This positive correlation does not equate a causal relationship, and our respondents did not explicitly link religious and political institutions.[6] However, they did not present them as in conflict either.

Given the data on religiosity and social activism, especially in postcommunist Orthodox countries, we can posit a link between this phenomenon, our respondents' ethical approach to politics, and their description of present-day Romanian politics as lacking a moral foundation. Since these women did not study ethics in school (under communism or since) and there are few public debates on ethics, we contend that our respondents' derive their ethical perspective on politics from customary and religious beliefs. Maternal and religious education function as the central conduits for the transmission of moral values and social norms. Thus, despite its negative impact on their own lives, our interviewees did not articulate an explicit desire to dislocate themselves from the patriarchal character of Romanian society.

Most of our respondents found the ethical approach to politics self-evident and normal. In their words, "real" politics and "true" democracy should focus preponderantly on citizens' needs and interests and cannot remain limited to party interests. This became apparent when they expressed frustration over how little concern political parties and candidates had for these women's interests and priorities and that democracy had been reduced to the ritual of voting due to the absence of a moral political model.

Communist generation women experienced much of Romania's turbulent political history, from the upheavals of war and fascism to the Soviet occupation and from the communist takeover and the development of national communism to the introduction of democracy. Through all of this, our interviewees described counting largely on other women for support and assistance in their daily lives. They relied far less on men, who generally assumed a secondary role in the home and were away at war (their fathers) or for work (their husbands). Despite these absences, men continue to enjoy their status as the head of the household, even if they have ceased to be the only, or primary, breadwinners. Many transition generation women have been their families' principal wage earners since the 1990s, when many men's jobs dried up. Yet some of these women continue to embrace a patriarchal-normative view of gender roles.

While women have begun to contest unequal gender relations more vocally in politics, they seldom explicitly question these dynamics in the home. We rarely heard direct references to gender justice from the communist generation, and they scarcely questioned the notion of men as domestic helpers (as opposed to fully responsible spouses and parents). They framed their stories as individual problems rather than social or political ones. Yet as they shared in the informal open focus groups, their attitudes and language shifted and bore a greater resemblance to the consciousness-raising groups conducted by second-wave American feminists. Transition generation respondents, in particular, made assertive political claims aimed at generating electoral and budgetary agendas that took their needs as citizens into account.

Different generations took one of two approaches to gender equality at home and in politics. While all of our respondents had a conservative[7] attitude about domestic gender norms, the transition generation more openly expressed frustration with sexism in politics. This divergence is not surprising, given the radical political and social changes they witnessed and the lack of an equally significant shift in domestic gender roles. Most of these women did not have direct or extensive exposure to feminist thought or activism; consequently, they offered intuitive critiques of patriarchy.

In both private and public life, our respondents' understanding of and assumptions about gender roles stem from an ethics of care and duty. Their views

Fig. 8.1 The transition generation group in June 2017. From among our interviewees, members of this generation have continued to meet and discuss personal, professional, and occasionally political matters at informal gatherings. Photo by Maria Bucur.

have little in common with the solipsistic individualism of nineteenth-century liberalism or contemporary neoliberalism (Soros 1998; Steger 2002). Their ideas more closely resemble concepts about the relational self and autonomy that integrate competition and cooperation (Hoagland 1990; MacKenzie and Stoljar 1999). Consequently, while these women believe that they are economically and professionally competitive, they feel alienated from a public sphere shaped not by responsibility and the duty to care for others but by personal and party interests. They are unable to reconcile the conflictual rhetoric and actions of Romanian politicians with their own tendency to problem solve through cooperation.[8]

Paradoxically, however, they are willing to make considerable compromises in familial relations but are far less willing to engage in compromises when it comes to politics. Inside the family and spousal relations, they display utilitarian and consequentionalist moral values; by contrast, in politics they show deontological ones. This is likely the consequence of having much richer experiences with familial institutions than with political ones.

Beginning with an ethics of care, women construct their gender roles in concentric circles of association. Instead of defining success as a vertical climb up the ladder, they understand it in relational, multidimensional terms. They often derive personal and professional satisfaction from their ability to multitask or perform as a "Jane of all trades," and from helping others realize their full potential (Benhabib 1992; Corrin 1992). This ethics of care includes consideration for the needs of other citizens and nurtures a propensity to identify solutions that simultaneously address multiple problems, improving lives in the community in a noncompetitive, comprehensive manner. They barely operate according to the abstract model of rational actors guided by self-interest.

These attitudes do not fit into a communitarian model of citizenship, however (Lister 2008; Tronto 1993, 2013). These women do not have the experience of the primacy of the ethics of rights in public life, a core element for developing democratic liberal citizenship. They come from a collectivist experience par excellence. Because of this and because of their historic and continued lack of political influence, we identify their approach not as a communitarian model but as a care-based model of democratic citizenship.

This model has failed to propel women through the glass ceiling. During the first postcommunist decade, women did not have a seat at the table when the budding male entrepreneurial class divided up the state's resources. The competitive and rapacious character of privatization did not resonate with women's cooperative and nonconflictual values. Over the next fifteen years, as Romania hitched its political and economic fortunes to neoliberal regimes in the EU and around the world, the male-dominated political elite dictated the country's economic priorities. As in much of Eastern Europe, they showed little concern for gender justice, especially when they dismantled social welfare programs (Dragolea 2016; Lukić et al. 2006). Without the sanctions of global justice movements, economic neoliberalism does not respond seriously to ethical concerns. This absence prevents our respondents from entering political life, since they feel an unethical politics is not for them.

Our findings lead us to draw broader conclusions about the necessary conditions for consolidating democratic citizenship (Diamond 2003; Dietz 1998; Krook 2009; Phillips 1991). They include an ethical approach that values active participation, responsibilization, and a good measure of public trust. Without a concerted effort to facilitate women's participation in politics, including policies aimed at creating gender parity, such values are not likely to become a core component of an electoral democracy (Dahlerup 2008; King and Marian 2015; Phillips 2003; Scott 2005; Wangnerud 2009). We believe their model of citizenship, based on an ethic of care applied in politics, represents both an extension of broader experiences as well as a normative preference. As Tronto states, "Political life is ultimately about the allocation of caring responsibilities, and that all of those relationships and people engaged in them need to be part of the ongoing political discourse" (2013, xiii).

This book has had a long journey from research and analysis to and writing. Its history coincides with a period of significant changes, some of them completely unexpected, in politics, both nationally and globally. Our respondents displayed a robust general optimism in describing progress toward democratization and the consolidation of democracy on ethical foundations, primarily by adapting Western values, specifically those embodied by the EU. At this point, Romania has had a decade of full membership in the "club" of Western democracies. The hopes expressed back in 2009 appear quite different; the optimism our respondents and we embraced in imagining that the moral consciousness of freedom would become a widely shared value seem more naive today. By 2016–17, some of the most established democracies in the world, such as the United Kingdom and the United States, had become vulnerable to populism and even antidemocratic radicalization. The results of such tendencies in neighboring postcommunist countries, such as Poland and Hungary, are worrisome for the prospect of maintaining a consolidated democracy.

The sources of this international trend seem to reach beyond economic processes and dissatisfaction. Cultural reasons appear just as relevant, with attacks on the part of right-wing parties against political correctness serving as the main expression of various frustrations (Inglehart and Norris 2016). Feminism has become a target in this larger offensive. In societies where misogyny and sexism have been deemed passé and that have entered a "postfeminist era," critiques of feminism have a type of purchase (Greer 2000; Wolf 1991). Yet in Romania and other postcommunist countries where antigenderism is becoming increasingly vocal, these criticisms against political correctness seem themselves a type of Western import, a type of populist correctness. Feminism has not become a hegemonic or even mainstream force in these countries, despite accusations to that extent. In the combined populist critique that wraps feminism, globalization, and the refugee crisis in the same blanket criticism of political correctness, Eastern Europe stands in clear contrast to the rest of the EU. None of these countries are in-takers of large numbers of refugees but instead are themselves the beneficiaries of much migrant work revenue that comes in from other parts of Europe and the world. And globalization has generated a great deal of economic growth rather than loss of status and economic power.

How well founded, then, is the cultural explanation regarding the rise of populism in Eastern Europe and, in our case, in Romania? Mainstream politics has not incorporated feminism beyond the legislative frameworks imposed by EU membership. Misogynist language is very present still without punitive consequences for politicians who engage in it. The same problem can be noted with regard to ethnic and sexual minorities. In short, the pretext that one of the cultural causes of populism is the "suffocation" felt against political correctness is laughable in this context (Inglehart and Norris 2016). On the other hand, an important similarity with populism in Western democracies is the revival of religious values and attitudes.

This explanation leads to a more general conclusion that transcends cultural differences. It is quite possible that beyond the populist inclination toward nativism and nationalism and against cosmopolitan neoliberalism with its attendant feminism, this trend represents a rejection of dirty or even "spotted hands" politics. It might be that voters are rejecting the separation between politics and morality. It remains to be seen what that closer relationship will look like. Our respondents' attitudes give us some continued hope for an ethics of care in this future political landscape. Yet their limited access to public fora for expressing these preferences remains an inauspicious context.

Notes

1. "Componența Consiliului Județean," accessed May 1, 2018, http://www.cjhunedoara.ro/index.php/componenta-consiliului.
2. "Consiliul local. Componență și competențe," accessed May 1, 2018, http://www.primariahd.ro/pagina/componen-539-a.
3. "Primarii județ Hunedoara," accessed May 1, 2018, http://www.portal-info.ro/primarii/primarii-judet-hunedoara.html.
4. After the 2012 elections, two women and one man represented Hunedoara County in the lower house, a rare gender distribution compared to the national average.
5. Oral communication with Mihaela Miroiu, June 2016.
6. Here we follow North's (1990) understanding of institutions as rules of the social game.
7. We define *conservative* here as a reluctance to openly question gender norms, primarily airing grievances in conversations with other women and hoping for, at best, their spouses' behavior to change incrementally.
8. A view that comes close to Aristotle's *Politics* and *Nicomachean Ethics*.

References

Achim, Viorel. 1998. *Țiganii în istoria României*. Bucharest : Editura Enciclopedică.
Adler, M. A. 1997. "Social Change and Decline in Marriage and Fertility in Eastern Germany." *Journal of Marriage and the Family* 59 (1): 37–49.
Alecsandru, Ioan I. [1865] 2011. *Codice Civile*. Bucharest: Nabu.
Almond, Gabriel, and Sidney Verba. 1989. *The Civic Culture: Political Attitudes and Democracy in Five Nations*. London: SAGE.
Antonovici, Valeriu. 2015. *Munca patriotică în comunism: Radiografia unui ideal falsificat*. Cluj: Eikon.
Ardelean, Ben-Oni. 2011. *Libertatea religioasă: O abordare normativă*. Bucharest: Editura Didactică și Pedagogică.
Axelrod, Robert. 1981. "The Emergence of Cooperation among Egoists." *American Political Science Review* 75 (2): 306–18.
Aspasia. "Is Communist Feminism a Contradictio in Terminis?" *Aspasia* 1 (2007): 197–246.
———. "Ten Years After: Communism and Feminism Revisited." *Aspasia* 10 (2016): 102–168.
Atkinson, Paul. 2006. "Rescuing Autoethography." *Journal of Contemporary Ethnography* 35 (August): 400–4.
Băban, Adriana. 1996. "Viața sexuală a femeilor: O experiența traumatizantă în România socialistă." In *Cine suntem noi? Despre identitatea femeilor din România modernă*, edited by Madalina Nicolaescu, 51–68. Bucharest: Anima.
Bader-Zaar, Brigitta. 2012. "Gaining the Vote in a World in Transition: Female Suffrage in Austria." In *The Struggle for Female Suffrage in Europe: Voting to Become Citizens*, edited by Blanca Rodriguez-Ruiz and Ruth Rubio-Marin, 191–206. Leiden: Brill.
Băluță, Oana, ed. 2006. *Gen și putere: Partea leului în politica românească*. Iași: Polirom.
Băluță, Oana, Alice Iancu, and Alina Dragolea, eds. 2007a. *Gen și interese politice: Teorii și practici*. Iași: Polirom.
———. 2007b. *Parteneri egali, competitori egali: Integrarea dimensiunii de gen în procesul de elaborare a politicilor publice*. Bucharest: Maiko.
Bănică, Mirel. 2007. *Biserica ortodoxă română: Stat și societate în anii '30*. Iași: Polirom.
Benhabib, Seyla. 1992. *Situating the Self: Gender, Community, and Postmodernism in Contemporary Ethics*. New York: Routledge.
Biebuyck, Erin. 2010. "The Collectivization of Pleasure: Normative Sexuality in Post-1966 Romania." *Aspasia* 4:49–70.
Bolovan, Ioan, Diana Covaci, Daniela Deteșan, Marius Eppel, and Elena Crinela Holom, eds. 2009. *Ciclul vieții familiale la românii din Transilvania în a doua jumătate a sec. al XIX-lea și începutul sec. XX*. Cluj: Presa Universitară Clujeană.
Blackden, C. Mark and Chitra Bhanu. 1999. "Gender, Growth, and Poverty Reduction: Special Program of Assistance for Africa, 1998 Status Report on Poverty in Sub-Saharan Africa." World Bank Technical Papers, no. 428. Washington, DC: The World Bank.
Brădeanu, Adina, and Otilia Dragomir, eds. 2002. *Femei, cuvinte și imagini: Perspective feministe*. Iași: Polirom.

Braga, Andreea. 2014. "Violența împotriva femeilor rome. Relații de putere între femei și bărbați în comunitatea cu romi din Valea Seacă." PhD diss., National School for Political Science and Public Administration, Bucharest.

Branea, Cristian. 2015. "Statul, politicile de mediu și activismul ecologist în Romania." In *Mișcări feministe și ecologiste în România*, edited by Mihaela Miroiu, 219–81. Iași: Polirom.

Brie, Mircea. 2011. "Ethnic Identity and the Issue of Otherness through Marriage in Northwest Transylvania (Second Half of the XIX–Early XX Century)." *Eurolimes* supplement: 89–104.

Brindley, Clare. 2005. "Barriers to Women Achieving Their Entrepreneurial Potential: Women and Risk." *International Journal of Entrepreneurial Behaviour and Research* 11 (2): 144–61.

Bucur, Maria. 1995. "In Praise of Wellborn Mothers: On Eugenics and Gender Roles in Interwar Romania." *East European Politics and Societies* 9 (1): 123–42.

———. 2000. "Between the Mother of the Wounded and the Virgin from Jiu. Romanian Women and the Gender of Heroism during the Great War." *Journal of Women's History* 12 (2): 30–56.

———. 2001a. "Birth of a Nation: Commemorations of December 1st, 1918, and the Construction of National Identity in Communist Romania." In *Staging the Past: The Politics of Commemoration in Habsburg Central Europe, 1848 to the Present*, edited by Maria Bucur and Nancy Wingfield, 286–325. La Fayette, IN: Purdue University Press, 2001.

———. 2001b. "Calypso Botez: Gender Difference and the Limits of Pluralism in Interwar Romania." *Jahrbücher für Geschichte und Kultur Südosteuropas* 3:63–78.

———. 2002. *Eugenics and Modernization in Interwar Romania*. Pittsburgh: University of Pittsburgh Press.

———. 2006a. "Ella Negruzzi." In *Biographical Dictionary of Women's Movements and Feminisms in Central, Eastern, and South Eastern Europe: 19th and 20th Centuries*, edited by Francisca de Haan, Krasimira Daskalova, and Anna Loutfi, 363–65. Budapest: Central European University Press.

———. 2006b. "Women's Stories as Sites of Memory: Remembering Romania's World Wars." In *Gender and War in Twentieth-Century Eastern Europe*, edited by Nancy M. Wingfield and Maria Bucur, 171–92. Bloomington: Indiana University Press.

———. 2007. "Between Liberal and Republican Citizenship. Feminism and Nationalism in Romania, 1859–1918." *Aspasia* 1:84–103.

———. 2008a. "An Archipelago of Stories: Gender History in Eastern Europe." *American Historical Review* 113 (December): 1375–89.

———. 2008b. "Gendering Dissent: Of Bodies and Minds, Survival and Opposition under Communism." In *Beyond Little Vera*, edited by Angela Brintlinger and Natasha Kolchevska, 16–32. Bloomington, IN: Slavica, 2008.

———. 2017. "The Economics of Citizenship: Gender Regimes and Property Rights in Romania in the 20th Century." In *Gender and Citizenship in Historical and Transnational Perspective: Agency, Space, Borders*, edited Anne Epstein and Rachel Fuchs, 143–65. London: Palgrave.

Bucur, Maria, and Mihaela Miroiu, eds. 2002. *Patriarhat și emancipare în istoria gîndirii politice românești*. Iași: Polirom.

Budeancă, Cosmin, and Florentin Olteanu, eds. 2009. *Stat și viață privată în regimurile comuniste*. Iași: Polirom.

Bulai, Alfred. 2000. *Focus-grup*. Bucharest: Paideia.
Cheşchebec, Roxana. 2005. "Feminist Ideologies and Activism in Romania (approx. 1890–1940s): Nationalism and Internationalism in Romanian Projects for Women's Emancipation." PhD diss., Central European University.
———. 2006. "Cantacuzino, Princess Alexandrina." In *Biographical Dictionary of Women's Movements and Feminisms in Central and South Eastern Europe, 19th and 20th Centuries*, edited by Francisca de Haan, Krasimira Daskalova, and Anna Loutfi, 89–94. Budapest: Central European University Press.
Chodorow, Nancy. 1999. *The Reproduction of Mothering: Psychoanalysis and the Sociology of Gender: With a New Preface*. Berkeley: University of California Press.
Ciocalteau, Michel. 1936. *Les régimes matrimoniaux dans le projet de code civil roumain*. Paris.
Cioflâncă, Adrian, and Luciana M. Jinga, eds. 2011. *Represiune şi control social în România comunistă*. Iaşi: Polirom.
Ciupală, Alin. 2003. *Femeia în societatea românească a secolului al XIX-lea: Între public şi privat*. Bucharest: Editura Meridiane.
CNCSIS. 2006–8. *Gen: Interese politice, şi inserţie europeană*, coordinated by Mihaela Miroiu and Ana Bulai. Bucharest.
Colescu, L. 1944. *Analiza rezultatelor recensămîntului general al populaţiei României din 1899*. Bucharest.
Comşa, Mircea, Dumitru Sandu, Alexandru Toth, Mădălina Voicu, and Ovidiu Voicu. 2006. *Barometrul de Opinie Publică, Mai 2006: Percepţii Despre Mass-Media*. Accessed August 27, 2017. http://www.fundatia.ro/sites/default/files/BOP-perceptii%20despre%20mass%20media.pdf.
Constituţia Republicii Socialiste România. 1965. Accessed August 27, 2017. http://legislatie.resurse-pentru-democratie.org/constitutie/constitutia-republicii-socialiste-romania-1965.php.
Constituţia României. 1991. Accessed August 27, 2017. http://www.cdep.ro/pls/dic/act_show?ida=1.
———. 2003. Accessed August 27, 2017. https://www.ccr.ro/constitutia-romaniei-2003.
Corrin, Chris. 1992. *Superwomen and the Double Burden: Women's Experience of Change in Central and Eastern Europe and the Former Soviet Union*. Toronto: Second Story.
Council of Europe. 2011. "Istanbul Convention: Action against Violence against Women and Domestic Violence." Accessed August 27, 2017. http://www.coe.int/en/web/istanbul-convention/text-of-the-convention.
Csizmadia, Andor, Alajos Degré, and Somfai Erika Filó, eds. 1979. *Etudes sur l'histoire du droit de mariage de Hongrie*. Hungary, Pecs.
Dahlerup, Drude. 2008. "Gender Quotas—Controversial but Trendy: On Expanding the Research Agenda." *International Feminist Journal of Politics* 10 (September): 322–28.
Daskalova, Krassimira. 2007. "How Should We Name the 'Women-Friendly' Actions of State Socialism?" *Aspasia* 1:214–19.
Deletant, Dennis. 2006. *România sub regimul comunist*. Bucharest: Editura Fundaţiei Academia Civică, 2006.
Diamond, Larry J. 2003. "Can the Whole World Become Democratic? Democracy, Development, and International Policies." *Center for the Study of Democracy*. Paper 03-05. Accessed August 27, 2017. http://repositories.cdlib.org/csd/03.
Dietz, Mary G. 1998. "Context Is All: Feminism and Theories of Citizenship." In *Feminism and Politics*, edited by Anne Phillips, 378–400. Oxford: Oxford University Press.

Dinculescu, Vasile, and Constantin Chirică. 1998. *Coordonate ale sărăciei în România*. Bucharest: Raport PNUD.

Doboș, Corina, Luciana M. Jinga, and Florin S. Soare, eds. 2010. *Politica pronatalistă a regimului Ceaușescu*. Iași: Polirom.

Dobrincu, Dorin, Vladimir Tismăneanu, and Cristian Vasile, eds. 2007. *Raport final: Comisia prezidențială pentru analiza dictaturii comuniste din România*. Bucharest: Humanitas.

Dragolea, Alina. 2007. "Dimensiunea de gen a pieței muncii." In *Parteneri egali, competitori egali: Integrarea dimensiunii de gen în procesul de elaborare a politicilor publice*, edited by Oana Băluță, Alice Iancu, and Alina Dragolea, 25–80. Bucharest: Maiko.

———. 2016. *Statul bunăstării după criza economică: Între realitatea austerității și necesitatea reformei*. Bucharest: Tritonic.

Economist. 2012. "Do Romanian Schools Produce Idiots?" *Economist*. August 7, 2012. Accessed August 27, 2017. http://www.economist.com/blogs/easternapproaches/2012/08/education-romania?zid=307&ah=5e80419d1bc9821ebe173f4f0f060a07.

Economist Intelligence Unit. 2010. *Democracy Index 2010: Democracy in Retreat*. www.eiu.com.

———. 2011–15. *Democracy Index*. www.eiu.com.

Einhorn, Barbara. 1993. *Cinderella Goes to Market: Citizenship, Gender, and Women's Movements in East Central Europe*. London: Verso.

Elliott, Joyce E., and William Moskoff. 1983. "Decision-Making Power in Romanian Families." *Journal of Comparative Family Studies* 14 (1): 39–50.

Elshtain, Jean Bethke. 1981. *Public Man, Private Woman: Women in Social and Political Thought*. Princeton, NJ: Princeton University Press.

Engels, Frederick. 1902. *The Origin of the Family, Private Property, and the State: in the Light of the Researches of Lewis H. Morgan*. Chicago: Charles H. Kerr.

Etzioni, Amitai, ed. 1995. *New Communitarian Thinking: Persons, Virtues, Institutions, and Communities*. Charlottesville: University of Virginia Press.

European Commission. 2015. *2017 Report on Equality between Women and Men in the EU*. Bruxelles: European Union.

European Institute for Gender Equality (EIGE). 2015. *Gender Equality Index*. Accessed August 27, 2017. http://eige.europa.eu/content/document/gender-equality-index-2015-measuring-gender-equality-in-the-european-union-2005-2012.

Eurostat. 2015. *Marriage and Divorce Statistics*. Accessed August 27, 2017. http://ec.europa.eu/eurostat/statistics-explained/index.php/Marriage_and_divorce_statistics.

Fábián, Katalin. 2007. "Making an Appearance: The Formation of Women's Groups in Hungary." *Aspasia* 1:103–27.

Ferree, Myra Marx. 1993. "The Rise and Fall of 'Mommy Politics': Feminism and Unification in (East) Germany." *Feminist Studies* 19 (1): 89–115.

Fidelis, Malgorzata. 2010. *Women, Communism, and Industrialization in Postwar Poland*. New York: Cambridge University Press.

Fitzpatrick, Sheila. 2000. *Everyday Stalinism: Ordinary Life in Extraordinary Times: Soviet Russia in the 1930s*. Oxford: Oxford University Press.

Forbrig, Joerg, and Pavol Demeš, eds. 2009. *Reclaiming Democracy: Civil Society and Electoral Change in Central and Eastern Europe*. Washington, DC: German Marshall Fund of the United States.

Fotino, George. 1925. *Contribution a l'étude des origines de l'ancien Droit coutumier roumain. Un chapitre de l'histoire de la propriété au Moyen Age*. Paris.

Friedan, Betty. [1963] 2001. *The Feminine Mystique*. New York: Norton.
Gheo, Radu Pavel, and Dan Lungu, eds. 2008. *Tovarășe de drum: Experiența feminină în comunism*. Iași: Polirom.
Gheorghe, Carmen. 2014. "O perspectivă feministă asupra identității și invizibilității femeilor rome în spațiul public." PhD diss., National School for Political Science and Public Administration, Bucharest.
Gherghina, Sergiu, and Sergiu Mișcoiu, eds. 2010. *Partide și personalități populiste în România postcomunistă*. Iași: Institutul European.
Ghimpu, Sanda, 1967. "Protecția femeii în dreptul muncii." *Revista Română de Drept* 8. Accessed August 27, 2017. http://www.costelgilca.ro/doctrina/document/1/19/#_ftnref7.
Ghodsee, Kristen. 2004. "Red Nostalgia? Communism, Women's Emancipation, and Economic Transformation in Bulgaria." *L'Homme* 15 (1): 23–36.
———. 2015. *The Left Side of History: World War II and the Unfulfilled Promise of Communism in Eastern Europe*. Durham, NC: Duke University Press.
Gilligan, Carol. 1993. *In a Different Voice: Psychological Theory and Women's Development*. Cambridge, MA: Harvard University Press.
Greer, Germaine. 2000. *The Whole Woman*. London: Transworld.
Grünberg, Laura. 2005. *Mass media despre sexe: Aspecte privind stereotipurile de gen în mass media din România*. Bucharest: Tritonic.
———. 2008. *biONGrafie: Istoria trăită a unui ONG de femei*. Iași: Polirom.
Gusti, Dimitrie, ed. 1938–43. *Enciclopedia României*. 4 vols. Bucharest: Imprimeria statului.
Habermas, Jürgen. 1989. *The Structural Transformation of the Public Sphere: An Inquiry into a Category of Bourgeois Society*. Cambridge: Polity.
Haney, Lynne. 2002. *Inventing the Needy: Gender and Politics of Welfare in Hungary*. Berkeley: University of California Press.
Hardin, Garrett. 1968. "The Tragedy of the Commons." *Science*, new series, 162 (3859): 1243–48.
Harsany Pasca, Doina. 1995. "Participation of Women in the Workforce: The Case of Romania." In *Family, Women, and Employment in Central-Eastern Europe*, edited by Barbara Łobodzińska, 54–66. Westport, CT: Greenwood.
Hartmann, Heidi. 1981. "The Unhappy Marriage of Marxism and Feminism." In *Women and Revolution: A Disscution of the Unhappy Marriage of Feminism and Marxism*, edited by Lydia Sargent, 1–42. Boston: South End Press.
Havelková, Hana. 1996. "Abstract Citizenship? Women and Power in the Czech Republic." *Social Politics* 3 (2–3): 243–60.
Hitchins, Keith. 1969. *The Rumanian National Movement in Transylvania, 1780–1849*. Cambridge, MA: Harvard University Press.
———. 1996. *The Romanians 1774–1866*. Oxford: Oxford University Press.
Hoagland, Sarah Lucia. 1990. *Lesbian Ethics: Toward a New Value*. Palo Alto, CA: Institute for Lesbian Studies.
Iluț, Petru. 1997. *Abordarea calitativă a socioumanului: Concepte și metode*. Iași: Polirom.
Inglehart, Ronald, and Pippa Norris. 2016. "Trump, Brexit, and the Rise of Populism: Economic Have-Nots and Cultural Backlash." HKS Faculty Research Working Paper Series RWP16-026. Accessed August 27, 2017. https://research.hks.harvard.edu/publications.
INSCOP. 2013. *Barometrul INSCOP*. Accessed August 27, 2017. http://www.inscop.ro.
———. 2015. *Barometrul INSCOP*. Accessed August 27, 2017. http://www.inscop.ro.

———. 2016. *Barometrul INSCOP*. Accessed August 27, 2017. http://www.inscop.ro.
Institutul Național de Statistică. 2012. *Evoluția natalității și fertilității în România*. Bucharest. Accessed May 1, 2018. http://www.insse.ro/cms/files/publicatii/Evolutia%20natalitatii%20si%20fertilitatii%20in%20Romania_n.pdf.
———. 2013. *Repere economice și sociale regionale: Statistică teritorială*. Bucharest. Accessed August 27, 2017. http://www.insse.ro/cms/files/publicatii/Statistica%20teritoriala/Statistica%20teritoriala%202013.pdf.
Jaggar, Alison. 1983. *Feminist Politics and Human Nature*. Totowa, New Jersey: Rowman & Allanheld.
Jeffee, Sara, and Janet Shibley Hyde. 2000. "Gender Differences in Moral Orientation: A Meta-Analysis." *Psychological Bulletin* 126 (September): 703–26.
Jinga, Luciana M. 2015. *Gen și reprezentare în România comunistă, 1944–1989*. Iași: Polirom.
Jinga, Luciana, and Ștefan Bosomitu, eds. 2014. *Între transformare și adaptare : Avataruri ale cotidianului în regimul comunist din România*. Iași: Polirom.
Jinga, Luciana, and Florin Soare, eds. 2011. *Politica pronatalistă a regimului Ceaușescu: Instituții și practici*. 2 vols. Iași: Polirom.
Karl, Terry. 2005. *From Democracy to Democratization and Back: Before Transitions from Authoritarian Rule*. Center on Democracy, Development, and the Rule of Law Working Paper 45 (September). Stanford, CA: Stanford Institute on International Studies.
Kessler-Harris, Alice. 2003. *Out to Work: A History of Wage-Earning Women in the United States*. 20th anniversary ed. Oxford: Oxford University Press.
Kideckel, David. 2008. *Getting by in Postsocialist Romania: Labor, the Body and the Working Class Culture*. Bloomington: Indiana University Press.
King, Gary, Robert O. Keohane, and Sidney Verba. 1994. *Designing Social Inquiry: Scientific Inference in Qualitative Research*. Princeton, NJ: Princeton University Press.
King, Ronald F., and Cosmin Gabriel Marian. 2015. "Representation, Incumbency and the Quality of Romanian Democracy." In *Post-Communist Romania at Twenty-Five: Linking Past, Present, and Future*, edited by Lavinia Stan and Diane Vancea, 149–70. Lanham, MD: Lexington Books.
Kligman, Gail. 1998. *The Politics of Duplicity: Controlling Reproduction in Ceausescu's Romania*. Berkeley: University of California Press.
Kligman, Gail, and Katherine Verdery. 2011. *Peasants under Siege: The Collectivization of Romanian Agriculture, 1949–1962*. Princeton, NJ: Princeton University Press.
Krastev, Ivan. 2009. "Where Next or What Next?" In *Reclaiming Democracy: Civil Society and Electoral Change in Central and Eastern Europe*, edited by Joerg Forbrig and Pavol Demeš, 235–44. Washington, DC: German Marshall Fund of the United States.
———. 2016. "What's Wrong with East-Central Europe: Liberalism's Failure to Deliver." *Journal of Democracy* 27 (1): 35–39.
Krook, Mona Lena. 2009. *Quotas for Women in Politics: Gender and Candidate Selection Reform Worldwide*. Oxford: Oxford University Press.
Leuștean, Lucian. 2009. *Orthodoxy and the Cold War: Religion and Political Power in Romania, 1947–65*. Basingstoke, UK: Palgrave Macmillan.
Leven, Bozena. 1994. "The Status of Women and Poland's Transition to Market Economy." In *Women in the Age of Economic Transformation*, edited by N. Aslanbeigui, Steven Pressman, and Gale Summerfield, 27–42. London: Routledge.
Levy, Robert. 2001. *Ana Pauker: The Rise and Fall of a Jewish Communist*. Berkeley: University of California Press.

Lister, Ruth. 1998. "Citizenship: Pushing the Boundaries." *Feminist Review* 60 (1): 28–48.
———. 2003. *Citizenship: Feminist Perspectives.* Basingstoke, UK: Palgrave Macmillan.
———. 2005. "Being a Feminist." *Government and Opposition* 40 (3): 442–63.
———. 2008. "Inclusive Citizenship, Gender and Poverty: Some Implications for Education for Citizenship." *Citizenship. Teaching and Learning* 4 (1): 3–19.
Loutfi, Anna. 2006. "Legal Ambiguity and the 'European Norm': Women's Independence and Hungarian Family Law, 1880–1913." *L'Homme* 13:507–15.
Lukić, Jasmina, Joanna Regulska, and Darja Zaviršek, eds. 2006. *Women and Citizenship in Central and Eastern Europe.* Aldershot: Ashgate.
MacIntyre, Alasdair. 1981. *After Virtue.* Notre Dame, IN: University of Notre Dame Press.
Mackenzie, Catriona, and Natalie Stoljar, eds. 1999. *Relational Autonomy: Feminist Perspectives on Automomy, Agency, and the Social Self.* New York: Oxford University Press.
Manolache, Anca. 1994. *Imaginea feminină în biserica lui Hristos.* Timişoara: Mitropolia Banatului.
Marea Adunare Naţională. 1972. "Codul Muncii (Legea nr. 10 din 25 noiembrie 1972)." *Buletinul oficial* 140 (December). Accessed August 27, 2017. http://www.monitoruljuridic.ro/act/codul-muncii-legea-nr-10-din-25-noiembrie-1972-emitent-marea-adunare-nationala-publicat-n-buletinul-oficial-296.html.
———. 1977. "Legea nr. 3 din 30 iunie 1977 privind pensiile de asigurări sociale de stat şi asistenţa socială." *Buletinul oficial* 82 (August). Accessed August 27, 2017. http://www.cdep.ro/pls/legis/legis_pck.htp_act_text?idt=1356.
Mărginean, Mara. 2015. *Ferestre spre furnalul roşu: Urbanism şi cotidian în Hunedoara şi Călan, 1945–1968.* Iaşi: Polirom.
Massino, Jill. 2007. "Engendering Socialism: A History of Women and Everyday Life in Socialist Romania." PhD diss., Indiana University.
———. 2009. "Workers under Construction. Gender Identity and Women's Experiences of Work in State Socialist Romania." In *Gender Politics and Everyday Life in State Socialist Eastern and Central Europe*, edited by Shana Penn and Jill Massino, 13–32. New York: Palgrave Macmillan.
Mateş, Adela-Ioana. 2012. "Fenomenul dezindustrializării din perioada de tranziţie şi impactul asupra geodemografiei şi al habitatului în judeţul Hunedoara." PhD diss., Babeş-Bolyai University.
Matland, Richard E., and Kathleen A. Montgomery, eds. 2003. *Women's Access to Political Power in Post-Communist Europe.* Oxford: Oxford University Press.
McBride, Dorothy E., and Amy Mazur, eds. 1995. *Comparative State Feminism.* Thousand Oaks, CA: SAGE.
Mihăilescu, Ştefania, ed. 2002. *Din istoria feminismului românesc: Antologie de texte (1838–1929).* Iaşi: Polirom.
———. 2006. "Sofia Nădejde." In *Biographical Dictionary of Women's Movements and Feminisms in Central, Eastern, and South Eastern Europe: 19th and 20th Centuries*, edited by Francisca de Haan, Krasimira Daskalova, and Anna Loutfi, 360–62. Budapest: Central European University Press.
Mill, John Stuart and Harriett Taylor Mill. 1982. *The Subjection of Women and Enfranchisement of Women.* London: Virago.
Millett, Kate. 1970. *Sexual Politics.* New York: Doubleday and Co..
Ministerul Muncii. 2013. "Pensii pe anul 2013." *Buletin statistic.* Accessed August 27, 2017. http://www.mmuncii.ro/j33/images/buletin_statistic/pensii_anul_2013.pdf.

Miroiu, Adrian, ed. 1998. *Învățământul românesc azi: Studiu de diagnoză*. Iași: Polirom.
——. 2016. *Fuga de competiție: O perspectivă instituțională asupra socităţii româneşti*. Iași: Polirom.
Miroiu, Adrian, and Iris Golopența, eds. 2015. *Acţiune colectivă şi bunuri commune în societatea romănească*. Iași: Polirom.
Miroiu, Mihaela. 1997. "Ana's Land. The Right to Be Sacrificed." In *Ana's Land, Sisterhood in Eastern Europe*, edited by Tanya Renne, 136–40. Boulder, CO: Westview.
——. 1999. *Societatea retro*. Bucharest: Editura Trei.
——. 2004a. "All in One: Fairness, Neutrality and Conservatism—A Case Study of Romania." *Prospects* 34 (March): 85–100.
——. 2004b. *Drumul către autonomie: teorii politice feministe*. Iași: Polirom.
——. 2004c. "State Men, Market Women." *Feminismo/s: Mujer y participation politica* 3 (June): 207–34.
——. 2011. "What Is Left from Democracy? Electoralism and Populism in Romania." *Perspective politice* 4 (2): 7–22.
——. 2013. "Morality in Politics, or the In Politics of Morality? 'Neo-Purification' in Romania." In *Applied Ethics: Perspectives from Romania*, edited by Valentin Mureșan and Shunzo Majima, 209–28. Sapporo, Japan: Center for Applied Ethics and Philosophy, Hokkaido University.
——. 2015a. "Despre metamorfozele feminismului recent." In *Mișcări feministe şi ecologiste în România*, edited by Mihaela Miroiu, 189–218. Iași: Polirom.
——, ed. 2015b. *Mișcări feministe şi ecologiste în România, 1990–2004*. Iași: Polirom.
——. 2015c. "On Women, Feminism and Democracy." In *Post-Communist Romania at Twenty-Five: Linking Past, Present, and Future*, edited by Lavinia Stan and Diane Vancea, 83–102. Lanham, MD: Lexington Books.
——. 2017. *Cu mintea mea de femeie*. Bucharest: Cartea românească.
Miroiu, Mihaela, and Otilia Dragomir, eds. 2010. *Nașterea: Istorii trăite*. Iași: Polirom.
Miroiu, Mihaela, and Mircea Miclea. 2005. *R'Estul Și Vestul*. Ego Grafii. Iași: Polirom.
Molocea, Andreea. 2015. "(Re)construcția feminismului românesc în cadrul mișcării de femei (1990–2000)." In *Mișcări feministe şi ecologiste în România*, edited by Mihaela Miroiu, 13–88. Iași: Polirom.
Monitorul Oficial. 1999. "Legea concediului paternal nr. 210/1999." Accessed August 27, 2017. http://www.mmuncii.ro/pub/imagemanager/images/file/Legislatie/LEGI/L210-1999.pdf.
Morteanu, Crina. 2014. "Mariajele timpurii în comunitățile de romi din România." PhD diss., National School for Political Science and Public Administration, Bucharest.
Mouffe, Chantal. 1993. *The Return of the Political*. London: Verso.
Muller, Anna. 2013. "Between Social and Individual Memory: Being a Polish Woman in a Stalinist Prison." In *Tapestry of Memory: Evidence and Testimony in Life-Story Narratives*, edited by Nanci Adler and Selma Leydesdorff, 55–76. New Brunswick: Transaction.
Muller, Wolfgang, ed. 1981. *History of the Church: The Church in the Age of Absolutism and Enlightenment*. New York: Crossroads.
Muravchik, Joshua. 2002. *Heaven on Earth: The Rise and Fall of Socialism*. San Francisco: Encounter Books.
Murgescu, Bogdan. 2010. *România și Europa: Acumularea decalajelor economice (1500–2010)*. Iași: Polirom.

Nădejde, Sofia. 1883. "Șicane bărbătești." *Contemporanul* 3 (8): 312–15.
Neaga, Diana Elena. 2013. *Gen și cetățenie în România: Intre formal și substanțial, normal și normativ*. Iași: Polirom.
Neculau, Adrian, ed. 2004. *Viața cotidiană în comunism*. Iași: Polirom.
Nicolae, Radu. 2010. *Corupția și politicile anticorupție*. Iași: Polirom.
North, Douglas. 1990. *Institutions, Institutional Change and Economic Performance*. Cambridge: Cambridge University Press.
Nussbaum, Martha. 2001. *Women and Human Development: The Capabilities Approach*. Cambridge: Cambridge University Press.
Okin, Susan Moller. 1987. *Justice, Gender, and the Family*. New York: Basic Books.
———. 1998. "Gender, the Public, and the Private." In *Feminism and Politics*, edited by Anne Phillips, 116–41. Oxford: Oxford University Press.
———. 2004. "Equal Citizenship: Gender, Justice and Gender. An Unfinished Debate." *Fordham Law Review* 72 (5): 1537–67.
Olteanu, Cristina Liana, Elena-Simona Gheonea, and Valentin Gheonea. 2003. *Femeile în România comunistă: Studii de istorie socială*. Bucharest: Politeia-SNSPA.
Open Society Foundation. 2000. *Barometrul de gen*. Bucharest: Gallup Organization of Romania.
Ostrom, Elinor. 1990. *Governing the Commons: The Evolution of Institutions for Collective Action*. Cambridge: Cambridge University Press.
———. 1998. "A Behavioral Approach to the Rational Choice Theory of Collective Action: Presidential Address, American Political Science Association." *American Political Science Review* 92 (1): 1–22.
Partidul Comunist Român. 1970. *Statutul Partidului Comunist Român*. Bucharest: Editura Politică.
Pasti, Vladimir. 1995. *România în Tranziție: Căderea în viitor*. Bucharest: Editura Nemira.
———. 2003. *Ultima inegalitate: Relațiile de gen în România*. Iași: Polirom.
———. 2006, *Noul capitalism românesc*. Iași: Polirom.
Pasti, Vladimir, Mihaela Miroiu, and Cornel Codiță. 1997. *România—starea de fapt*. Bucharest: Nemira.
Pateman, Carole. 1988. *The Sexual Contract*. Stanford, CA: Stanford University Press.
———. 1989. *The Disorder of Women: Democracy, Feminism, and Political Theory*. Stanford, CA: Stanford University Press.
———. 2006. "The Patriarchal Welfare State." In *The Welfare State Reader*, edited by Christopher Pierson and Francis G. Castles, 102–19. Cambridge: Polity.
Paul, Andreea, ed. 2011. *Forța politică a femeilor*. Iași: Polirom.
———. 2016. *Forța economică a femeilor*. Iași: Polirom.
Păltineanu, Oana Sinziana. 2015. "Converging Suffrage Politics: The Romanian Women's Movement in Hungary and Its Allies before World War I." *Aspasia* 9:44–64.
Păunescu, Ramona. 2012. *Evoluții politice ale maternității: Perspective feministe*. Iași: Polirom.
Phillips, Anne. 1991. *Engendering Democracy*. University Park: Pennsylvania State University Press.
———. 1997: *Engendering Democracy*. Cambridge: Polity Press.
———, ed. 1998. *Feminism and Politics*. Oxford: Oxford University Press.
———. 2003. *The Politics of Presence: The Political Representation of Gender, Ethnicity, and Race*. Oxford: Oxford University Press.

Playboy. 2000. "Cum să îți bați nevasta fără să lași urme." *Playboy* 1 (April).
Plumwood, Val. 1993. *Feminism and the Mastery of the Nature*. London: Routledge.
Popa, Raluca Maria. 2016. "'We Opposed It.' The National Council of Women and the Ban on Abortion in Romania (1966)." *Aspasia* 11:152–60.
Popescu, Liliana. 2004. *Politica sexelor*. Bucharest: Maiko.
———, ed. 2006. *Guvernare pentru șanse egale*. Bucharest: Tritonic.
Preda, Marian. 2002. *Politica socială românească între sărăcie și globalizare*. Iași: Polirom.
———, ed. 2009. *Riscuri și inechități sociale în România: Raportul comisiei prezidențiale pentru analiza riscurilor sociale și demografice*. Iași: Polirom.
Putnam, Robert, Robert Leonardi, and Raffaella Y. Nanetti, eds. 1994. *Making Democracy Work: Civic Traditions in Modern Italy*. Princeton, NJ: Princeton University Press.
Rădoi, Cristina. 2011. "Apărare și război din perspectivă feministă. Studiu de caz: impactul femeilor în instituțiile militare din România." PhD diss., National School for Political Science and Public Administration, Bucharest.
Rădulescu, Andrei, et al., eds. 1962. *Îndreptarea legii, 1652*. Bucharest: Editura Academiei Republicii Populare Romîne.
Roman, Denise. 2003. *Fragmented Identities: Popular Culture, Sex, and Everyday Life in Postcommunist Romania*. Lanham, MD: Lexington Books.
Roman, Monica, and Cristina Voicu. 2010. "Câteva efecte socioeconomice ale migrației forței de muncă asupra țărilor de emigrație. Cazul României." *Economie teoretică și aplicată* 7 (7): 50–65.
Rostaș, Zoltan, and Theodora-Eliza Văcărescu. 2008. *Cealaltă jumătate a istoriei: Femei povestind*. Bucharest: Curtea veche.
Rubin, Herbert, and Irene Rubin. 2005. *Qualitative Interviewing: The Art of Hearing Data*. 2nd ed. London: SAGE.
Schatz, Edward, ed. 2009. *What Immersion Contributes to the Study of Power*. Chicago: University of Chicago Press.
Scott, Joan Wallach. 2005. *Parité! Sexual Equality and the Crisis of French Universalism*. Chicago: Chicago University Press.
Sen, Amartya. 1999. "Democracy as a Universal Value." *Journal of Democracy* 10 (3): 3–17.
Shapiro, Virginia. 1998. "When Are Interests Interesting? The Problem of Political Representation of Women." In *Feminism and Politics*, edited by Anne Phillips, 161–92. Oxford: Oxford University Press.
Slote, Michael. 1983. *Goods and Virtues*. Oxford: Clarendon.
Smith, S. A., ed. 2014. *The Oxford Handbook of the History of Communism*. Oxford: Oxford University Press.
Solinger, Rickie. 2016. "Bleeding across Time: First Principles of U.S. Population Policy." In *Reproductive States: Global Perspectives on the Invention and Implementation of Population Policy*, edited by Rickie Solinger and Mie Nakachi, 63–97. New York: Oxford University Press, 2016.
Solinger, Rickie, and Mie Nakachi. 2016. *Reproductive States: Global Perspectives on the Invention and Implementation of Population Policy*. New York: Oxford University Press.
Soros, George. 1998. *The Crisis of Global Capitalism: Open Society Endangered*. New York: Public Affairs.
Stahl, Henri. 1980. *Traditional Romanian Village Communities: The Transition from the Communal to the Capitalist Mode of Production in the Danube Region*. Cambridge: Cambridge University Press.

Stan, Lavinia, and Lucian Turcescu. 2007. *Religion and Politics in Post-Communist Romania*. Religion and Global Politics Series. Oxford: Oxford University Press.
Stănculescu, Manuela, and Ionica Berevoescu. 2004. *Sărac lipit, caut altă viață!: Fenomenul sărăciei extreme și al zonelor sărace în România 2001*. Bucharest: Nemira.
Ștefan, Cristina. 2006. *Familia monoparentală: O abordare politică*. Iași: Polirom.
Steger, Manfred. 2002. *Globalism: The New Market Ideology*. New York: Rowman and Littlefield.
Tannen, Deborah. 2001. *You Just Don't Understand: Women and Men in Conversation*. New York: Quill.
Tipei, Alex. 2016. "For Your Civilization and Ours: Greece, Romania, and the Making of French Universalism." PhD diss., Indiana University.
Tismăneanu, Vladimir. 2003. *Stalinism for All Seasons: A Political History of Romanian Communism*. Los Angeles: University of California Press.
Tronto, Joan. 1993. *Moral Boundaries: A Political Argument for an Ethic of Care*. New York: Routledge.
———. 2013. *Caring Democracy: Markets, Equality and Justice*. New York: New York University Press.
Tudosoiu, Silvia. 2010. "Educația în sistemul comunist din România (anii 1965–1989)." PhD diss., University of Bucharest.
Utrata, Jennifer. 2015. *Women without Men: Single Mothers and Family Change in the New Russia*. Ithaca, NY: Cornell University Press.
Văcărescu, Theodora-Eliza. 2014. "Educația femeilor în provinciile locuite de români și în România între anii 1880 și 1930. Studiu de caz: Universitatea din București." *Cooperativa Gusti* (November). Accessed August 27, 2017. http://www.cooperativag.ro/educatia-femeilor-provinciile-locuite-de-romani-si-romania-intre-anii-1880-si-1930-studiu-de-caz-universitatea-din-bucuresti/.
Verdery, Katherine. 1996. *What Was Socialism, and What Comes Next?* Princeton, NJ: Princeton University Press.
Vincze, Enikő. 2006. "Romanian Gender Regimes and Women's Citizenship." In *Women and Citizenship in Central and Eastern Europe*, edited by Jasmina Lukić, Joanna Regulska, and Darja Zaviršek, 21–38. Aldershot: Ashgate.
———, ed. 2011. *Equality through Differences: Roma Women's Access to the Labor Market*. Cluj: Desire.
Vintilă-Ghițulescu, Constanța. 2004 "Divorce and Divortiality in Eighteenth-Century Romanian Society." *Südost-Forschungen* 63–64 (2004): 188–210.
———. 2009. "Marriage Strategies, Women's Dowries and Conflicts between Relatives in Romanian Society (18th Century)." In *The Transmission of Well-Being: Gendered Marriage Strategies and Inheritance Systems in Europe (17th–20th Centuries)*, edited by Margarida Durães, Antoinette Fauve-Chamoux, Llorenç Ferrer i Alòs, and Jan Kok, 123–44. Bern: Peter Lang.
Vlad, Ioana. 2015. "Dezvoltări în mișcarea românească de femei după 2000." In *Mișcări feministe și ecologiste în România*, edited by Mihaela Miroiu, 89–188. Iași: Polirom.
Vlad, Ioana, and Katalin Fabian, eds. 2015. *Democratization Through Social Activism: Gender and Environmental Issues in Post-Communist Societies*. Bucharest: Tritonic.
Vlăsceanu, Lazăr, and Gabriel Hâncean. 2014. *Modernitatea românească*. Pitești: Paralela 45.
Vlăsceanu, Lazăr, Adrian Neculau, and Adrian Miroiu. 2002. *Școala la răscruce: Schimbare și continuitate în curriculumul învățământului obligatoriu; Studiu de impact*. Iași: Polirom.

Voinescu, Alice. 1997. *Jurnal*. Bucharest: Editura Albatros.
Walker, Lenore E. 1987. *The Battered Woman*. New York: Harper and Row.
Walzer, Michael. 1974. "Political Action: The Problem of Dirty Hands." In *War and Moral Responsibility*, edited by Marshall Cohen, Thomas Nagel, and Thomas Scanlon, 62–82. Princeton, NJ: Princeton University Press.
———. 1995. "The Communitarian Critique of Liberalism." In *New Communitarian Thinking: Persons, Virtues, Institutions, and Communities*, edited by Amitai Etzioni, 52–70. Charlottesville: University of Virginia Press.
Wangnerud, Lena. 2009. "Women in Parliaments: Descriptive and Substantive Representation." *Annual Review of Political Science* 12:51–69.
Wollstonecraft, Mary. (1792) 2004. *A Vindication of the Rights of Woman*. Harmondsworth: Penguin.
Wolf, Naomi, 1991. *The Beauty Myth: How Images of Beauty Are Used Against Women*. New York: HarperCollins.
World Economic Forum. 2014. *Global Gender Gap Report*. Accessed August 27, 2017. www.weforum.org.
Young, Iris Marion. 1990. *Justice and the Politics of Difference*. Princeton, NJ: Princeton University Press.
Zanoschi, Delia, and Cristina Deteșan. 2012. "Educația din România la standarde europene în 6 ani: este oare posibil?" Accessed August 27, 2017. http://www.europuls.ro/societate-sp-1187835791/educaie-i-cultur/613-educaia-din-romania-la-standarde-europene-in-6-ani-este-oare-posibil#_ftn1.
Zielińska, Katarzyna. 2013. "Concepts of Religion in Debates on Secularization." *Approaching Religion* 3 (1): 16–24.
Zimmermann, Susan, and Borbala Major. 2006. "Schwimmer, Róza." In *A Biographical Dictionary*, edited by Francisca de Haan, Krassimira Daskalova, and Anna Loutfi, 484–89. Budapest: Central European University Press.

Index

abandonment, 20, 127
abortion, 65, 81, 124–25, 126–27. *See also* pronatalism
abuse, 20, 21, 29, 40n24, 52, 53, 62n8, 70, 71, 123. *See also* domestic violence
Acqui Communitaire, 36
agriculture, 45, 131, 138, 158; collectivization and, 7, 90; women's work and, 35, 79, 84, 91
alcoholism, 28. *See also* drinking
American, 16n6, 22, 56, 84, 114, 140, 164. *See also* United States
Antonovici, Valeriu, 105, 109
atheist, 70, 110n6, 163
Austro-Hungarian Empire. *See* Austria-Hungary
Austria-Hungary, 24, 25, 26, 27, 32, 33
authoritarian, 2, 3, 16n6, 65, 129, 136, 145
authority, 24, 25, 72, 73, 89, 96; in the family, 20, 42, 46, 47, 49, 54, 71, 76, 77, 92n3; political, 31, 155, 162
autonomy, 4, 14, 16n8, 18, 37, 157; economic, 21, 24; personal, 52, 87, 98, 112, 113, 165

Băluță, Oana, 7
Baptist, 8, 32, 70, 99, 100, 103
Barometrul de gen, 5, 6
Băsescu, Traian, 55, 62n11
beating, 20, 21, 39n7, 51, 52, 53, 71, 117. *See also* domestic violence
Beijing Platform, 36
Bergen, Adriaan, van, 106
Bilcescu, Sarmiza, 22
birth, 1, 30, 40n14, 58, 63, 64, 77n2, 82, 123; control, 115, 124, 125, 126, 127, 134n15, 142; rate, 38, 61n2, 64, 65. *See also* childbearing; maternity leave; pronatalism
Botez, Calypso, 16n9, 22–23, 28
bourgeois, 31, 40n20, 103
boyar, 20, 21, 25, 39n1, 39n3
Brăescu, Smaranda, 31
breadwinner, 51, 55, 57, 85, 164

Breaking the Silence, 77n8
bribe, 77n3, 85, 121, 122. *See also* corruption
Bucharest, 10, 22, 24, 28, 32, 34, 68, 71, 101, 115, 116, 129, 130, 1334n13, 136, 150
Bulgaria, 5, 29, 36, 40n22
Bureau of the Base Organization (BOB), 113, 114, 117
byzantine symphony, 100

Călan, 86, 99
candidates, 31, 72, 160n10, 164; women, 85, 154, 161, 162
Cantacuzino, Alexandrina, 22
campaign, 15, 25, 27, 28, 37, 92n4, 141, 142, 145, 146, 147, 154, 162
capitalism, 38, 98, 117, 130, 135, 136, 137, 139, 140, 141, 143, 144, 158, 159, 160n3. *See also* free market; neoliberal
caregiver, 36, 149. *See also* caretaking
caretaking, 14, 15, 17n23, 44, 48, 50, 57, 61, 66, 82, 92n3, 116, 138, 140, 149, 166; paid work and, 37, 69, 77n7, 80, 88, 89. *See also* childcare; mother; parenting
Carol II, King, 28
Catholic, 7, 8, 9, 19, 24, 32, 39n10, 99, 100, 105. *See also* Greek Catholic
Ceaușescu, Nicolae, 29, 60, 63, 73, 75, 103, 114, 116, 123, 124, 128, 148. *See also The Politics of Duplicity: Controlling Reproduction in Ceausescu's Romania*
censorship, 75, 134n13
charity, 93, 101, 105; work, 106, 197, 110. *See also* organizations, charitable
childbearing, 63, 66. *See also* birth
childcare, 3, 16n5, 17n23, 35, 36, 37, 44, 61, 64, 65, 67, 69, 81, 87, 89, 91, 92, 92n3, 98, 110, 121, 124, 150, 154. *See also* crèche; kindergarten; mothering; parenting
children, 9, 12, 14, 15, 16n19, 39n3, 41, 43, 49, 52, 56, 57, 58, 62n8, 63, 64, 68, 71, 72, 73, 74, 77, 77n6, 82, 86, 88, 90, 95, 97, 100,

181

102, 103, 105, 107, 109, 114, 125, 127, 129-30, 132, 134n16, 136, 139, 140, 141, 142, 145, 153, 158, 159; education and, 30, 42, 47, 48, 50, 66, 67, 69, 70, 75, 76, 81, 85, 112, 116, 118, 149. See also childcare; kids; legal issues, guardianship
church, 11, 64, 69, 76, 93, 99, 107, 109, 126, 150. See also Baptist; Catholic; clergy; Greek Catholic; Lord's Army; Orthodox; Pentecostal; Protestant; Seventh-Day Adventist
citizen. See citizenship
citizenship, 8, 17n20, 24, 28, 37, 54, 77, 93, 107, 109, 137, 143, 148, 150, 152, 157, 164; democratic, 2, 4–5, 12, 35, 71, 112, 135, 162, 163, 166; education and, 64, 72, 74, 75; feminist definitions of, 2–3, 26; gender and, 6, 13, 41, 42, 46, 49, 59, 60, 79, 84, 142; participatory, 15, 147; rights, 30, 32, 136, 143; under communism, 113, 115, 117, 118, 119, 121, 124, 129, 133; women and, 1, 11, 14, 16n19, 17n23, 21, 25, 27, 29, 43, 50, 63, 73, 80–81, 92n3, 159
city hall, 140, 147, 148, 151, 152, 155. See also municipal
civic issues, 2, 48, 54, 55, 59, 70, 83, 109, 117, 127, 133n3, 142, 152, 153; action, 3, 12, 13, 60, 61, 73, 93, 143, 156, 162; activism, 7, 16n19, 37, 99, 110, 132, 133; rights, 1, 4, 71, 72; values, 63, 64, 74, 75, 76. See also education
civil code, 21, 23, 25, 28, 30
class, 3, 18, 19, 21, 23, 24, 26, 31, 32, 33, 36, 73, 77n5, 85, 86, 89, 99, 110n8, 116, 127, 144, 152, 166; enemy, 102, 103, 114, 118; working-, 28, 30, 45. See also bourgeois; boyar; elite; peasant; proletariat
clergy, 40n20, 84, 103
clientelism, 36, 37, 149
Cluj, 71, 102
collective farm. See collectivization
collectivization, 7, 34, 35, 67, 87, 90, 91, 99, 116, 118, 119, 128, 138, 139
common good, 15, 69, 73, 93, 105, 110, 111n11, 144
communism, 3, 8, 9, 10, 12, 13, 15, 16n10, 17n22, 21, 31, 32, 33, 40n17, 44, 50, 57, 76, 89, 90, 91, 98, 99, 101, 103, 106, 122, 136, 139, 149, 154; education and, 30, 31, 67, 74, 118, 119; gender roles and, 4, 5, 6, 14, 16n11,

17n23, 29, 36, 42, 45, 49, 53, 61, 80, 81, 82, 83, 85, 91, 92n2, 92n3, 113, 120, 124, 125, 126, 127, 133n3, 163; industrialization and, 34, 38, 94, 160n4; regime, 1, 2, 7, 16n14, 35, 40n22, 65, 66, 72, 73, 75, 77, 77n2, 77n3, 108, 110n2, 111n14, 121, 134n5, 134n18, 140, 144, 153. See also authoritarian; Ceaușescu, Nicolae; citizenship, under communism; generation, communist; organizations, communist; postcommunism; proletariat, dictatorship of the; Romanian Communist Party (RCP)
community, 1, 2, 9, 10, 14, 16n17, 17n20, 21, 26, 27, 32, 39n9, 40n13, 50, 53, 54, 55, 61, 70, 80, 83, 88, 91, 95, 96, 99, 106, 110, 140, 142, 143, 151, 155, 156, 159, 166; informal, 6, 15, 93, 98; political, 2, 11; religious, 100, 101, 103, 105, 107, 109, 110n7, 163. See also neighborhood
commute, 51, 87, 120
competition, 32, 40n17, 85, 98, 99, 105, 106, 122, 129, 131, 140, 142, 143, 156, 158, 159, 165, 166
competitiveness. See competition
constitution, 2, 27, 35, 36, 119, 135, 136, 142
corruption, 79, 85, 111n18, 121, 136, 137, 141, 144, 145, 152, 157, 158, 159, 160n6, 162. See also bribe
crèche, 67. See also kindergarten
crime, 38, 53
cultural. See culture
culture, 5, 13, 18, 20, 26, 40n13, 69, 73, 75, 82, 102, 104, 107, 110, 111n16, 122, 134n13; activities, 87, 105, 106, 119; differences, 95, 167; hearth, 99, 100
Czech, 25, 29, 36, 67, 134n20

deindustrialization, 38, 138, 158
democracy, 1, 14, 38, 73, 76, 102, 109, 128, 131, 135, 138, 140, 142, 144, 145, 146, 157, 159, 164; consolidated, 143, 167; electoral, 166; illiberal, 2, 37; liberal, 15, 36. See also citizenship, democratic; generation, democracy; Democratic Liberal Party (DLP); Democratic Party (DP)
Democratic Liberal Party (DLP), 145
Democratic Party (DP), 37, 137, 155

Deva, 32, 34, 86, 149, 153
dictatorship, 13, 28, 35, 114, 119. *See also* authoritarian; proletariat, dictatorship of the
disabled persons, 139, 148
discrimination, 1, 2, 36, 40n20, 40n23, 70, 102, 110n8; gender, 4, 15n1, 26, 30, 31, 32, 37, 79, 87, 88, 90, 136, 155. *See also* misogyny
divorce, 30, 39n4, 41, 48, 51, 52–53, 62n7, 73, 105, 136, 154
domestic violence, 6, 36, 40n24, 51, 52, 53, 70, 71, 77n8, 98, 117. *See also* abuse; beating; Istanbul Convention
double burden, 14, 17n23, 29, 36, 44, 48, 49, 57, 61, 80, 81, 82, 83, 92, 115, 124, 138
double workday. *See* double burden
dowry, 19, 20, 23, 24, 29, 30
drinking, 46, 47, 52, 86, 107, 143. *See also* alcoholism

Easter, 69, 103, 104
Eastern Bloc. *See* Eastern Europe
Eastern Europe, 5, 6, 8, 29, 38, 40n22, 114, 133n3, 142, 166, 167
East Germany, 41, 92n2
Economist Intelligence Unit, 36, 37, 142
economy, 2, 7, 15, 24, 25, 33, 34, 53, 66, 73, 80, 84, 92n1, 110n2, 115, 118, 128, 130, 131, 133, 149, 157, 161, 162, 166; cash, 21, 46; command, 6, 31, 50, 119, 139, 158; crisis, 9, 28, 112, 113, 125, 132, 137; gender inequality and, 3, 4, 13, 14, 18, 19, 20, 23, 26, 27, 29, 32, 35, 37, 42, 51, 69, 79, 81, 83, 85, 86, 87, 89, 90, 92n3, 92n7, 94, 120, 123, 141, 165; market, 13, 106, 135, 145. *See also* agriculture; autonomy, economic; breadwinner; capitalism; communism, industrialization and; deindustrialization; gray market; free market; industry; inequality, economic; neoliberal
education, 1, 11, 12, 25, 27, 33, 43, 44, 50, 68, 72, 78n9, 80, 83, 86, 87, 110n1, 133, 137, 145, 149, 157, 158; civic, 63, 64, 76; gender and, 6, 9, 14, 18, 22, 26, 28, 29, 31, 32, 35, 37, 49, 54, 57, 63, 65, 81, 163; moral, 70, 107, 163. *See also* children, education and; citizenship, education and; communism, education and; employment assignment; illiteracy; PISA; school; women's education

elected officials, 3, 6, 11, 35, 40n22, 51, 55, 56, 109, 111n18, 113, 117, 136, 145, 148, 149, 152, 155, 159, 160n9, 161, 163
election, 1, 2, 21, 29, 35, 72, 106, 113, 137, 143, 146, 147, 153, 159, 162, 168n4; local, 151, 161; municipal, 27; national, 28, 135. *See also* elected officials; electoral
electoral, 15, 147, 148, 150, 154, 161, 162, 164, 166; promises, 37, 143, 145, 159. *See also* democracy, electoral
elite, 18, 24, 39n1, 39n10; political, 36, 141, 159, 166
empathy. *See* leadership, political and leadership and empathy
employment, 27, 28, 31, 35, 38, 50, 51, 65, 67, 69, 75, 77n7, 80, 81, 84, 90, 91, 97, 99, 102, 110, 119, 120, 121, 122, 123, 150; assignments, 85, 86, 132. *See also* unemployment
entrepreneur, 25, 36, 37, 117, 137, 140, 141, 142, 143, 161, 162, 166
environment, 15, 26, 47, 69, 73, 80, 83, 84, 86, 87, 88, 93, 97, 134n13, 147, 149, 152, 158, 160n12. *See also* environmental
environmental, 107, 108, 109
equality, 22; gender, 1, 2, 15n1, 29, 42, 47, 58, 60, 81, 133n3, 164; legal, 142, 163. *See also* equal opportunity; inequality
equal opportunity, 4, 36, 37, 40n23. *See also* Law for Equal Opportunity for Women and Men
ethical. *See* ethics
ethics, 5, 54, 56, 76, 136, 141, 142; in politics, 4, 61, 91, 135, 143, 145, 147, 159, 163, 167; of care, 164, 165, 166, 168
ethnicity, 1, 3, 6, 11, 12, 17n20, 18, 24, 25, 26, 36, 40n16. *See also* minorities, ethnic
eugenics, 28, 92n3, 124
Europeanization, 135, 157
European Union (EU), 2, 6, 11, 13, 31, 35, 36, 37, 40n23, 41, 53, 61n2, 61n3, 62n7, 62n9, 66, 71, 78n9, 79, 90, 137, 141, 145, 149, 155, 156, 157, 158, 159, 160n10, 161, 162, 163, 166, 167. See also *Acqui Communitaire*

family, 6, 9, 10, 12, 14, 16n19, 23, 26, 28, 30, 40n20, 45, 48, 49, 51, 53, 55, 56, 58, 66, 72, 84, 85, 86, 86, 90, 93, 95, 97, 98, 102, 103,

104, 107, 110, 110n2, 112, 116, 119, 121, 123, 125, 127, 129, 134n14, 134n18, 149, 154, 157, 163, 165; civic values and, 63, 64; network, 65, 67, 71, 82, 94, 130, 132; responsibilities in the, 42, 43, 44, 46, 47, 50, 57, 83, 109. *See also* divorce; domestic violence; double burden; husband; kinship; marriage; wife

fascism, 28, 164

father, 20, 21, 28, 39n3, 42, 45, 46, 48, 50, 52, 57, 64, 66, 73, 77n4, 85, 92n3, 100, 102, 116, 150, 164

fear, 52, 69, 76, 115, 125, 127, 137

femininity, 54, 56, 58, 59, 60, 63

feminism, 4, 5, 36, 40n23, 92n5, 167, 168. *See also* Beijing Platform; citizenship, feminist definitions of

Fidelis, Malgorzata, 5, 40n19

foreign capital, 139

freedom, 2, 4, 76, 113, 128, 129, 136, 141, 144, 157, 167; of information, 74, 75, 131 (*see also* censorship)

free market, 98, 99, 136, 137, 139, 140, 141. *See also* capitalism, neoliberalism

friend. *See* friendship

friendship, 10, 13, 21, 58, 63, 80, 84, 93, 97, 98, 99, 101, 104, 106, 107, 109, 130, 131, 132, 143, 144

gender, 4, 11, 16n3, 21, 35, 40n16, 40n17, 40n18, 43, 51, 62n10, 64, 75, 83, 88, 109, 115, 116, 120, 124, 128, 136, 140, 149, 168n4; analysis, 5, 6, 18; bias, 141, 156, 161; desegregation, 87; disparity, 89, 90, 91, 162; justice, 164, 166; norm, 10, 14, 17n23, 19, 45, 49, 50, 54, 55, 56, 65, 66, 70, 72, 76, 82, 112, 134n7, 145; parity, 48; policy, 92n2, 133; power, 3, 123; regime, 23; role, 6, 13, 39n8, 41, 44, 59, 67, 69, 71, 77, 84, 85, 165. See also *Barometrul de gen*; citizenship, gender and; communism, gender roles and; discrimination, gender; domestic violence; economy, gender inequality and; equality, gender; femininity; husband; inequality, gender; masculinity

generation, 5, 8, 9, 14, 17n21, 22, 34, 43, 49, 50, 60, 61, 63, 64, 65, 72, 74, 77n2, 80, 82, 85, 87, 97, 126, 131, 137, 145; communist, 12, 13, 54, 58, 84, 94, 95, *95*, 97, 99, 102, 109, 110n6, 112, 114, 118, 119, 121, 127, 128, 129, 132, 138, 143, 148, 158, 164; democracy, 12, 13, 67, 94, 98, 101, 104, 112, 123, 129, 133; transition, 12, 13, 36, 42, 45, 55, 56, 57, 58, 59, 67, 84, 98, 99, 100, 102, 104, 105, 106, 110, 110n6, 112, 114, 115, 121, 123, 127, 128, 130, 132, 138, 140, 142, 152, 158, 161, 164, *165*

German, 7, 9, 22, 24, 25, 26, 27, 29, 32, 40n13, 40n20, 107. *See also* East Germany, West Germany

Gheorghiu-Dej, Gheorghe, 34

globalization, 135, 157, 158, 167

god, 57, 64, 69, 70, 76, 95, 102, 125, 154

governance, 6, 135, 147, 149, 158

grandmother, 42, 65, 66, 67, 68, 69, 77, 82, 83, 84, 92, 109, 124

gray market, 90

Great Britain. *See* United Kingdom

Greek Catholic, 15n14, 100, 102, 104, 114

Habsburg Empire, 18, 24, 39n10, 39n10. *See also* Austria-Hungary

household, 20, 21, 42, 44, 48, 52, 56, 57, 58, 61, 69, 81, 82, 94, 99, 118; decision-making, 43, 49; head of, 19, 41, 47, 164; manager, 24, 29, 41, 46, 91. *See also* double burden; family

heteronormativity, 41

hospital, 34, 49, 50, 63, 84, 101, 113, 122, 125, 126, 150, 153

housing, 34, 94, *95*, 96, 100, *122*, 133, 134n18; benefits, 35, 118, 119, 121, 123, 132, 150

Hungarian, 7, 9, 26, 27, 29, 32, 33, 39n11, 40n13, 40n20, 116, 145, 153. *See also* Hungary

Hungary, 26, 28, 29, 40n12, 40n22, 65, 134n20, 167. *See also* Austria-Hungary, Transylvania

Hunyadi Castle, 106, 111n15, 149, *151*

Hunedoara, 3, 12, 16n14, 17, 24, 26, 33, 37, 61, 67, 68, 70, 80, 90, 94, 95, 99, 100, 107, 108, 110n1, 128, 137, 142, 158; city, 7, 8, 9, 32, 33, 34, 86, 87, 105, 106, *108*, 109, 110n5, 111n14, 111n16, 111n18, 114, 121, *122*, 126, 134n4, 134n8, 134n15, 149, 150, *151*, 155, 161, 162; county, 1, 7, 8, *27*, 34, 38, 40n24, 85, 87, 90, 92n10, 120, 136, 161, 168n4 husband, 12, 15, 19, 20, 21, 22, 23, 24, 28, 41, 42, 43, 45, 49, 50, 61, 64, 66, 69, 70, 71, 80, 85, 90, 91, 100, 104, 115, 116, 117, 122, 123, 125, 129, 140, 142; household chores and, 46, 48, 67, 82, 87, 154, 164; ideal, 54, 55, 57. *See also* divorce; domestic violence; household head; household, decision-making; marriage

Iași, 22
illiteracy, 20, 23, 30, 118
Îndreptarea legii: Pravila cea mare (Setting the law: The great codex), 19, 20, 21, 39n7
industry, 33, 38, 91; heavy, 38, 86, 107, 148; service, 68, 69, 99. *See also* communism, industrialization and; deindustrialization; mining; steel works
inequality, 53, 139; economic, 79, 81, 85, 86, 132, 160n3; gender, 3, 26, 46, 61, 82. (*see also* communism, gender roles and)
inheritance, 19, 20, 21, 24, 25, 27, 30, 39n3
Institute for Social Assistance, 28
International Monetary Fund (IMF), 145, 157, 158
Isac, Victor, 105, 111n14
Istanbul Convention, 53
Italy, 33, 129

Jewish, 7, 25, 26, 40n16. *See also* Jews; Judaism; synagogue
Jew, 19, 24, 28, 32, 40n20, 65
Jinga, Luciana, 115
Judaism, 100
justice, 7, 25, 144, 160n12; social, 93, 110. *See also* gender, justice; law

Kant, Immanuel, 4, 147
kids, 42, 46, 47, 51, 64, 67, 69, 82, 84. *See also* children
kindergarten, 69, 82, 88, 114, 149. *See also* crèche
kinship, 49, 50, 101. *See also* family

law, 20, 22, 23, 30, 31, 32, 36, 40n13, 53, 68, 79, 81, 83, 89, 92n3, 114, 116, 124, 127, 134n18, 140, 142, 147, 152, 154, 163; for Equal Opportunity for Women and Men, 36, 136; for Preventing and Combating Domestic Violence, 71; rule of, 2, 111n18, 135, 138, 144, 157, 159. *See also Acqui Communitaire*; civil code; constitution; *Îndreptarea legii: Pravila cea mare*; justice; legal issues; penal code; work code
leadership, 48, 96, 100, 110n3, 116; male, 141, 145, 161; political, 37, 59, 74, 80, 81, 85, 107, 112, 114, 115, 119, 120, 137, 142, 143, 154, 162; caretaking and, 89; empathy and, 56; integrity and, 55; intelligence and, 56; transparency and, 55; trust and, 43
legal issues, 2, 19, 20, 21, 22, 23, 24, 25, 28, 30, 35, 53, 65, 79, 81, 98, 115, 127, 142; guardianship, 92n3; personhood, 18; protection, 1, 32
leisure, 6, 58
liberal, 4, 16n7, 26, 39n9, 131, 133, 165. *See also* democracy, Democratic Liberal Party (DLP); National Liberal Party (NLP); neoliberal
Lister, Ruth, 2, 3, 97
local, 10, 18, 33, 39n1, 99, 103, 106, 110n7, 111n14, 112, 113, 125, 141, 142, 150, 153, 154, 156, 161; administration, 9, 11, 34, 35, 37, 93, 96, 101, 107, 108, 114, 115, 116, 119, 121, 122, 136, 145, 149, 160n4; budget, 147, 148; policy, 37, 105. *See also* elections, local; politics, local
Lord's Army, 9, 16n17, 100, 101, 102, 103, 107, 110n4, 110n7
Love, 42, 52, 53, 55, 64, 69, 84, 86, 102, 150
Lutheran, 32, 100, 104

Macovei, Monica, 6, 7
Magyarization, 25, 40n13
marriage, 19, 24, 30, 35, 39n4, 41, 47, 48, 55, 60, 61n2, 61n3, 65, 72, 77, 104, 111n10, 121, 122–23, 134n13; as partnership, 42, 43, 50, 53, 54, 58; women's rights in, 21, 27, 29. *See also* abandonment; divorce; domestic violence; dowry; husband; wife; widow
masculinity, 45, 56
Massino, Jill, 5, 92n4
maternity leave, 45, 67, 81, 91
Marxism, 16n7, 81, 135, 136

Index

membership, 1, 2, 13, 37, 40n23, 53, 71, 157, 159, 167. *See also* party, membership

men, 4, 11, 13, 14, 15, 19, 20, 21, 23, 24, 25, 27, 29, 30, 31, 33, 35, 37, 38, 39n3, 39n8, 48, 60, 61, 61n10, 65, 70, 75, 79, 83, 86, 87, 88, 89, 90, 92n7, 92n10, 96, 99, 109, 110n8, 114, 120, 122, 124, 128, 132, 137, 141, 142, 143, 148, 152, 153, 154, 156, 159, 160n5, 162, 164; and homemaking, 17n23, 43–44, 45, 66, 81, 92n4; ideal, 54, 55, 56, 58. *See also* alcoholism; breadwinner; divorce; domestic violence; drinking; father; gender; household, head of; leadership, male; marriage; masculinity

migration, 33, 34, 35, 38, 43, 67, 68, 77n7, 99, 100, 122, 149, 150, 161

military, 25, 39n2, 117; women and, 30, 31, 61, 87, 88, 89, 92n6

Mill, John Stuart, 4, 16n9

mining, 31, 33, 38, 40n19, 120, 155

minorities, 16n3, 105, 136; ethnic, 7, 24, 27, 32; racial, 93; religious, 7, 16n14, 19, 32, 100, 104, 114; sexual, 93

misogyny, 26, 156, 167

mobility, 106, 121, 122

modernization, 22, 35, 38, 65

Moldavia, 18, 21, 24, 25, 34

money, 42, 43, 46, 47, 54, 56, 57, 66, 96, 97, 99, 101, 103, 118, 119, 122, 128, 130, 138, 139, 144, 147, 148, 149, 150, 152, 153, 155, 156, 158, 162. *See also* local budget; salary; savings

moral, 1, 2, 42, 60, 71, 93, 141, 142, 147, 164, 167, 168; code, 21, 70, 105, 144; values, 14, 19, 64, 72, 77, 102, 152, 163, 165. *See also* education, moral

mother, 13, 16n19, 29, 42, 44, 45, 46, 48, 52, 56, 57, 58, 59, 60, 63, 64, 65, 66, 67, 68, 69, 70, 71, 72. *See also* maternity leave

mothering. *See* mother

municipal, 27, 28, 95, 107, 109, 111n16, 114, 154, 160n9

Muscă, Mona, 156, 160n11

Muslim, 19

National Women's Council, 124
NATO, 13, 31, 35, 145

National Peasant Party (NPP), 111n14, 137, 153, 154

National Salvation Front (NSF), 137, 141, 158

nationalist, 25, 26, 28, 29n11, 111n11, 116, 137, 114, 168

nationalization, 34, 118, 121

Neaga, Diana, ix, 10, 45, 104

Negruzzi, Ella, 22, 23

neighborhood, 3, 11, 15, 94, 95, 96, 130, 148

neoliberal, 4, 6, 16n10, 35, 36, 37, 38, 66, 108, 135, 138, 158, 159, 165, 166, 168

network, 5, 15, 29, 42, 67, 71, 89, 91, 97, 107, 110n7, 130, 133, 149. *See also* family network

North America, 31, 77n7

nobility, 24, 39n1. *See also* boyar

Oltenia, 34

Open Society Foundation, 6, 75

Orăștie, 117

Organization for Democracy and Socialist Unity, 113

organizations, 94, 106, 158; charitable, 107, 109; civic, 72, 93; communist, 40n17, 40n18, 112, 113, 114, 133; nongovernmental (NGO), 6, 105, 110; political, 51, 137; professional, 25, 83; women's, 71, 115, 133n3, 153, 154. *See also* Bureau of the Base Organization (BOB); National Women's Council; Organization for Democracy and Socialist Unity; Open Society Foundation

Orthodox, 7, 9, 16n14, 19, 20, 21, 24, 25, 32, 39n8, 39n10, 40n20, 70, 99, 100, 101, 102, 103, 104, 105, 110n4, 110n5, 110n7, 111n10, 163. *See also* Îndreptarea legii: Pravila cea mare; Lord's Army

Ostrom, Elinor, 95

Ottoman Empire, 18

paternity leave, 77n4. *See also* maternity leave

parenting, 14, 41, 44, 45, 47, 48, 50, 57, 59, 61, 63, 65, 66, 69, 71, 72, 77, 82, 92n3, 133n3. *See also* father; mother

parish council, 101, 102

parliament, 23, 26, 28, 29, 35, 36, 37, 40n22, 56, 90, 93, 101, 142, 145, 155, 158, 162, 163

party, 1, 6, 15, 20, 97, 130, 135, 146, 152, 156, 164, 165; hierarchy, 113, 134n10; leader, 40n16, 81, 119, 120, 154, 161, 162; membership, 31, 113, 114, 115, 116, 117, 131, 133, 153, 163. *See also* Democratic Liberal Party (DLP); Democratic Party (DP); National Liberal Party (NLP); National Peasant Party (NPP); National Salvation Front (NSF); organizations, political; Romanian Communist Party (RCP); Social Democratic Party (SDP)
paternalist, 4, 28, 113, 117, 136, 139, 140. *See also* patriarchy
Pateman, Carol, 97
patriarchy, 2, 6, 61, 121, 135
Paul, Andreea, 142
Pauker, Ana, 29, 40n16, 114, 115
peasant, 21, 27, 39n8, 116, 118. *See also* National Peasant Party (NPP)
penal code, 53
pensioner, 89, 106, 109, 116, 138. *See also* pension; retirement
pension, 23, 38, 69, 79, 81, 89, 91, 118, 132, 138, 140, 146, 150; survivor, 51, 90
Pentecostal, 8, 16n14, 100
pioneer, *68*, 112, 114
PISA, 78n9
pleasure, 58, 106, 127
pluralist, 2, 35, 159
Poland, 5, 17, 29, 40n19, 40n22, 134n20, 167
police, 31, 40n17, 53, 83, 87, 88, 105, 121, 133n3, 139, 147; secret, 94, 100, 110n7, 125, 132, 134n10, 134n18, 160n11. *See also* Securitate
political, 5, 6, 13, 16n6, 18, 31, 39n10, 40n13, 49, 54, 63, 71, 72, 79, 92n5, 93, 102, 112, 114, 127, 129, 139, 140, 144, 147, 151, 157, 160n12, 160n13, 165, 168; control, 113, 115, 121, 124, 127, 133n3, 136; correctness, 167; dissent, 124; participation, 2, 3, 12, 17n20, 17n23, 29, 51, 132, 133, 146, 152, 154, 155, 163; persecution, 28, 111n10; power, 3, 15, 21, 141; prisoner, 103, 111n14, 115; representation, 11, 25, 26, 27, 36, 133, 156; right, 1, 4, 14, 22, 24, 132, 133n3, 135. *See also* authority, political; elite, political; leadership, political; organizations, political; party; Political Executive Committee; politician; politics; time, political participation and

Political Executive Committee, 124
politician, 2, 53, 54, 74, 83, 136, 137, 142, 143, 145, 146, 147, 148, 159, 165, 167; female, 6, 48, 151, 155, 156, 162; male, 15, 42, 55, 152, 162
politics, 2, 3, 12, 14, 15, 36, 48, 50, 51, 54, 56, 59, 60, 61, 64, 72, 73, 76, 79, 91, 92, 97, 112, 115, 123, 131, 133, 134, 135, 136, 137, 138, 141, 142, 143, 144, 145, 146, 147, 152, 153, 154, 156, 159, 161, 163, 164, 165, 166, 167, 168; global, 15n1; international, 11; local, 6, 161–62; national, 7, 155. *See also The Politics of Duplicity: Controlling Reproduction in Ceausescu's Romania*
The Politics of Duplicity: Controlling Reproduction in Ceausescu's Romania, 126
populism, 37, 145, 147, 162, 167
postcommunist, 4, 7, 14, 35, 38, 41, 61n3, 62n7, 67, 74, 78n9, 79, 109, 126, 127, 135, 137, 141, 163, 166, 167; transition, 5, 13. *See also* neoliberal
pornographic material, 74
poverty, 6, 25, 36, 89, 90, 101, 106, 123, 129, 134n14, 137, 138, 139, 140
private, 2, 15, 28, 29, 49, 58, 66, 67, 93, 94, 110n1, 111n17, 117, 118, 122, 132, 135, 137, 139, 148, 150, 164; sphere, 3, 6, 14, 42, 56, 57, 77, 134n6
proletariat, 112; dictatorship of the, 13, 114, 119
pronatalist, 63, 65, 74, 81, 113, 124, 125, 126, 132, 133
propaganda, 131, 132, 137, 144
property, 30, 39n8, 94, 129; nationalization of, 118; restitution of, 154; rights, 18, 21, 23, 25, 27, 28, 36, 92n3, 132, 141. *See also* civil code; dowry; inheritance; marriage
Protestant, 19, 24, 25. *See also* Baptist; Lutheran; Pentecostal; Seventh-Day Advantist
public, 7, 9, 15, 16n16, 20, 23, 28, 31, 40n16, 54, 56, 57, 59, 71, 75, 84, 87, 92n3, 92n4, 99, 107, 108, 111n16, 124, 137, 146, 147, 156, 160n11, 163; policy, 2, 36, 138, 142, 148, 152; resource, 3, 136, 150, 154, 155; service, 34, 50, 77n3, 92, 105, 111n11, 111n17, 118; sphere, 3, 6, 14, 42, 55, 63, 74, 77, 93, 109, 113, 134n6, 143-4, 162, 164, 165, 166, 168; spending, 22, 148, 149; trust, 137, 142, 145, 166

quota, 115; gender, 31, 116; work, 90

Rădoi, Cristina, ix, 10
rape, 21
religious, 11, 18, 24, 40n15, 63, 69, 70, 74, 76, 100; attitude, 9, 77, 99, 167; diversity, 7, 8; group, 12, 15, 19, 25, 32, 40n20, 101, 102, 103, 104, 107, 110, 114, 163. *See also* Catholic; church; clergy; community, religious; Jew; Jewish; Judaism; minority, Muslim; Orthodox; Protestant, religious
reform, 21, 145
reproduction, 20, 41, 63, 64, 65, 124, 126. *See also* abortion; birth; pronatalism; sex
revolution, 17, 41, 141, 144, 148
retirement, 9, 38, 51, 68, 81, 87, 89, 90, 92n7, 104, 109, 111n17, 139, 160n5. *See also* pensioner
Reuss-Ianculescu, Eugenia, 16n9, 22
Roma, 7, 17n20, 21, 24, 25, 32, 39n9, 65, 107, 111n19
Romanian Communist Party (RCP), 16n14, 29, 30, 34, 85, 100, 110n6, 112, 113, 114, 115, 116, 117, 118, 124, 129, 133n3, 134n7, 137, 154, 155, 158, 163. *See also* Bureau of the Base Organization (BOB); communist; organizations, communist; Political Executive Committee

salary, 47, 86, 114, 115, 117, 134n18
Sâncrai, 7, 9, *10*, *91*, 99, 100, 103, 107, 110n7, 116, 138, 145, 146, 161
savings, 29, 47, 89
scarcity, 97, 127, 129, 130, 131, 133
school, 8, 17n22, 26, 27, 28, 32, 34, 40n13, 40n21, 42, 44, 46, 48, 56, 63, 64, 68, 72, 73, 74, 75, 76, 84, 85, 86, 99, 101, 110n1, 112, 113, 122, 123, 149, 163; admission, 22, 25, 116; day, 67, 77n5; dropout, 38; teacher, 8, 9, 22, 28, 48, 69, 75, 76, 84, 87, 88, 90, 97, 99, 102, 113, 115, 120, 140, 153; vocational, 31, 118, 119. *See also* education.
Schwimmer, Rózsa, 26
secularization, 25, 77, 110n6, 163
Securitate, 40n18
Sen, Amartya, 146
Seventh-Day Adventist, 8, 16n14, 70, 100, 103

Serb, 24, 25, 40n13
serf, 21, 39n8
sex, 36, 39n8, 40n16, 60, 63, 83, 122, 124, 125, 127, 134n11, 156, 164; activity, 19, 21; orientation, 3, 36, 61n1, 93, 167; violence, 53. *See also* abortion; birth control; domestic violence; heteronormativity; minorities, sexual; pornographic material; rape; reproduction
sexism. *See* sex
slave, 21, 39n8, 45, 130
social, 2, 7, 15, 18, 20, 21, 24, 25, 36, 38, 41, 42, 59, 60, 64, 70, 71, 73, 77, 79, 80, 81, 97, 102, 107, 109, 110n8, 114, 119, 121, 132, 134n13, 138, 139, 142, 143, 156, 160n3, 164, 168n6; contract, 133, 159; justice, 93, 110; norm, 13, 53, 55, 57, 58, 63, 72, 76, 89, 101, 104, 134n7, 163; program, 4, 36, 61, 66, 77n3, 91, 123, 148, 150, 166; right, 4, 29; solidarity, 10, 129, 130, 131. *See also* Institute for Social Assistance; Social Democratic Party (SDP); welfare, social
Social Democratic Party (SDP), 35, 141, 145, 154
socialism, 86, 160n3. *See also* Romanian Communist Party (RCP); Social Democratic Party (SDP); state patriarchy
Soviet Union, 41, 94, 128, 134n20, 164
Spain, 66
steel plant, 33, 38, 105, *108*, 111n13
synagogue, 32

Temesvár. *See* Timișoara
television (TV), 60, 71, 74, 75, 98, 130, 131, 136
Teorodoriu, Ecaterina, 31
time, 1, 6, 7, 9, 11, 12, 14, 15, 15n1, 17n21, 23, 24, 28, 35, 39n8, 40n20, 42, 43, 44, 45, 46, 48, 50, 51, 52, 56, 57, 63, 64, 65, 66, 68, 69, 70, 72, 73, 74, 80, 82, 84, 85, 86, 87, 89, 96, 97, 98, 102, 103, 106, 115, 116, 119, 123, 124, 125, 127, 130, 131, 132, 133, 134n18, 135, 138, 139, 142, 143, 145, 147, 148, 149, 150, 152, 154, 155, 158; political participation and, 17n23, 29, 49, 77, 83, 92, 105, 110, 156, 162. *See also* leisure
Timișoara, 26, 125, 130, 134n15

tradition, 6, 9, 19, 22, 24, 25, 31, 45, 49, 57, 61, 67, 69, 76, 77, 81, 85, 86, 88, 92, 89, 100, 101, 122, 154
Transylvania, 8, 14n16, 16n15, 18, 19, 24, 25, 26, 28, 30, 32, 33, 40n12, 40n14, 153
Tronto, Joan, 16n7, 16n9, 147, 166
trust, 37, 43, 74, 94, 97, 98, 99, 100, 102, 104, 109, 157; and elected politicians, 55, 66, 146, 152; and the state, 87, 127, 160n6. *See also* leadership, political and trust; public trust

Udrea, Elena, 156
Ukrainian, 24, 40n22, 102
unemployment, 13, 38, 77n4, 92n10, 103, 137, 139, 140, 143, 147, 150, 158
United Kingdom, 16n6, 167
United States, 4, 10, 16n6, 67, 92n1, 113, 156, 167
university admission. *See* school
urbanization, 25, 34, 35, 38, 49, 94, 120

Visegrád group, 134n20, 137
Voinescu, Alice, 28
voluntary associations, 93, 98
volunteering, 105, 106, 110, 150, 159

wage, 28, 30, 50, 62n5, 79, 80, 81, 164
Wallachia, 18, 20, 21, 24, 25
Weber, Renate, 6, 7
welfare, 4, 19, 139, 140, 152; policy, 92n3, 113, 147, 148, 160n3, 166; service, 35, 135, 150; social, 36, 159
Western Europe, 21, 22, 31, 77n7, 92n1, 134n20

widow, 3, 9, 20, 90, 95, 99, 105, 150
wife, 19, 20, 23, 39n7, 46, 47, 48, 53, 54, 55, 56, 57, 71, 90, 117, 125
women's, 20, 23, 30, 39n9, 40n18, 40n24, 48, 51, 54, 56, 57, 58, 59, 60, 61, 63, 64, 65, 66, 68, 69, 70, 77, 77n1, 79, 80, 8284, 91, 92, 93, 94, 96, 103, 117, 120, 124, 126, 141, 142, 152, 154, 155, 156, 160n14, 162, 163, 166; education, 18, 22, 85; emancipation, 81, 83; identity, 124; interests, 24, 29, 36, 159, 164; organizations, 115, 133n3, 153; professions, 28, 84, 87, 88; rights, 21, 25, 26, 27, 35, 49, 71, 92n3, 105, 110; shelters, 40n24. *See also* candidates, women; femininity; military, women and; National Women's Council; organizations, women's
World Bank, 145
World War I, 18, 22, 23, 24, 25, 26, 64, 65
World War II, 7, 29, 16n40; 40n20, 44, 92n1
work, 29, 30, 35, 39n8, 43, 46, 48, 49, 50, 51, 54, 56, 57, 58, 61, 62n6, 63, 65, 66, 67, 68, 73, 74, 75, 77n3, 80, 86, 87, 88, 91, *91*, 92n1, 96, 97, 98, 101, 104, 105, 111n11, 113, 115, 117, 119, 120, 122, 123, 125, 127, 131, 132, 133, 136, 138, 139, 140, 142, 143, 144, 145, 146, 147, 148, 149, 151, 152, 153, 154, 156, 161. 163, 164, 167; as vocation, 83, 84; charity, 106, 107, 110; domestic, 44, 46, 69; satisfaction and, 64, 79, 83, 89, 92; unremunerated, 81, 89. *See also* breadwinner; double burden; employment; household economy; quota, work; salary; unemployment; wage; work code
work code, 81, 85

MARIA BUCUR is John V. Hill Chair of East European History and Professor of Gender Studies at Indiana University. She has written extensively on the history of eugenics in Eastern Europe, gender history in Romania, and war and memory in twentieth-century Europe. Her books include *Eugenics and Modernization in Interwar Romania*; *Heroes and Victims: Remembering War in Twentieth-Century Romania*; and *The Century of Women: How Women Have Transformed the World since 1990*.

MIHAELA MIROIU is Professor of Political Science at the National School for Political Studies and Public Administration, Bucharest, Romania. Her research area encompasses the fields of political theory, feminist political theories and political ethics, postcommunist transition, and gender and politics. Her books include *Convenio. Despre natură, femei și morală* (Convenio. On nature, women and morals), *Guidelines for Promoting Equity in Higher Education*, *Drumul către autonomie: Teorii politice feministe* (The road to autonomy: Feminist political theories), and *Neprețuitele femei* (Priceless women).

www.ingramcontent.com/pod-product-compliance
Lightning Source LLC
Chambersburg PA
CBHW070316240426
43661CB00057B/2661